The Politics of
Affirmative Action

Back in The Cottage, the three women prowl around the garden identifying plants. 'I know there's a lot of weeding to be done,' acknowledges Flora, 'but how do you tell a weed from a plant?' Her desperation is born of many hours trying to work out the difference.

'You don't, really,' says Olga unhelpfully. 'It's civilization again. Some things are *defined* as weeds. Myself, I let them grow if I like the look of them. To hell with the definition. This here' – she plants a stout foot in the red earth – 'would be called a weed by some. But I like it. It's up to you, my dear; it's your garden.'

Ann Oakley, *Scenes Originating in the Garden of Eden*, 1994: 95

The Politics of Affirmative Action

'Women', Equality and Category Politics

CAROL LEE BACCHI

SAGE Publications
London • Thousand Oaks • New Delhi

SAGE Publications Ltd
6 Bonhill Street
London EC2A 4PU

SAGE Publications Inc
2455 Teller Road
Thousand Oaks, California 91320

SAGE Publications India Pvt Ltd
32, M-Block Market
Greater Kailash – I
New Delhi 110 048

British Library Cataloguing in Publication data

A catalogue record for this book is
available from the British Library

ISBN 0 8039 8792 7
ISBN 0 8039 8793 5 (pbk)

Library of Congress catalog card number 96–070154

Typeset by Mayhew Typesetting, Rhayader, Powys
Printed in Great Britain by Biddles Ltd, Guildford, Surrey

to Joan

Contents

Preface

In 1991 I began a major research project, examining affirmative action theory and practice in six countries – the United States, Australia, Canada, Norway, Sweden and the Netherlands. These countries were selected because they were reputed to be leading the world in affirmative action. I wished to find out more about practice and rationale. My particular focus was affirmative action for women.

This project took place during a period in which affirmative action was facing increasing opposition, particularly in the United States where it originated. Criticism came from those who located themselves on the political right on the grounds that affirmative action meant equal results and hence was antithetical to American political culture. Some who located themselves on the political left described the reform as elitist and assimilationist, since it asked no more than inclusion in existing social structures.

The project also ran concurrently with a growing concern among many feminist theorists that the category 'women' was problematic because it presumed an ahistorical essence and/or falsely universalized women's experiences. Other groups, including groups of Aboriginal peoples, were troubling over problems with appeals to identities deemed essentialist. Since affirmative action targeted just such categories, it seemed to be open to this kind of criticism.

Many feminists, myself included, support forms of affirmative action. Hence, I found myself investigating a reform many feminists agreed was necessary, but a reform targeting 'women', a category many feminists were eschewing. I puzzled over the tension between practice and theory.

I asked a group of feminists attending an International Political Science Association Conference in Buenos Aires in 1991 how to resolve this dilemma. I was met with a sympathetic shrugging of the shoulders. In a 1993 seminar at the Australian National University, Iris Young again problematized the category 'women'.[1] She usefully distinguished between women as a group and women as a series, drawing on Sartre's notion of seriality. Young emphasized that 'the group is necessarily partial' and '. . . will have particular objectives or purposes that cannot encompass or even refer to the totality of the condition of women as a series'. I asked where this left reforms like affirmative action for women. Young replied: 'That's politics!' This book shows that Young is right. It also spells out the implications for the ways we think about affirmative action and about 'women' which accompany this realization.

It is difficult to offer a working definition of affirmative action since part of the purpose of the book is to point out that there are several possible interpretations of affirmative action and the reforms it should encompass. Politics, as we shall see, is involved in the very act of definition. Roberta Ann Johnson's definition is useful because of its open-endedness:

> Affirmative action is a generic term for programmes which take some kind of initiative either voluntarily or under the compulsion of law, to increase, maintain, or rearrange the number or status of certain group members usually defined by race or gender, within a larger group. (1990: 77)

This captures the intention that affirmative action be proactive, that it not wait upon a complaint of discrimination, and that it be forward-looking, as well as redressing past and present discrimination. In Canada, affirmative action has been renamed 'employment equity'; in Europe the phrase 'positive action' is used to describe this type of reform initiative.

As Chapter 2 explains, most people talk about two kinds of affirmative action programmes, 'soft' programmes and 'hard' or 'strong' programmes. The former refers to programmes which increase the possibility that members of underrepresented groups be hired, appointed, or promoted. These include initiatives such as targeted recruiting policies or training programmes. The latter refers to policies which specify that being a member of an underrepresented group counts in assessing candidates for appointments and promotions. I use the terms 'targeted hiring' or 'targeted promoting' to describe policies of this sort instead of the more commonly used phrase 'preferential hiring/promoting' because of the implication of favouritism in the latter. Quotas are one form of targeted hiring/promotion.

Language is important here. In the constructed categories 'hard affirmative action', 'soft affirmative action' and 'preferential hiring/ promoting', terms have been devised which have particular effects. 'Soft' and 'hard' programmes are differentiated in ways which suggest that the former are acceptable while the latter are illegitimate. In addition, the phrase 'preferential hiring/promotion' implies that the targets of the reform are recipients of special favours. This understanding produces affirmative action as 'reverse' or 'positive discrimination'.

Programmes, as Johnson states, identify group members generally by race or gender, though affirmative action programmes have also been devised for the disabled in some countries. The targeting of separate groups creates a number of problems. It compels people to campaign on behalf of one of their identities, forcing them to privilege a part of themselves and to deny other parts. It also sets groups in competition with each other. In addition, since 'women' is often one target group, other groups come to be spoken about as if they were constituted by men. Hence, multiply-oppressed women fall through the cracks in many programmes.

I have coined the term 'category politics' to talk about the ways in which categories figure in affirmative action debates. The idea of category politics builds upon social construction theory as is explained in Chapter 1. The position is developed that the concepts and categories used in political debate are constructed and deployed for political purposes. I distinguish between conceptual categories which are to do with ideas like 'equal opportunity', 'preferential hiring/promoting', 'reverse discrimination', and identity categories, such as 'women', 'Aborigines', 'men', and so on. From this starting place I highlight the importance of what I refer to as 'the practices of category politics', the variety of ways in which categories are marshalled in political debate for political effect. Such a focus directs attention away from some presumed abstract content to the political uses of categories.

This book examines the political uses of both conceptual and identity categories in affirmative action theory and practice. It shows how conceptual categories such as 'equal opportunity', 'equal results', 'political culture', 'public' and 'private' are defined and positioned to delegitimize targeted hiring/promotion, to minimize public supervision of affirmative action initiatives, to sequester the domestic domain from examination, and so to contain the effects of affirmative action. Generally the reform has been transformed into a species of philanthropy. This makes it unattractive to many in the targeted groups since it identifies recipients as the ones who need reforming. It is also confined to 'public' or 'working life'. Some supporters of the reform, I argue in Chapters 2 and 3, by accepting and working within this constructed conceptual terrain, have diluted the potential impact of affirmative action. The case is also made that, among identity categories, 'women' is seen as less 'needy' and hence as less 'deserving' than other claimant groups.

Val Plumwood (1995) identifies a link between the privatizing of employer–employee relations in the discourse around affirmative action and the displacement of 'women' as an important political category. Connections between these two themes become clear in discussions about the place of the family in workplace reform and the tendency to keep 'intervention' to a minimum through allocating responsibility in this domain to women. As Plumwood says (1995: 116), the privatizing of these two domains – the household and the economy – keeps these areas outside public supervision and accountability.

Focusing on the ways in which conceptual and identity categories are deployed in political debate allows us to see several things. Looking at the uses of conceptual categories points to the role of theorists in shaping political argument. The importance of recognizing political and other social theorists as political actors is a key argument in the book.

Examining the uses of identity categories highlights their political character both for those who campaign on their behalf and for those who deny their relevance. I argue that an awareness of the political character of identity categories takes the sting out of accusations that some, such as 'Aborigines' or 'women', are essentialist. Such categories seem essentialist only because those campaigning on their behalf have felt impelled to give these groups definition. They have been impelled to do this because they are positioned as outgroups, inhabiting the borderlands of power and influence.[2] Ingroups such as 'men' are seldom called upon to specify just who 'men' are. Existing power relations hence are responsible for the *appearance* of essentialism in these claims.

The first two chapters in the book provide an introduction to theory and argument. Chapter 1 elaborates the notion of category politics and explores its implications, particularly for understandings of the category 'women'. Chapter 2 previews the central theoretical debates surrounding affirmative action and offers pointers to problems with current dominant understandings.

The rest of the book is organized around interpretive themes which allow a close examination of the practices of category politics in particular contexts. To facilitate this approach the experience in one of the countries studied is taken as a primary illustration in each case. This kind of historical specificity is required to see how context affects the shape of category politics in particular circumstances though, as we shall see, many of the themes repeat themselves.

In Chapter 3 we tackle 'The Politics of (Mis)representation', with the United States providing the focus. An analysis of the theoretical debates in the United States illustrates how affirmative action has been contained through the creation and positioning of conceptual categories. Affirmative action is equated with 'equal results' which is set against 'equal opportunity', declared to be the core of American 'political culture'. Distinctions between 'public' and 'private' restrict reform to 'working life' and limit severely 'public' monitoring of 'private' enterprise. Moves to replace affirmative action with 'diversity management' follow logically from this construction of affirmative action as inappropriate and excessive 'intervention'.

Links between the historical legacy of slavery and meanings of affirmative action are striking in the United States. The resultant emphasis on racial identity categories causes problems for those who wish to campaign for 'women'. It causes particular problems for Black women who are impelled to select *an* identity around which to mobilize and hence to choose *between* their Blackness and their womanness.

Chapter 4, 'The Politics of Displacement', provides a close study of the way in which 'women' has been displaced from the affirmative action/ employment equity agenda in Canada. Here the historical legacy of the British conquest has produced a tension between English and French Canada, a tension the federal government has at times sought to dispel through encouraging the emergence of new identity categories. An initial commitment to affirmative action for 'women' has been replaced by 'employment equity' for four targeted groups – 'visible minorities', 'Aboriginal peoples', 'the disabled', and 'women'.

In 'The Politics of Incorporation' (Chapter 5) the Australian experience is used to illustrate how 'women' can gain categorical recognition without the anticipated changes in their status. For historically specific reasons Australia's federal affirmative action legislation targets only 'women'. This, however, has not meant that 'women' as a category is considered politically important. Almost perversely, targeting 'women' allows a diminution of attention to women.

'The Politics of Solidarity' (Chapter 6) examines another kind of identity politics, this time in Sweden, which proves equally problematic for women. The historical background to affirmative action, or positive action as it is called, charts new terrain due to the social democratic heritage and the commitment from the 1920s to facilitate the combining by women of workforce participation and domestic responsibilities. 'Class', not race or gender, is talked about as the most important factor distinguishing groups of people. This has produced a narrow space within which claims can be made for 'women', and a gender-neutral approach to affirmative action. Corporatist politics operate to protect the prerogative of industry and unions in deciding just which 'positive actions' they will accept.

'The Politics of Transformation' (Chapter 7) tells the story of conceptual revision which occurred in the Netherlands. An early (1970s) commitment to 'affirmative action', meaning targeted hiring/promotion, in the public sector has been diluted into widespread endorsement of something called 'positive action', meaning little more than targeted recruiting and training. The clientele, which originally was 'women', now includes 'ethnic minorities'. For the private sector affirmative action is restricted to incentives and voluntary programmes.

'The Politics of Difference' (Chapter 8) looks at the attempt by Norwegian women to call upon 'women's' traditional category status as mothers and keepers of the hearth to demand affirmative action. Quotas are in place to increase the representation of women in political parties and government committees. Women activists have achieved this recognition through appealing to a common understanding that 'women' as a group or category see the world differently because they are the nurturers and carers, and hence their views need to be represented. Other kinds of claims for 'women', particularly claims which would interfere with the operations of the private sector, receive short shrift. There are also indications that reliance on an image of 'woman' as nurturer is creating the conditions for a discursive shift to 'family' which will further reduce the openings for claims for 'women'.

As noted earlier, the countries researched were selected because they were seen to be leaders in affirmative action. These close studies show that this impression is delusive because of the ways in which affirmative action is being contained. In each case, albeit to different degrees in the different countries, demarcations between 'public' and 'private' are operating to limit the extent to which change will take place. 'Private' life is deemed outside the purview of government concern. 'Private' enterprise is *de facto* left to define the degree of its involvement.

Affirmative action programmes are classified as 'soft' and acceptable, or 'strong' and less so or unacceptable. In the United States, Canada and Australia, targeted hiring and promotion, which have the greatest chance of altering the material distribution of power and influence, have been damned as antidemocratic. Outreach policies, which position claimants as those needing 'help' and hence as the problem, receive some support. In the process affirmative action is constituted 'beneficence' to the 'needy' and ingroups are kept invisible in their positions of privilege.

'Strong' affirmative action has been accepted at times for the public sector in the Netherlands and Norway, and for the public and private sectors in Sweden. In Norway and the Netherlands, there has been a trend away from such measures. In Sweden quotas are more often talked about than used. When they are applied, they are applied in a gender-neutral fashion.

In all the countries studied the consistency with which 'women' and 'women's issues' are side-stepped or displaced from the political agenda is striking. Even in countries where 'women' is given categorical legitimacy, this is no guarantee that meaningful change for women will follow. Category politics tells us something about why this is so. It shows that 'women' as a political category does not rate much importance and that other agendas dominate. In the main these are agendas to do with economic stability and political survival; often the two are connected. The category 'women' is also interpreted at times in ways which work against particular groups of women.

A key point to note here is that the category 'women' already operates in political discourse. Hence I argue that it can neither be ignored nor eliminated. It follows, I suggest, that it is at least as important to examine its uses in particular contexts as to speculate upon its abstract content. I should note that there is no sense in which I mean to suggest that theoretical debates about abstract meanings of 'women' are not useful. In fact, I believe they are crucial because they assist in drawing attention to inadequacies in the ways in which 'women' is treated as an homogeneous category in some policy. The project, as I see it, is in each case contesting uses of categories, including 'women', which undermine desired objectives. My hope is that, by suggesting a shift in focus from women to 'women', I offer a way to talk about the variety of women's experiences without presuming that all women 'are' a particular way, or that all women see the world or social relations in the same way.

This approach opens up a space for asking somewhat different questions about women than those addressed in much feminist theory, and for asking some familiar questions differently. It asks where 'women' is positioned in political debates around affirmative action. Through this focus, it raises a broader question about the discursive location of 'women' in political debate generally and the effects of this location. This kind of analysis provides a rationale for pressing to increase the representation of women, those identified as members of the category 'women', in places where this discursive locating takes place – universities, boardrooms, work councils, unions, parliaments, the media.

I want to stress that what I am offering here is not an answer to a problem; it is a way of exposing an often-ignored part of the puzzle. My argument, put simply, is that discussions about meanings of 'woman'/ 'women' and other abstract categories need to give attention to the political uses of these categories. Without this awareness, or wariness, we fall into many traps. We need to see these before, with Judith Butler (1992b: 84), we can 'work' them.[3] In the Conclusion, 'No Final Curtain', I expand upon the strategic implications for reformers of category politics.

Notes

1 The seminar presentation outlined the argument in Young, 1994. The first quotation is from this article.

2 Lerner (1980: 16) borrows the terminology of ingroup and outgroup from Tajfel (1970) who referred to the general process, at least in Western societies, 'of coding people along dimensions of similar to me, different from me, belonging to my categories, belonging to others.'

3 I would like to thank Sarah Zetlein for bringing this reference to my attention.

Acknowledgements

There are many people I wish to acknowledge for their assistance in the genesis of this book. I owe a particular debt to a large number of people in Australia and in the countries visited who gave of their time to speak to me about their experience, practical and/or theoretical, with affirmative action. The research trip to Canada in 1994 was facilitated by a Canadian Studies Faculty Research Award from the Canadian High Commission in Canberra.

I would also like to thank colleagues at the Research School of Social Sciences in the Australian National University and in the Politics Department, University of Adelaide, for helpful, probing comments on drafts of some of the material. Here I would like to mention Barry Hindess and Doug McEachern. Carol Johnson, whose work is drawn upon extensively in Chapter 5, provided valuable feedback on the entire manuscript. Thanks also to Paul Corcoran for his encouragement.

Most especially, I want to thank Joan Eveline for providing the essential sounding-board for ideas in the crucial last six months of writing. Joan has co-authored one chapter (Chapter 5), but my indebtedness to her work and insights pervades the other chapters as well. I have seldom experienced such an exhilarating and productive friendship.

I am also grateful to the three readers who offered such useful suggestions, and to Chris Hill and Natalie Mahoney for assisting in the production of the final draft.

Catharine, Sarah, Thomas and Ron Gladman provided indispensable support on the home front. My dear son, Stephen, enlivened the task and made it seem worth while.

1

The Political Uses of Categories

Affirmative action is a controversial reform. Or, at least, it is a reform which attracts great controversy. Its critics describe it as at odds with notions of equal opportunity and as undermining procedures designed to appoint the best person for the job. Its supporters often, even usually, feel the need to qualify their support – to specify that *their* form of affirmative action does not undermine merit. Affirmative action for 'women' is even more controversial than affirmative action for some other groups. 'Women', it is frequently argued, are not really 'disadvantaged'. In some ways, the case is put, they are advantaged by the 'special treatment' they receive from chivalrous men, and now through affirmative action. Besides, it is added, the women who benefit from affirmative action are already an elite who have no need of 'assistance'.

This at least is the scenario in Australia, where I live and work. The evidence in this study is that these attitudes appear frequently in all the countries in my sample. These – the United States, Canada, Australia, Sweden, the Netherlands and Norway – are the countries reputed to be leading the way in affirmative action for 'women', which is the reason they were selected for scrutiny.

As we shall see, these understandings of affirmative action hinge upon the meanings imputed to terms like 'equal opportunity' and 'merit' among others. I will be arguing that these meanings are contestable and hence so too are dominant understandings of affirmative action.

The notion of 'essentially contested concepts' has a long history. W.B. Gallie (1955–56) first used the phrase. Christine Swanton (1985) elaborates the different kinds of claim attached to the phrase and the implications of those claims. As will become clearer, I am suggesting neither that there are differences of opinion about concepts which possess an uncontestable core, nor that concepts are linked to incommensurable theories. Rather I see concepts and categories as shaped by political goals and intentions. Contests over the meaning of concepts, it follows, are contests over desired political outcomes. On the grounds that one can argue for or against particular social visions, I accept with Connolly (1993: 227) that '[T]here is no contradiction in first affirming the essential contestability of a concept and then making the strongest case available for one of the positions within that range. That's politics.'

This book therefore sets out to discern how the understandings of affirmative action outlined above have assumed the status of common sense and to challenge them. I use the notion of category politics to this end.

By category politics I mean the deployment of categories for political purposes. The term 'deployment' is meant to capture two related processes: the imputing of meaning to concepts and analytical categories for political purposes; and the positioning of these categories for political effect. The intention here is to highlight the malleability of concepts and hence to shift the focus from their 'meaning', implying that there are set meanings, to contests over meaning, and the way politics figures in those contests. This shift, I suggest, has significant implications for feminist theory.

I am invoking a rather conventional notion of politics here as the play of power relations in the decision making which affects people's lives. And I am primarily concerned with traditional political venues, parliaments, public bureaucracies, union and business organizations, and the people who inhabit them, though I include social theorists as political actors, for reasons which will be explained below. As the term 'deployment' suggests, I am primarily interested in instrumental political activity.[1]

By focusing on the political uses of categories, I am accepting Tanesini's (1994) emphasis on the inferential-justificatory role of kinds of expressions. According to Tanesini, we need to become aware of the fact that concepts are not descriptive of anything, but that they are 'proposals about how we ought to proceed from here.' The purpose of concepts or categories is 'to influence the evolution of ongoing practices.' Hence, they can be defined to certain purposes and redefined to other purposes. As Tanesini says, paraphrasing Wittgenstein, 'to make a claim about the meaning of a certain word is to make a claim about how the word ought to be used, it is not to describe how the word is used.'

I draw a simple distinction between what I call 'conceptual categories' and 'identity categories'. Conceptual categories refer to terms or concepts which are based on ideas. Here I would include notions like 'equal opportunity' and 'merit'. Identity categories refer to terms associated with people's identities, for example 'women', 'Blacks', 'ethnic minorities', 'Australian', 'British'. Some might wonder why a concept like 'merit' should be deemed a 'category'. Here, I take my cue from George Lakoff (1987: xii) who wrote, '[M]ost of our words and concepts designate categories.' To call something a 'tree' or to say something has 'merit' is in both instances making a case that the things so labelled have characteristics in common and hence form a category. I am particularly interested in constructed binaries such as 'equal opportunity' and 'equal results', 'individualism' and 'collectivism', and 'public' and 'private' which are clearly intended to categorize approaches to social organization.

In a sense identity categories like 'women', 'Blacks' and so on are also conceptual categories, since they feature in theoretical analysis. Indeed, a good deal of this book is about the analytic uses of 'women' as a category. Identity categories, however, deserve to be separated off because of the part they play in constituting people's identities. Jan Pettman (1992a: 131) puts the point simply and clearly: '. . . that experience and identity, while not transparent, are not simply fictions; that who you are (seen to be) does matter.'[2]

In analytical discourse, concepts like 'women', 'men' and 'Blacks' are grounded in commonly assumed biological differentiations among people. Concepts like 'equal opportunity' and 'merit' are grounded in commonly assumed political belief systems. The point here is the need to pay more attention to the ways the terms are marshalled and the political purposes they serve than to any presumed ontological foundation.

This analysis builds upon developments in social construction theory. At its simplest, as Jackson and Penrose (1993: 21) explain, 'social construction theory is concerned with the ways in which we think about and use categories to structure our experience and analysis of the world.' While recognizing that 'human thought requires categories as fundamental communicative devices', this understanding challenges their 'taken-for-grantedness'. Martha Minow describes the way we have tended to 'treat the categories we use as dictated by the essence of things rather than established by our decision to focus on one trait rather than another':

> We conceive of our placement of an item in one category instead of another as obvious or self-evident instead of recognizing our decision to shape a category to access or reject a new item. We select the particular features to focus upon in building categories for the world, and then we attribute to the whole consequences related to those selected features. (Minow, 1990: 233)

The point is not that some categories are 'true' while others are 'false', or that some categories are more 'real' than others. The categories are 'real' to the extent that they operate as signifiers in the 'real world'. But they are also constructs, reflecting specific combinations of historical and political experience. Even the *tendency* to categorize shows a historical dimension. Sarah Hoagland (1988: 224; quoted in Eveline, 1994c: 455, fn. 3) draws attention to the fact that over the last centuries users of the English language 'focus more on categories and classifications which define a thing and fix its nature for all time, and are less concerned with processes, movement, and change.'

Authors working with this understanding have taken to putting quotation marks around the notion of 'race' to indicate its historical contingency (Donald and Rattansi, 1992; Jackson and Penrose, 1993). Vron Ware (1992: xii) states the new orthodoxy that 'race' is a 'socially constructed category with absolutely no basis in biology.'[3] Incorporating this insight, Donald and Rattansi (1992: 1) state that '[O]ur pragmatic starting point here is not whether "race" exists. Instead, we rephrase the question and ask how the category operates in practice'. My project is to apply this approach to 'women' and 'men'.

There has been a reluctance, however, to look at 'women' or 'men' in this way, reflecting the continuing strength of a biological imperative in attitudes on gender issues. It seems to me there is adequate evidence that the tendency to try to place all human beings into two categories, 'women' and 'men', has meant either ignoring those who do not fit or labelling them 'freaks'. This strong focus on 'women' and 'men' as some sort of natural couplet/couple has also contributed to the stigmatizing of those who are not heterosexual. I am not of course alone in this conclusion. Monique Wittig (1982), as Diana Fuss (1989: 41) points out, insists that 'men' and 'women' are political and not natural categories. Marjorie Garber (1992) talks about the 'constructedness of gender categories'. And many theorists have taken to using quotation marks around 'women', though the same seldom happens to 'men'. With Butler, I use this convention to 'denaturalize the terms, to designate these signs as sites of political debate' (Butler, 1992a: 19).[4]

It is quite a simple project to point to the large amount of effort which goes into the reinforcement of what appear to be biological givens. If indeed 'boys' were boys and 'girls' were girls, there would not be the amount of disquiet generated by attempts to challenge gender-specific hair styling (long hair for boys and short hair for girls), or attempts to challenge dress codes (Garber, 1992). A good deal of research illustrates the role of the law and other professions in reinforcing these gender[5] distinctions (Naffine, 1994).

Clearly, this reinforcement has effects. As Diana Fuss (1989: 91) says with regard to 'race', '[T]o say that "race" is a biological fiction is not to deny that it has real material effects in the world.' Gill Bottomley (1994: 67) notes, that 'gender, class and ethnicity are experienced as natural attributes.' And since the designation 'female' and 'male' is the first and strongest attribution of identity we are assigned, it is not surprising that we seldom question the material significance of the designation. Even Lakoff (1987: 99) accepts the uses of 'male' and 'female' as 'a standard contrast in categorization systems around the world.'

That this organization is based upon physiological characteristics is significant, but not as significant as the social and cultural interpretations applied to physiological differences. That is, if the identification of 'women' by their capacity to give birth was accompanied by a valuing of that capacity and its product, the results for women would be fortuitous rather than devastating. The fact that this is not the case, and the recognition that the physiological categorization of the species has uneven effects for women and men grounds a demand that women – those the category 'women' is deemed to represent – need greater representation in positions of influence to contest these effects.

Importantly, we do not all experience the effects of gender categorization in the same ways. How we live these effects is connected to other messages we receive about what it means to be a 'white woman' (or 'Black woman'), a 'heterosexual' (or 'homosexual'), and so on. As an example, Nitya Duclos (1993: 34) points out that '[T]here is a marked difference in treatment of white women and black women as sex symbols in mainstream American popular culture.' How we live these effects is also affected by our material circumstances and our cultural location. As Anne Marie Goetz (1988: 492) says, with respect to Third World women, their conditions may mean struggling 'for freedom from personal oppression within the family while at the same time engaging in a common project with men to protect the integrity of traditional economies.' Clearly the categories 'women' and 'men' are not the only, nor necessarily the most important, categories for many women and men.

In a variety of political circumstances, some identity categories have provided and are providing the grounds for political mobilization among outgroups. In some ways, these categories may appear to be limited conceptually, to the extent that their constructed status is ignored. They may in fact cause problems for individuals endeavouring to take up *an* identity. Black women, for example, may be pressed to support 'women' *or* 'Blacks' (see Chapter 3). Still, any intervention intended to draw attention to these limitations must remain sensitive to the political effects of this intervention. Recognizing that these identity categories play a part in constituting identities, a point raised earlier, means respecting the ways in which these groups choose to represent them. As Jan Pettman (1992b: 127) says, '[I]t is . . . necessary to contest the "naturalisation" of categories and boundaries, especially those imposed on subordinate groups, without denying the validity of identities based on shared experiences and common social location.'

Moreover, I would suggest that a greater awareness of the practices of category politics gives a certain legitimacy to identity categories like 'women' and 'Aborigines'. Helen Meekosha and Jan Pettman (1991; see also Pettman, 1992b: 126) express concern about the ways in which formerly oppressed groups come to have a vested interest in keeping the boundaries between groups firmly in place. While I agree that we need to realize that '[I]dentities as homogeneities block alliances across lines of race/ethnicity, gender/sexuality, class and generations' (Bottomley, 1994: 65), I argue that once we recognize that the demarcations between groups are *products of a particular constellation of power relations*, it becomes possible to play with, through and around them. This point will be made clearer when we discuss the meanings of 'women' later in this chapter.

Moving to a consideration of *conceptual* categories, I wish to emphasize the lack of content of political concepts and to draw attention to the ways they are used to shape and constrain understandings of social 'problems'. I would therefore stress how concepts are created and used for political purposes rather than suggesting that they depend upon ontological disagreements. Stephen Mulhall (1987) clarifies the argument:

> The liberal does not advocate a certain societal structure because he has a certain concept of the person: rather, one way of emphatically illustrating or expressing his view about the way society ought to be organized in the interests of its members is to advocate a certain way of viewing the nature of those members.

A good deal of my thinking on this matter was stimulated by Murray Edelman (1988). I certainly agree with Edelman (1988: 11) that the 'denotations of key political terms' in specific situations are 'strategies, deliberate or unrecognized for strengthening or undermining support for specific courses of action', though I would query his contention that these terms are also marshalled to support 'particular ideologies'. Rather I would suggest that 'ideologies' themselves prove useful in defending particular courses of action. This will become clearer when we see how appeals to 'equal opportunity' have functioned to delegitimize affirmative action in the United States (Chapter 3), and how 'social democracy' has been invoked in ways which place limits on the political space available for claims on behalf of 'women' in Sweden (Chapter 6).

This kind of analysis does not rule out the importance of studying ideology but it adds a dimension to that study; it suggests that we should not take ideology all that seriously when politics is involved. I am trying here to inject a counterbalance into the overreliance on ideology as explanation. While my particular target here is ideological 'isms', such as liberalism or socialism, I mean to capture any use of the term 'ideology' which implies coherence in beliefs or belief systems.

This does not mean that ideologies have no effects. In fact, people and societies are constituted to some extent by beliefs they hold about themselves. Barry Hindess (1990: 120) makes a related point about the effects of 'ideas concerning the workings of particular institutions', such as ideas about 'the rational actor' or the 'welfare state'. As Hindess says, '[T]hese words may not be descriptively accurate but they play an important part in the way these societies operate.' This insight draws attention to the role of political theorists in channelling political debate. While Stanley Fish (1989: 14) disputes that theory can have consequences, he admits that 'theory talk' can 'do work' and in 'doing work' can have 'consequences of a nontheoretical (and therefore real) kind.' David Held (1991: 15) makes the same point in a more positive way when he argues that the 'interpretive framework we employ determines what we apprehend, what we notice and what we register as important.' Kristie McClure (1992: 365) usefully suggests that we start thinking about theory as a verb rather than as a noun, so that 'theorizing' is seen as 'a contingent and located social practice without the security of foundations, as well as a political practice always and inescapably implicated with power.'

Political theory constructs the categories through which we are meant to understand power struggles in society (see Cockburn, 1991). And, as Steven Lukes (1991) says, in the hands of many political theorists, it tends to reduce complexity and ambiguity. Whereas the social psychologists, Michael Billig et al. (1988: 147, 163), point out that ideologies are not internally consistent and hence people must 'impose an assessment of conflicting values', much political theory presents us with limited, often dichotomized options – a 'small set of stock texts', to borrow Edelman's phrase (1988: 112). The fact that to date most political theorists have been men has meant that many of these options sit uneasily with many women's understandings of their lives. The implications of this point for feminist theory is a major theme in this text.

Avtar Brah (1992: 138) suggests that there is a need to 'focus on a given context and differentiate between the demarcation of a category as an object of social discourse, as an analytical category, and as a subject of political mobilisation without making assumptions about their permanence or stability across time and space.' While I agree that it is certainly useful to pay attention to the different kinds of role categories play and their instability, in a sense I wish to blur the distinctions Brah draws in order to highlight the political character of categories in all these roles. Like Brah, Pettman (1992a) wishes to distinguish between the analytical and the political uses of categories, a distinction which I feel downplays the politics of interpretation. The case I make throughout is that theoretical analysis and hence the construction of analytical categories is indeed a highly political process.

While all this may sound like manipulation, we need to recognize that this is simply what political debate is about. This means that participation in category politics is unavoidable. Every person who wishes to engage in politics, defined traditionally, will need to invoke categories. Hence they would do well to develop a sharpened awareness of the practices of category politics. A major argument in this book is that an awareness of category politics opens up new kinds of strategies for change.

Others, sensitive to the constructed nature and malleability of concepts, have warned against setting one's argument in the established terms of political discourse, and have invested some hope in conceptual revision.[6] While I endorse the first warning, I am more sceptical about the recommended response. As will be seen throughout this volume, concepts – new and old – are susceptible to uses not intended by their initiators. Hence I prefer to emphasize the need *to keep a careful watch on and to expose the practices of category politics.*

These practices can involve the encouragement of the proliferation of categories or can mean a strategy of smoothing over categorical distinctions, or the two can be worked together. Bills of Rights illustrate how this works for identity categories. On the one hand they allow space for the articulation of the 'interests' of particular groups; on the other hand they are often introduced as symbols of national integration. Cynthia Williams (1986) discusses this blending of purposes in the promotion of a Canadian Charter of Rights.

Any of these approaches – promoting identity categories, denying identity categories, or attempting to do both at the same time – can have regressive or, conversely, progressive effects. We shall see in several chapters (Chapters 3, 4, 7) how the listing of separate identity categories as affirmative action targets can limit change in some ways. We shall also see, however, that suggestions to replace the emphasis on groups with a focus on 'individual enablement' ignore group-based power relations. This insight is important for those who prefer to draw attention to problems only with the first of these approaches. It leads to the conclusion drawn by Patricia Williams (1991: 102): '[we need] to acknowledge the utility of such categories for certain purposes and the necessity of their breakdown on other occasions.'

Chapters 2 and 3 illustrate politics at work in the shaping of conceptual categories central to the affirmative action debate. An umbrella concept 'equality' is bifurcated into oppositional halves 'equal opportunity' and 'equal results', with affirmative action subsumed beneath the latter. The category 'equal opportunity' is then declared coterminous with something called American 'political culture'. Affirmative action is cast as foreign. Trying to save it from this negative characterization, its defenders alter its content to make it compatible with 'equal opportunity'.

The playing out of these dramas can be understood only in context. With Paul Bagguley et al. (1990: 183, 210), I wish to stress 'the complexity of interactions between various factors within the political environment' and hence the extent to which 'place matters'. That is, historically and politically specific configurations will mean that appeals are made to different conceptual and identity categories at times and there will be different inflections in responses to these categories. As an example, the notion of solidarity which accompanies Sweden's social democratic background has no near cousins in the United States. Appeals to this notion, as we shall see in Chapter 6, have particular effects on the ways in which affirmative action is translated into policy. They also have important effects on the positioning of 'women' in the reform.

The focus on context is crucial in any attempt to develop strategies for change. Several authors have made the point that 'discourses should be evaluated not in the abstract but always in a social context' (Pringle and Watson, 1992: 68; Weedon, 1987). Applying this approach to the study of affirmative action means examining the debates around the reform with a focus on the conceptual categories and identity categories invoked both by opponents and supporters. The task is to see how, and with what effects, these categories are positioned in specific contexts –

here the United States, Canada, Australia, Sweden, the Netherlands and Norway.

In this project it is useful to follow two trajectories and mark their intersections. The first involves understandings of affirmative action generally – How is it described in political discourse? What kinds of arguments are made for and against it? The second looks specifically at how 'women' is treated as a claimant group. Chapter 2 tracks the first trajectory. Here we will proceed along the second. The chapters that follow mark the intersections.

There is much debate within the feminist community about the status of the category 'women' and whether efforts to defend reforms targeting this category are in fact misguided, because they assume a degree of commonality among women which does not match experience. There is an increased feminist sensitivity to the constructed nature of the category 'woman' and the way in which it commonly subsumes racial, ethnic, class, sexual identity and 'ability' differences. As Ngaire Naffine (1994: 11, fn. 10) puts it: '[T]he problem with the idea that "woman" is a coherent and unified category is that such insistence denies and suppresses "the multiplicity of cultural, social and political intersections in which the concrete array of 'women' are constructed"'.[7] As Denise Riley (1988: 111, 66) says, the problem is larger than 'there being different sorts of women on this earth'; the conundrum is the 'designation' 'women', and the historical and cultural baggage attached to it. Because the word 'women' is 'imbued in all political languages with domesticity in a broad sense', this means that the term could seem a 'dubious rallying-point' for progressive use. Riley (1987) also shows that, because the construction 'woman' has a concrete impact on women's lives, it is also impossible to speak about 'women' as some sort of ahistorical collectivity.

To some this sensitivity has created a feminist conundrum, undermining feminism's *raison d'être*. Naomi Schor (1994: xiii) puts the question thus: 'do politics precede alliance . . . or does commonality ground politics?' Or, put another way, 'can there be a feminist politics that dispenses with the notion of Woman?' Hence, there has emerged an almost insurmoutable rift between some feminist policy makers and some feminist theorists, with the former group campaigning for 'women' and the latter disputing the legitimacy of the project. Riley (1988: 98) notes the policy dilemma created by the debate – what to do about 'legislation for equal rights and educational chances, which must name the social grouping that they help?' Affirmative action provides an ideal opening for considering this problem, since 'women' is a frequent affirmative action target.

Understanding the practices of category politics provides a different way to approach debates about meanings of 'women'. There are four major points introduced here which will be developed throughout the text. First, it is important to note that 'women' already operates as a key political signifier. Hence, feminists have little option but to engage in contests over its signification.

More disturbing perhaps is the second discovery – that, when the category 'women' appears to gain recognition, this is often part of a political manoeuvre to limit political change for women. This is not a new insight. In 1934 Winifred Holtby (quoted in Riley, 1988: 63) heralded the warning: '[T]oday, whenever women hear political leaders call their sex important, they grow suspicious.'

The major finding in this study is that, despite commitments to 'women' in the form of affirmative action policies, women rate little political attention. The evidence in the six countries studied is that indeed assumptions about 'women' vary across national boundaries, and the variations reflect the historical and political constitution and positioning of a variety of interest groups. However, the evidence also shows a disturbing commonality – that 'women' as a political category is accorded little importance. I am reminded here of Pringle and Watson's (1992: 68, 57) conclusion that 'women have in common a discursive marginality'. Hence, they continue, '[W]hat feminists are confronted with is not a state that represents "men's interests" as against women's, but government conducted as if men's interests are the only ones that exist.'

Third, representations of 'women' and of 'men' can serve to narrow a political agenda and limit change more generally. In previous work (Bacchi, 1990) I focused on how representations of 'women' as 'different from' or 'the same as' 'men' operate to divert attention from certain social problems, such as the need to rethink the way certain Western societies handle child and elder care. In this volume we see how 'buying into' existing identity categories such as 'women' can leave some problems unaddressed – for example, the needs of multiply-oppressed women. However, insisting upon the recognition of sub-categories of 'women' is not always an answer to this dilemma, since these categories are similarly homogeneous and can similarly be invoked to protect rather than challenge the status quo. In Canada (see Chapter 4), for example, Vickers, Rankin and Appelle (1993: 165) describe the efforts of the Conservative Mulroney Government to divide women by 'courting' groups representing visible minority and rural women. The approach suggested in this volume is to pay close attention to the politics behind the mobilization and deployment of identity categories in specific cases.

The fourth insight is the most important. This is that feminists have been impelled to assign a meaning to 'women' because women have been asked to provide grounds to defend an increase in representation in positions of influence. Groups of women who have tried to broaden the political space available for 'women' have had to choose whether to try to use 'women's' traditional status as carers and nurturers – Naffine

(1994: 12) refers to an archetype of 'woman' – to achieve other kinds of influence, or to find other bases for the claim that 'women' constitute a category deserving political attention. Often they appeal to what I call 'anomalous analogies', drawing comparisons between 'women's' situation and understandings of the situations of other kinds of categories, such as classes, castes, races, geographical areas, and so on.

These efforts have had mixed results and these results have a great deal to do with context. In the United States, as we shall see in Chapter 3, the archetypical 'woman' is posited in such a way as to maintain the status quo. In Sweden and Norway (see Chapters 6 and 8) appeals to this model have led to certain political gains. Feminists need to recognize that their interventions are strategic, to be sensitive to context in selecting strategies, and to be willing to change course when a given strategy ceases to work or backfires. The close study of successful and failed interventions in the following chapters will provide some pointers to the factors which need to be watched. One lesson here, as with the discussion earlier of the possibilities of conceptual revision, is that a discursive opening can also be a discursive trap.

This kind of analysis allows feminists to see that their internal debates about the ontological status of 'women' are produced by a political dynamic which locates 'women' as 'other'. The finding here is similar to that in *Same Difference* (Bacchi, 1990) – feminist debates to an extent are generated by the power arrangements we wish to challenge. Showing this means that we can shift the focus of our analysis from talking about who 'women' are or are not, to the practices which have made this question *appear* to be one we needed to answer.

The point to remember here is that appeals to the category 'women' have been necessary because women (and other outgroups) are located outside positions of power and influence. Hence, appeals to 'women' (and 'Aborigines' and so on) are practical and strategic, not ontological. There are no similar debates about the ontological status and content of 'men' because men have seldom been asked to justify their privilege. In a sense, we need to say that it is unnecessary for women to justify demands on behalf of 'women' since the practices of category politics which locate us as 'other', as 'outsider', are what have made this justification seem necessary.

This is not to suggest that feminists should refuse the meanings assigned to 'women'; we have just seen how invoking these meanings may be necessary strategically. However, we should refuse the 'felt need' to give the category meaning and recognize the source of this 'felt need'. My point, therefore, is not that essentialist appeals may be necessary or strategic (compare de Lauretis, 1989), but that appeals which *appear* essentialist seem so because those in power demand that women give themselves definition. It is the power of the insiders – who remain invisible – to define 'women' and to demand that women define themselves which needs to be challenged.

Numerous feminist authors, from the time of de Beauvoir (1952; see also Black and Coward, 1981; Eveline, 1994c: 22 ff.; Jay, 1981), have noted that 'man' remains the 'unremarked standard' in discussions about the 'woman problem/question',[8] that political discourse allows men to represent themselves as 'people', 'humanity', 'mankind'. Daphne Patai (1983) spells out the problem: 'men's gender is simply not attended to, it obeys a rule of irrelevance.' This has meant that women are eternally on the defensive, eternally the ones to be explained and justified. According to Murray Edelman (1988), the way in which a social 'problem' is conceived and/or represented limits the range of possible responses. He goes further to suggest that this sequence is not coincidental but serves the purposes of those who wish to moderate change to protect their status and power. Making 'women' the 'problem' has had the effect of diverting attention from the processes which are problematic and from those defining the nature of the 'problem'. Eveline (1994c) makes the important point that this strategy is so successful that feminists also avoid an analysis of, or refrain from talking about, men's advantage.

One response here is the kinds of reversal both Patai (1983) and Eveline (1994c) recommend. Patai suggests making 'men' visible; Eveline emphasizes drawing attention to the advantages men reap from the social status quo. Drawing attention to 'men' and to 'men's advantage' positions 'women' and 'women's disadvantage' differently. It alters women's status as supplicants and damages the attempt by some men to portray themselves as benefactors. Importantly, it also allows us to see that some men have imposed upon women the preoccupation with just who 'women' are.

While engaging in these strategic reversals, it is important to avoid 'making' 'men' a homogeneous category. Such a move would ignore important differentiations among men. It would also imply an overly simple explanation, a kind of patriarchal conspiracy, for women's inequality. That some men have a stake in denying some women access to power is clear. But the reasons for doing so are complex. The examples in this study reveal that it is often because some men have constructed political investments in other identity categories, especially class and the organizations representing class, for example employer organizations or unions. The fact that some *women* have political investments in identity categories other than 'women' also figures largely in category politics.[9]

Suggestions that constituting 'men' a category will alter power relations ignore the fact that 'men', like all other categories, can be deployed in ways which limit change. The recent campaign to label affirmative action discrimination against 'men' is only the most obvious of these. We return therefore to the central thesis – the importance of drawing attention to the political uses of categories and working to produce understandings of categories which have effects we deem desirable. Patricia Williams (1991: 102) makes the important point that 'Categorizing is not the sin; the problem is the lack of desire to examine the categorizations that are made.' To this I would add '. . . and the uses these categorizations serve.'

Feminists should not be seeking a single meaning of 'women'; nor should we engage in endless internal disputation about the legitimacy of invoking a collective notion 'women'. Rather we need to keep looking at how various meanings of 'women' have been and are being produced, and for which political ends. The message is that feminists must continue to insist upon the political relevance of 'women' but contest interpretations and deployments of the category which minimize progressive developments for women and other outgroups. The category 'women' will not go away. Hence we are obliged to monitor the effects which accompany its invocation.

By drawing attention to the political effects of different deployments of 'women', we can bring other items onto the agenda. With Meekosha and Pettman (1991), we can draw attention to the ways in which identity categories are themselves formed by their boundaries, by what they exclude. We can also show how talk about 'women' can leave some women's needs unaddressed. This can produce a more reflexive, responsive and progressive agenda. With Tanesini (1994: 213) I believe that it is 'important that feminists contribute to the construction of new uses for the concept "woman", instead of abandoning the concept altogether.'

What follows is the importance of having more women in politics and in positions of influence to engage in examining the uses of 'women' and other categories. Those whom the category is deemed to represent need to be present in numbers to debate its uses. This is the argument I advance for affirmative action.

Notes

1 I would like to thank Doug McEachern for suggesting this way to describe my project.

2 Jan Pettman (1992a, 1992b; see also Meekosha and Pettman, 1991) has used the term 'category politics' in ways which capture part of what I intend by the term, though her primary interest is the play of politics around identity categories like 'Aborigines' and 'women'. She also talks about the state 'responding' to 'mobilised political identities', adapting and reworking them 'as needs and administrative categories'. This book, by contrast, stresses an interactive relationship between those who inhabit state structures and those active in social groups, with the former at times facilitating and hence contributing to the mobilization of identity categories. I use the somewhat awkward phrase, 'those who inhabit state structures', to indicate that it is overly simple to personify the state as actor.

3 This is a different issue about biology from the issue that could arise in native title claims which relate to a community's biological descendence from traditional owners. I would like to thank Carol Johnson for this point.

4 Since in this study I wish to highlight the effects of invoking a category 'women', I will reserve quotation marks for this purpose. Generally then when I talk about the numbers of women in the labour force or the numbers of women on welfare, and the like, I

will not problematize the category, though I will insert qualifiers such as 'some' or 'many' when these will help clarify which representatives of the category are being considered. As it will become exceedingly tedious to have quotation marks around every social category to signal their constructed nature, I ask readers to insert them mentally.

5 It has become increasingly difficult to use the terms 'sex' and 'gender' to designate anything in particular given the theoretical implications of separating the concepts. That is, it is clear that every aspect of what is acknowledged or described as sexual identity is influenced by social norms. More than this, our whole way of knowing sexual identity is affected by those norms. So there is no way of speaking of sex outside of gender. Hence the term gender will be used throughout, except when it is necessary to explain this theoretical point.

6 Here it is important to quote Connolly (1993: 203), to do justice to his argument: '[C]onceptual revision is not, then, a sufficient condition of political change, but it is indispensable to significant political change.'

7 The words quoted by Naffine are from Butler, 1990: 22.

8 The 'woman question' was a common epithet in nineteenth-century Anglo-Saxon countries, used to describe the increasing disquiet of some women and some women's groups (see Bacchi, 1986).

9 By suggesting that people's actions are affected by their connections to particular identity categories (including those of class, job description, and so on), I am not suggesting that these connections determine their actions. I am saying that they are one factor influencing those actions. Jenny Ozga (1987: 146) notes the need to pay attention to the 'reality where individual personality and personal relations were vital in affecting policy outcomes', and warns against treating people solely as 'occupants of roles which largely determine their behaviour.'

2

Setting the Stage

This chapter offers necessary background information – What is affirmative action? What reforms does it encompass? Where does it come from? Its purpose is broader than this, however. It foreshadows themes taken up in subsequent chapters and provides a backdrop to them. Specifically, it introduces some of the central theoretical debates about affirmative action. It also shows where 'women' is located within those debates. The direction of the central argument of the book – that it is essential to expose the implications of the ways conceptual and identity categories construct affirmative action and 'women' in order to develop strategies for change – is established.

What's in a name?

Affirmative action, a term which originated in the United States, refers to a range of programmes directed towards targeted groups to redress their inequality. Broadly it takes two forms: policies to alter the composition of the labour force, and/or policies to increase the representativeness of public committees, political parties, and educational institutions.[1]

Arguments about affirmative action differ slightly, depending upon whether the reform is addressed to the labour market or to political and educational institutions. For the latter the claim is often made that these institutions ought to reflect, to an extent, the composition of the population. There are those who would protest that 'objective' representatives are preferable to 'interest group' representatives, and that education, at the tertiary level at least, ought to be available only to those with 'talent'. Still, there is an opening here for claims less readily available in the labour market sector debate where, it is argued, jobs should go to those with 'merit'.

Public bureaucracies are somewhat anomalous since they offer jobs and yet can be expected to be representative of the population to an extent.[2] This explains in part why governments generally have been more willing to centre reform efforts on their own bureaucracies. The other reason, of course, is that 'interference' with 'free market forces' is always more controversial.

This study is primarily concerned with labour market affirmative action for both the public and private sectors, though in the case of

Norway the success some women have had with quotas in political parties will be examined in some detail. Here I am more interested in what unites these disputes rather than in what distinguishes them. In both cases, outgroups are asked to justify their inclusion. This, I suggest, puts an onus of proof on them which impels certain kinds of arguments – arguments about the commonalities of members of their group. It is positioning outside power which in effect compels outgroups to *appear* essentialist.

The stated goals of most labour market affirmative action programmes are to encourage 'women' into nontraditional jobs, that is, jobs traditionally performed by men, and to increase their access to positions of higher pay and higher status. The means to these ends can include training courses, review of personnel procedures to remove obvious and/or indirectly discriminatory practices, the setting of goals to increase the representation of targeted groups and, most controversially, targeted hiring, promoting or appointing, sometimes with quotas applied. Commonly, though this labelling is itself contentious, these proposals are categorized as 'soft' or 'hard' options. 'Soft' reforms include attempts to remove structural impediments which affect particular groups, and strategies, such as training schemes, to assist 'disadvantaged' groups to compete more effectively. 'Hard' or 'strong' options would include reforms which make membership of a designated group one or the only criterion for access to jobs and positions of influence.

As mentioned, the term 'affirmative action' originated in the United States and, due largely to the experience there and the controversy surrounding the reform, policy activists and administrators elsewhere often felt it wise to distance themselves from the American terminology. This is clearest in Canada where Judge Rosalie Abella, who headed the Royal Commission into Equality in Employment (1984), stated explicitly that she was avoiding the phrase 'affirmative action' because of the negative connotations associated with it in the United States. The phrase she chose to describe Canada's reform approach and which remains in use is 'employment equity'.

It is equally clear that in Australia there was concern about distancing the affirmative action proposal from the American initiative. Here it was felt adequate to add to the 1986 Affirmative Action Act a parenthetical qualification, Equal Employment Opportunity for Women. In Sweden, Norway and the Netherlands currently the phrase 'positive action' is most commonly used, as it is throughout Europe (Serdjenian, 1994), though it is important to note that in the Netherlands the term 'affirmative action' was adopted in the 1970s.

In the countries in this sample, it is generally accepted that there are two domains where labour market affirmative action is needed, in the public sector and in the private sector. Policies differ for the two domains, with governments generally being willing to impose stricter obligations on the public sector.[3] There are differences in the degree of supervision of these policies. As we shall see, the recent trend towards decentralization has meant that more authority is being devolved from the centre to the branches of government.

Approaches to the private sector vary to an extent, but the general trend is voluntarist. The 'great debate' about affirmative action in all the countries studied has been about whether legislation *of any kind* is justified in this area. In the early stages of the debate, in the United States, Canada and Australia, employers were vociferous in their opposition, claiming unnecessary interference in market forces. In Sweden, Norway and the Netherlands, the case was put that the government ought not to intervene in collective agreements between employers and unions.

In the United States, Canada and Australia reporting mechanisms have emerged. These have been criticized for being difficult to enforce and impossible to monitor. There has also been an overreliance on the reporting of statistics. Sanctions vary by country, with the most stringent being the withholding of government contracts from companies which refuse to comply with a government directive to analyse workforce figures and set targets.

In Sweden and Norway, attempts to encourage the introduction of positive action have been contained by provisions which exempt collective agreements from scrutiny by outside bodies.[4] The Netherlands has felt it adequate to offer government grants to employers as an incentive towards reform.

Of the countries studied here, Australia, Canada and Sweden have legislation calling for the introduction of affirmative action. In the United States, affirmative action policies have emerged by way of Executive Orders. In the Netherlands and Norway the chief focus is on increasing women's representation in political processes and in the public bureaucracy. Specific legislation has been unnecessary to promote these goals.

From antidiscrimination to affirmative action

Labour market affirmative action[5] needs to be understood as a response to identified inadequacies in antidiscrimination legislation. These are generally claimed to be the reactive nature of antidiscrimination policies and the reliance on individual complaint. Affirmative action, by contrast, is described as proactive intervention to create a nondiscriminatory environment. This means, however, that affirmative action is situated within an antidiscrimination discourse, and suffers from all the limitations of that discourse.

Antidiscrimination legislation is similar in form in all the countries studied. There are either specific Acts condemning kinds of discrimination, most often racial or sexual discrimination, or omnibus pieces of legislation with closed or open-ended lists of the kinds of discrimination disallowed. Initially antidiscrimination laws focused upon behaviours resulting from malice or evil motive. This is commonly called direct or 'facial' discrimination and occurs, for example, when an employer adopts a policy which 'treats certain classes of workers differently from other classes of workers on the grounds of race, religion, national origin, or gender' (Wendy Williams, 1981). Other commonly enumerated grounds, depending on country or jurisdiction, include sexual preference, Aboriginality, marital status and disability.

The foundational assumption here is that society's rules are generally functioning fairly, but that a particular attitude produces an unfair behaviour called 'discrimination' which requires 'intervention'. Donald Black (1989) challenges this notion that law is primarily an affair of rules and that discrimination is an aberration. He shows that many factors – such as the social elevation of each party, the social distance between them, whether they are individual or corporate beings – influence who will win and what the punishment will be. If discrimination is not an aberration, treating it as such necessarily hides the way in which 'social differentials pervade law.'

'Intervention' is kept to a minimum by waiting upon an individual complainant to use the court processes to draw attention to the discrimination. Margaret Thornton (1994: 219) outlines the limitations of complaint-based mechanisms. In her view they 'represent no more than a halting and ephemeral step in the direction of EEO [Equal Employment Opportunity]' since the lodgement of a complaint 'requires both perspicacity and fortitude [and leaves complainants] always vulnerable in the face of corporate power.'

The scope of 'intervention' is further minimized through both an explicit and an implicit invocation of notions of the 'public' and the 'private'. Margaret Thornton (1991: 453) describes the operation of the 'public'/'private' dichotomy in antidiscrimination law at length, concluding that in some respects 'the legislation is almost schizophrenic in endeavoring to decide where the line of demarcation between public and private should run.' Private schools and single-sex clubs are considered outside the ambit of the legislation due to their 'private' character. More subtly, the 'actual mode of dispute resolution' encourages the settling of disputes 'within the privatized setting of conciliation, preferably without lawyers.' Such 'privatized procedures' are potentially dangerous since the fact that 'the process cannot be scrutinized renders it immune from public accountability.' Most noticeably, the family and the work performed in the family, mainly by women, are considered outside the ambit of the legislation (Thornton, 1991).

There are subsidiary effects to the thinking which informs legal responses to direct discrimination. As Julian Henriques et al. (1984) have explained, the idea of prejudice which underlies the legislation reduces racism and sexism to individual aberration and suppresses recognition of the institutional and structural dimensions of discrimination. The argument runs that individuals should not be judged by unsubstantiated generalizations, but by their personal abilities. The model is an individualistic one. It also seems to suggest that, since discrimination is due to a mistaken belief that people are 'different', 'differences' do not exist, making it difficult to address the 'differences' which result from social and economic causes, and biological and cultural 'differences'. The model is assimilationist. The goal becomes some notion of equal treatment which ignores 'difference'.

There is often a shift in focus from the perpetrators to the 'objects' of prejudice, producing a preoccupation with just what it is about 'these people' which causes others to perceive them as 'different'. The model therefore casts the victims of discrimination as the problem. They are labelled 'disadvantaged', which becomes almost an explanation of their social location. As Didi Herman (1994: 45) explains, antidiscrimination law constructs a 'classification of identities', categories of person who are, in some way, 'lesser than' the unstated norm. It is not surprising then that antidiscrimination laws contribute 'to a low sense of self-worth in victims of discrimination and to the public impression of them as inferior' (Edelman, 1988: 26; Bumiller, 1988).

Some authors draw attention to a fundamental ambiguity in antidiscrimination discourse. Kimberle Crenshaw (1988) for one feels that it can accommodate conservative as well as liberal views of race and equality. In her view, it is not clear if the goal of the American Civil Rights Act is a 'mere rejection of white supremacy as a normative vision' or if the goal may be expanded to include 'a societal commitment to the eradication of the substantive conditions of Black subordination.' This tension between what Crenshaw calls a 'restrictive' and an 'expansive' view is clearer when one looks at the way in which affirmative action is 'allowed', but only through an exemption from the antidiscrimination provision, about which more will be said later.

The discursive and ideological openings identified by Crenshaw and others (Howe, 1991; McCrudden, Smith and Brown 1991; Taylor, 1991) create a space for making particular kinds of political claims. The notion of indirect discrimination made its way onto the political agenda through these openings. The idea of indirect discrimination is one important outgrowth of experience with the inadequacy of the direct discrimination model.[6] Indirect discrimination can be claimed if it can be shown that an apparently neutral rule, such as a height or weight requirement not necessary for job performance, has a disproportionate adverse impact on one of the groups enumerated in antidiscrimination legislation. This adverse impact can, at least theoretically, be demonstrated statistically (Wilenski 1977, 180).[7]

As Chris Ronalds describes, using the example of Australia's Sex Discrimination Act, the definition of indirect discrimination 'considerably widens the impact of the legislation by recognising that discrimination occurs beyond an individual's behaviour or actions.'[8] Hence, it purportedly recognizes that '[D]iscriminatory decisions are often based on policies and practices which form the structures and patterns of an organisation in particular, and society as a whole' (Ronalds, 1987: 99).

This recognition of what has been called 'structural' or 'systemic' discrimination opens the door to examining a wide range of work practices. It also provides opportunities to raise questions about the impact of deeply entrenched institutional practices upon individuals and groups of individuals.

It is important to recognize, however, that the notion of structural discrimination can be taken in a number of directions. As Connolly (1993: 198–203) correctly points out, it can become a way of confronting the managerial elite with responsibility for altering dated administrative and personnel policies. However, the lack of a need to identify a perpetrator creates problems. By making everything structural, it in fact becomes difficult to find someone to hold responsible for the discrimination (see Thornton, 1994). The power relations which install and maintain inequitable organizational systems become difficult to discern. It is also but a short step from 'structural discrimination' to the suggestion that organizations are best placed to 'sort out' this kind of problem themselves. The argument here is that, since the practices at issue are parts of an organization's systems of operation, good personnel practices are all that is required to 'update' administrative procedures. Regulation is described as unnecessary and intrusive.

This ambiguity about how best to address structural discrimination lies behind much of the debate about affirmative action. Notionally, affirmative action was introduced because of identified limitations in complaint-based approaches to structural discrimination. The argument was put that companies and large public organizations needed to confront *proactively* the systemic barriers in their rules and practices which effectively barred 'women' and other groups from access and promotion. However, the degree to which companies ought to be held *accountable* for change remains hotly contested.

From affirmative action to 'reverse discrimination'

In all the countries studied here, there has been concern about the relationship between affirmative action and antidiscrimination policies. Because antidiscrimination legislation is couched in race- and sex-neutral language, it has been possible to argue that legislation like affirmative action which targets 'women' or 'Blacks' is a kind of discrimination, albeit 'reverse discrimination'. Because of this concern, the United States, Canada, Australia and Norway have included exemptions in their anti-discrimination legislation to 'allow' affirmative action for designated groups. Section 33 of Australia's *Sex Discrimination Act* (1984), for example, stipulates that 'Nothing in Division 1 or 2 [the antidiscrimination clause] renders it unlawful to do an act a purpose of which is to ensure that persons of a particular sex . . . have equal opportunities with other persons in circumstances in relation to which provision is made by this Act' (cited in Leon, 1993: 92–3). Similarly, in European law, which currently affects the Netherlands and Sweden, an exemption 'permits' Member States to adopt 'measures to promote equal opportunity for men and women, in particular by removing existing inequalities which affect women's opportunities' (Docksey, 1987: 17). Notably Sweden's 1980 Equality Act (see Dahlberg, 1982) created a separate directive for positive action, not tying it to antidiscrimination in the ways other countries have done. However, as we shall see in Chapter 6, this has had minimal impact on the effectiveness of the legislation.

Antidiscrimination laws generally have a number of exemptions. Most, for example Australia's Federal *Sex Discrimination Act* (1984; see Ronalds, 1987), exempt what is referred to as 'special treatment' for pregnancy. Zillah Eisenstein (1988) notes that such an exemption reveals the implicit male norm structuring the legislation. Similarly, the way in which affirmative action is 'allowed' in antidiscrimination legislation highlights the conceptual limitations surrounding it.

Christopher Docksey (1987) identifies two approaches: actions falling within the principle of equality and those falling outside. The former, he argues, would include policies which either advise or compel employers to take measures to 'encourage' women to come forward or which remove 'obviously discriminatory' hiring policies. The latter would go further, says Docksey, to 'permit derogation from the principle of equal treatment by way of so-called reverse or positive discrimination.' This could mean 'single-sex recruitment' or quotas. According to Docksey (1987: 17), 'action falling within the principle of equality is normally to be preferred and should be used as far as possible.'

We should recognize here the distinction drawn earlier between 'soft' and 'hard' affirmative action, and the implied condemnation of the latter. A recent ruling by the European Court of Justice condemning a Bremen law which required city agencies to hire female candidates over male candidates with the same qualifications for posts where women were underrepresented indicates that the narrow definition of 'equality' is being upheld. The Court ruled that the Bremen law constituted sex discrimination (Case C-450/93; 17 October, 1995; Reuters).

Here, we have entered a legal and conceptual minefield. In this 'equality' discourse, by definition, strong measures to redress 'women's' (or other targeted groups') inequality are placed on the defensive. They are seen as in themselves discriminatory, since they treat one sex differently from the other, and hence are considered exceptional. The labelling of such measures as 'positive discrimination' or 'reverse discrimination' ensures that they will be seen this way.

The relationship between equal treatment/equal opportunity and affirmative action is thus central to the affirmative action controversy.

Most often, a comparison is drawn between 'equal opportunity' and 'equal results', with the implication that affirmative action has the latter as its goal. This dichotomy is then used to delegitimize 'strong' affirmative action, including targeted hiring/promoting. The favoured target of opponents is quotas.

Elsewhere (Bacchi, 1990; 1992b) I have written about the problems with this understanding. Among other things, I point out that such an approach is based on the view that all that people require to succeed is the opportunity to do so. The removal of obvious impediments, such as discrimination, is considered adequate to this task. A focus on expanding opportunities in this way in effect disaggregates social categories into competing individuals. The impression is left that we are dealing with barriers to individual achievement rather than unequal power relations between and among groups.

Those who need 'more' are automatically labelled as 'wanting' in some way. The targets become the 'problem', because of their presumed lack of expertise or initiative. Attempts to alter their status become 'handouts', to be severely restricted given their 'exceptional' nature and their 'contravention' of a basic equal treatment rule. Given this starting point, it is not surprising that the 'dominant ordinary-language view' often identifies recipients as receiving 'assistance' beyond genuine 'need', and therefore paradoxically as 'advantaged' (Radin, 1991). All these terms imply that otherwise 'undeserving' recipients are being 'privileged'. There is no way within these terms to question the standards which were applied to those currently holding positions of power and authority, or which continue to be used in hiring and promotion. Nor is there any way to address the relationship between domestic responsibilities and 'value' as an employee.

Positioning affirmative action as an exemption to discrimination has placed severe limitations on the ways in which it can be used and has left even modest attempts to implement change open to challenge. For example, in 1992, women's health services in Australia (see Chapter 5) came under attack as discrimination against 'men'. The current campaign against so-called 'reverse discrimination' in the United States is simply the clearest illustration of the way in which current conceptualizations of affirmative action lead in a sense to its destruction.

To the charge that 'equal results' mean 'quotas', and 'quotas' mean hiring people regardless of their 'qualifications', some feminists have replied that only 'qualified' women would be hired. Others, however, have gone further and suggested the need to question the standards by which people are assessed (Game, 1984). In a pamphlet published early in the life of the Affirmative Action Agency, set up by the Australian government to monitor compliance with the Affirmative Action Act, Clare Burton, for example, called for a 'redefinition' of 'merit' (Burton, 1988). At one level drawing attention to the meaning of 'merit' means ensuring only that unfair stereotypes are not imported into supposedly objective assessment. To those who wish to promote more dramatic change in social structures, this acquiescence to traditional standards of assessment tars affirmative action as assimilationist. However, problematizing the meaning of merit can open the door to all sorts of questions about desert in job selection and status in hierarchies. As Clare Burton correctly points out,

> When we refer to equitable organisational arrangements, we are not restricting our view to 'narrow, distributive concerns of equity' (Pateman, 1981, p.36) which address who has which job, nor to the formal rules governing the allocation process, but to the exercise of power at the work place, how jobs are organised and practised and the fundamental preconditions for the development of alternative arrangements. (Burton, 1987: 432)

Dominant understandings of affirmative action stop short of this kind of analysis. As with understandings of antidiscrimination, the focus is on barriers to achievement and to an extent those barriers are seen to inhere in outgroups. Though groups form the basis of policy design, such an interpretation effectively constitutes recipients as competing *individuals*.

The way in which current understandings of affirmative action disaggregate targeted categories into numbers of individuals has been a first step in the integration of affirmative action into management practices. Initially, as has been mentioned, when the reform was proposed there was a great deal of hostility among employers, on the grounds that the government ought not to intervene in business matters (the United States, Australia, Canada), or in business and union matters (Sweden, Norway, the Netherlands). More recently, however, it is easy to find positive endorsement from business leaders. The fact that business spokespeople in the United States undercut President Reagan's attempts to end affirmative action is only the most obvious example (*Harvard Law Review*, 1989).

Part of the reason for this shift is due to the way in which affirmative action has been implemented. Whether we look at Sweden, where it was made explicit that decisions by the Equal Opportunity Ombudsman could not override collective agreements, or at the minimal reporting requirements of Canadian and Australian legislation, it is clear that affirmative action has not undermined management prerogative. Rather it has been absorbed into management practice through incorporation in human resource planning. This trend sees its apotheosis in 'managing diversity' programmes, about which more will be said in later chapters.

Missing the target

Targeted groups vary depending on country and jurisdiction. In Northern Ireland affirmative action is used by American companies to increase the proportion of Catholic workers. A recent book (Wyzan, 1991) examines the impact of similar programmes on, among other groups, gypsies in Eastern Europe. In post-World War II India affirmative action, which involved the reservation of government positions for members of the so-called 'backward classes', was introduced (Chandran, 1990).

All the countries which appear in this study target 'women', though they do so in different ways. Some, like Australia and Norway, target 'women' primarily.[9] Others, like the United States, Canada and, recently, the Netherlands, include 'women' alongside other claimant groups. Canada targets 'women', visible minorities, the disabled and Aboriginal peoples. In the United States, Blacks, ethnic minorities, the disabled and 'women' are most commonly identified as targets. Recently, the Netherlands has addressed the needs of ethnic minorities, whereas previously there were policies only for 'women'. Sweden's gender-neutral approach to 'sex equality' means that, in effect, 'positive action' targets both 'women' and 'men'.

An interactive relationship is established between the state, here constituting members of bodies which formulate and enforce affirmative action laws, and members of targeted social groups. As with rights struggles (see T. Williams, 1990: 758–9), making use of affirmative action legislation requires taking up the identity categories made available. This means working within discrete categories which pay little attention to the fact that lives are not lived in neat packages as 'women', 'Blacks', and so on. It also means emphasizing commonalities and downplaying differences within these categories.

Meanwhile, outgroups are constituted as 'interest groups' and are set in competition with each other. Cynthia Chertos (1983: 240) talks about the way in which a 'zero-sum mentality' is created which suggests that 'there is a finite number of opportunities for "others", and if a member of one group obtains a position, it is at the expense of another group.' This creates problems both for groups facing multiple forms of oppression, and for reformers trying to initiate meaningful change.

While both rights and antidiscrimination discourses make it necessary to campaign for homogeneous identity categories, Pringle and Watson (1992: 61) show that making a claim under one of these discourses usually means surrendering a claim to the other. Instead of citizens with rights, those who appeal to antidiscrimination provisions become '"disadvantaged groups", mostly women, who fall outside of the contract.' For them, 'a social justice strategy is offered which effectively entrenches them in a position of disadvantage.'

In all this, little attention is directed to those doing the categorizing, those defining just what the 'problem' is. Nitya Iyer (1993: 185) describes how being in the speaker's position, to be the categorizer or comparison maker, is to occupy a position of power: '[A]s categorizer, I can make myself absent from the process. I can create one side of the comparison as "a difference", while constituting my particular constellation of attributes as the invisible background norm.' Iris Young (1990: 123) makes a similar point: 'The dominant group need not notice their own group being at all; they occupy an unmarked, neutral, apparently universal position.' Jackson and Penrose (1993: 18) also identify the way that 'dominant groups still manage to efface their own actions by implying that they are somehow outside the process of definition.'

Importantly, categorizers are also in charge of offering 'solutions'. Richard Delgado makes this point convincingly:

> A 'we-they' analysis . . . justifies a disadvantage that we (the majority) want to impose on ourselves to favor them (the minority). This type of thinking, however, leaves the choice of remedy and the time frame for that remedy in the hands of the majority; it converts affirmative action into a benefit, not a right. (1984: 570–1)

One of the effects of being constituted an outgroup is the tendency to set arguments within existing terms of reference. For example, affirmative action is debated within the terms of already existing theoretical and ideological categories (individualism/collectivism, freedom/equality, hierarchy/equality), instead of showing that these concepts are used by social actors to put a particular case. Attempts to make affirmative action fit notions of equal opportunity leave the outgroup open then to attacks along the lines that affirmative action is excessive intervention. More will be said about this in Chapter 3.

Importantly, as Iyer (1993: 186) again notes, 'it is not just anyone who gets to do the categorizing. The categorizer in antidiscrimination law has a particular social identity shared, in varying degrees, by members of the dominant groups in Canadian society.' What Iyer says about Canadian society applies to all the countries which are studied here. And in all these countries most of the categorizers are men.

Where is 'women'?

This study documents the implications of current theorizing of affirmative action for the social category 'women'. The major argument in this book is that the category 'women' receives different and less favourable treatment than other social/identity categories in the philosophical debates around and in the implementation of affirmative action. This treatment takes a number of forms and is integrally related to the conceptual categories structuring understandings of affirmative action.

When opponents and supporters of the reform canvas the types of argument which might be made in favour of affirmative action, these are generally classified as compensatory, redistributive or utilitarian. The first suggests the need to compensate some groups for discriminatory treatment in the past. The second recommends some redistribution of monetary and status rewards in the present. The third builds upon the argument that society will be well served if social divisions are dulled. These arguments have in-built logics which produce problems for their defenders. 'Compensation' claims almost invariably lead to disputes about why contemporary 'innocents' should pay dues for their 'sinning' parents. A focus on redistribution means being challenged to explain why poverty is not or should not be the distinguishing characteristic of recipients. A utilitarian argument runs up against the counter-claim that affirmative action *increases* rather than *reduces* social tensions and divisions. The kinds of defences available therefore are compromised by the larger framework of beliefs structuring the arguments.

This is particularly relevant for 'women'. On one side, when 'women' is compared to other claimant groups, using the kinds of defences above, presuppositions about 'women' position them as less deserving. On the other side, supporters of affirmative action for 'women', who try to use these arguments, find themselves making uncomfortable theoretical claims. The problems posed for feminist theory by the conceptual schema of emergent arguments for legal and political reform is a major theme in this book.

A compensatory defence of affirmative action is commonly tied to an acknowledgement of past discriminatory behaviour. The classic case, and the one commonly used to defend affirmative action in the United States, is the experience there of slavery. 'Women', it is argued, cannot possibly claim that historically they have been treated like slaves and hence they are less deserving of affirmative action. However, trying to analogize 'women' to 'Blacks', which defenders of affirmative action for 'women' have felt impelled to do, means that Black women disappear from the analysis (see Chapter 3 for more detail).

If 'women' face any kind of historical legacy of 'disadvantage', it is claimed, mainly by men theorists, that this is due to their 'choice' of role. The argument is if, in fact, 'women' earn less than 'men', or find themselves underrepresented in positions of power or overrepresented in poorly paid occupations, this is because they 'choose' to so locate to fit in with 'their' domestic responsibilities. As Peattie and Rein (1983) point out, this domestic role is often 'naturalized' to support the argument that these results are inevitable and/or desirable. Liberals add that 'women's' current inequality is an artifact which will disappear as women 'choose' from the new opportunities available to them.

This particular representation of a division of responsibilities between 'public' men and 'private' women has a long history, as has been ably demonstrated by a number of feminist philosophers (Gatens, 1991; Lloyd, 1984; Okin, 1989). And there are clear connections between this representation and the archetypical 'woman' introduced earlier. In effect then, the basis for the traditional category 'woman' – her domestic role – is held to be synonymous with and the reason for 'women's' inequality. This has made it difficult for some feminists, particularly in the early stages of second-wave feminism, to insist that indeed the division of domestic responsibilities is a major cause of 'women's' inequality. As Carl Cuneo (1990: 149–50) says, this kind of argument had a ready response – it is no one's 'fault' that 'women' mother.

The particular effects of this discourse, instantiating the current sexual division of labour, suggest one reason why affirmative action for 'women' is seen (by some men) in a different light from affirmative action for other categories. They also suggest that the way in which certain understandings of affirmative action could destabilize expectations surrounding sex roles is one reason some men oppose it.

'Women' is also differently placed in the redistribution debate, and for related reasons. The tendency to see 'woman' as tied to a supporting spouse has been used both to discriminate against some women, and to argue that 'women' are not discriminated against. The presumption is and has been that 'women' is a dependent category. Its class location is ambivalent, but generally it is assumed that 'women' carry the class of their spouse. Hence it is assumed that if 'disadvantaged' men are catered for, 'their women' will benefit by default.

Opponents of affirmative action emphasize that the reform benefits better-off individuals within the categories targeted. This is the main objection raised by John Edwards (1987: 99–100). He states that he would be willing to see affirmative action for those genuinely in need but the focus on groups means that some who are not needy will receive unnecessary benefits. In this sense, it is argued that affirmative action is overinclusive. While this criticism affects all the recipient categories, 'women' is particularly affected by the presumption that 'women' have access to the resources and assets of their spouses. In a similar fashion, when 'poor white men' are described as 'disadvantaged' by reforms targeting 'women', there is a presumption that these 'poor white men' are bearers of family responsibilities, while the 'women' could easily be supported (if they so 'chose').

Iris Young (1990) has pointed out that the argument that the poor ought to be targeted rather than categories like 'women' or 'Blacks' is tied to an understanding of inequality as economic in nature. She details the inadequacy of the distributive paradigm which informs this analysis and identifies five factors of oppression which stand outside of or alongside poverty: exploitation, marginalization, powerlessness, cultural imperialism and violence. On these grounds, she defends affirmative action for Blacks, the elderly, Native Americans and 'women', among others. In Young's analysis, 'women' becomes one among a number of outgroups. Similarly, in utilitarian debates about social cohesion and social tension, it has been seen to be necessary to locate 'women' as 'like' 'other' cultural 'minorities'. While 'women' is acknowledged as not quite fitting this characterization, it is placed there nonetheless. As not quite a true 'minority', however, the category is deemed somewhat anomalous, and any sympathy attached to minority status is placed elsewhere.

The attempt by Helen Hacker (1951) to make 'women' a minority shows the kinds of problems involved in this claim. Hacker followed the lead of sociologist Gunnar Myrdal (1946) and compared 'women' to 'Negroes'. She concluded that 'women's' privileges exceed those of

'Negroes', and that marriage can act as a 'social elevator' for 'women', but not for 'Negroes'. This kind of comparison has at least two problems: it collapses 'women' into 'relationships' without reflecting upon the nature of those relationships; and it completely ignores the existence of Black women. This makes it difficult to consider 'women's' position *within* cultural minorities, a theme pursued in Chapter 4.

It is clear that feminists are engaged here in a rhetorical contest and that they have tended to use the claims of other groups as discursive openings to make claims for 'women'. Part of the purpose of this book is to sensitize feminists to the effects, some unintended, of these kinds of claims, which I call anomalous analogies. Instead of arguing that 'women' are like or different from other claimant groups, I think it more useful to expose how 'women' is positioned in affirmative action discourses and how this positioning needs to be challenged, not accepted. For example, the targeting of discrete groups – such as 'Aborigines', 'women', 'the disabled' – has a number of effects. Because 'women' is singled out, there is a presumption that the other categories must be composed of 'disadvantaged' 'men'. As a result, women who experience multiple oppression disappear from the analysis.

In addition, the listing of separate groups suggests the possibility of assessing *degrees* of 'disadvantage'. In this assessment, 'women', which in many analyses becomes 'white women' or even 'white middle class women', are described as 'less disadvantaged'. A study I conducted of staff and student attitudes to affirmative action at the University of Adelaide (Bacchi, 1991a, 1991b, 1991c) revealed that, when compared to 'Aborigines', 'the disabled' and 'the poor', 'women' were not considered to be particularly 'disadvantaged'. In fact, the effect I noted above – the way in which an understanding of affirmative action as 'handouts to the needy' translates perversely into a characterization of recipients as advantaged – was confirmed in this survey. Forty-seven per cent of men staff who responded to the survey and 39 per cent of men students felt that women received 'discrimination in their favour' to a large or moderate extent (Bacchi, 1991c: 3).[10]

A recent Equity Review prepared by Clare Burton for the University of South Australia (1995: 28–9) found similarly that the view that women are advantaged, in access to scholarships and promotion, 'is commonly expressed by men.' Some recent surveys in the Netherlands suggest that this perception is common elsewhere. Lie and O'Leary (1990: 53) show that many men academic staff in the Netherlands believe that women are indeed advantaged by current 'equal opportunity' hiring practices. In all the countries studied, 'men' or 'white men' or 'poor white men' are described as the 'invisible victims', the 'truly disadvantaged' (see Lynch, 1989).

Challenging the positioning of 'women' in affirmative action debates means challenging the positioning of other outgroups, but it does not mean arguing that 'women' are 'like' other outgroups. We need to find ways to speak about the specificity of forms of oppression while identifying what oppressed groups share in common. Here, we need to focus upon the power relations that constitute outgroups in ways which minimize change.

Along similar lines, I feel that feminists need to be careful that they do not uncritically accept the assimilationist *version* of affirmative action as an accurate reflection of what affirmative action involves. Rather they should be pointing out how that version has gained ascendancy. That is, they need to show how the debate has been structured in such a way that reform has been contained. By accepting that there is a necessary correspondence between the assimilationist version and the reality of affirmative action, some feminists have given away their opportunity to theorize what affirmative action means.

Here I tend to think that Iris Young (1990: 198 ff.) has let the game slip away by accepting, rather than contesting, the terms of the debate set by the assimilationist version of affirmative action. Cynthia Cockburn (1991), by contrast, shows that it is possible to develop egalitarian versions of affirmative action. Margaret Radin (1991: 133) also develops a model of affirmative action which accepts diversity.

Conclusion

In this chapter we learn that the progressive potential of affirmative action has been thwarted by a conceptual sleight of hand. The kind of real material change which would accompany targeted hiring and promoting has been rendered illegitimate by being defined as outside 'equality'. Less challenging incorporationist measures, such as training sessions, are seen as a species of beneficence. We learn also that 'women' as an identity category is given less weight and status than other identity categories, with adverse effects for most women.

These lessons highlight the need to engage in category politics. Engagement means disputing rather than working within the existing terms of political debate. Engagement also means drawing attention to the practices that have produced these results.

The chapters that follow elaborate upon these themes. They draw attention to a cast of political actors who have played a part in shaping affirmative action in different contexts. In this way we can see the importance of historical specificity while drawing a larger picture of the practices which contain reform and which contain 'women'.

Notes

1 In educational institutions affirmative action can operate as a labour market policy, affecting the hiring of teaching or administrative staff, and/or as a policy designed to affect the composition of the student body, encouraging students from certain social or ethnic backgrounds, or encouraging women into certain areas of study.

2 Clare Burton (1991) discusses the rationale behind descriptive representation in bureaucracy.

3 I say generally because in Canada it has proved very difficult to impose externally audited affirmative action on the federal bureaucracy. Despite numerous studies and reports confirming that reform is seriously needed (Morgan, 1988; Canada, 1990), the Canadian bureaucracy has to date (1994) successfully fended off supervision of their affirmative action processes.

4 Since Sweden joined the European Community in January 1995, collective agreements can no longer relieve employers from observing Sections 4–11 of the Swedish Equal Treatment Act, covering *inter alia*, positive action (correspondence, Directorate General V Employment, Industrial Relations and Social Affairs, European Commission, 28 February 1996).

5 Unless otherwise indicated, subsequent references to affirmative action will be references to labour market affirmative action.

6 Wendy Williams (1981) includes an intermediate category which would still be called direct discrimination but which involves the use of an apparently neutral policy as a 'mere pretext for forbidden discrimination'.

7 In fact, the means of proving indirect discrimination has become a political battleground. In the United States the pendulum has swung away from the possibility of using a statistical discrepancy to prove the discriminatory impact of a particular rule. In *Wards Cove* (1989) the US Supreme Court held that 'disparate impact' plaintiffs cannot rely solely on statistics to establish a prima-facie case of discrimination. Without invoking statistics, it is difficult to see how indirect discrimination can be proved. For the details on *Wards Cove*, see Francis, 1993: 15–16.

8 It should be noted that the countries in my sample have added indirect discrimination to their legislation at different times. The addition has been most recent in Sweden (Nielsen and Halvorsen, 1992: 9).

9 In Australia, public authorities have 'equal opportunity' policies for several groups, Aborigines, people of non-English-speaking background, the disabled and 'women', but only 'women' is targeted by the private-sector-oriented Affirmative Action Act (1986).

10 I received 320 completed returns from full-time academic staff, a return rate of 40 per cent; 36 per cent of men staff and 56 per cent of women staff. Completed surveys from students totalled 1191 (666 men students and 525 women students), more than 10 per cent of the student population.

3

The Politics of (Mis)representation

Debates about the legitimacy of affirmative action have a surprising degree of similarity in all of the countries selected for this study. Basically, affirmative action is positioned as in opposition to and incompatible with equal opportunity. This has led its proponents to reshape its content, softening reform proposals and repositioning their targets as the 'problem'. At times, as in Sweden (Chapter 6) with its social democratic political heritage, some of this replication is surprising.

Within these conceptual understandings, and in the implementation of affirmative action, 'women' is located as an afterthought.[1] Even where 'women' appears to be prominent in the design of the reform (see Australia in Chapter 5, Sweden in Chapter 6, the Netherlands in Chapter 7, and Norway in Chapter 8), the ways in which it is interpreted place severe constraints on the kinds of change permitted. This book focuses attention on the positioning of 'women' in these debates to tease out some of these effects.

These developments are most easily traced in the United States which deserves a key place in any discussion of affirmative action because of the early introduction there of reforms designated 'affirmative action'. Affirmative action has struggled against accusations that it undermines 'fair play' and that it sits uncomfortably with the American way of doing things. A campaign to eliminate it is currently underway.[2] Moreover, key interpretive debates about affirmative action which originated here have subsequently been transported to Canada, Australia and Europe via mass media links and American multinationals.

This chapter traces the political history of affirmative action in the United States. Its primary concern is the conceptual understandings which have framed this history, rather than specific legislative instruments. The chief focus is the location of 'women' within these conceptual understandings.

To begin, I look at the ways in which meanings of affirmative action have been shaped by the attempts of proponents to make the reform legitimate given popular understandings of the United States as the land of equal opportunity. Attempting to present affirmative action as compatible with or even as 'parasitic on' (Rosenfeld, 1991: 295–6) equal opportunity has meant that affirmative action is produced as 'preferential treatment' of the 'disadvantaged'.

I then examine the widespread tendency to see 'women' as less worthy recipients of affirmative action 'handouts'. This argument depends in large part on comparisons between 'Blacks' and 'women' which find 'women' less 'needy'. It is important here to see how the category 'woman' is used in these debates to delegitimize affirmative action for 'women'.

I proceed to show that comparisons between 'women' and 'Blacks' are inadequate conceptually since they ignore Black women or force them into categories which fail to address the nature of their oppression. While current understandings of categories of oppression as separate and homogeneous are clearly inadequate, however, recent moves to displace these categories through appeals to a more 'inclusive' 'class' 'disadvantage' or to a desire for 'diversity' are, if anything, more problematic.

As mentioned in Chapter 1, category politics can involve either accentuating or blurring categorical distinctions, or doing both simultaneously. The point is that categories themselves are not the problem, but that we need to keep a sharp eye on the political uses of categories and the politics behind the claims that categories either are or are not important. This means, and the point will be made several times, that it is necessary to continue to campaign for 'women' as a first step towards challenging the uses to which that and other categories are put.

What is affirmative action?

In American law, as Fania Davis (1993: 5) outlines, the term 'affirmative action' first appeared in the 1935 Wagner Act, 29 USC section 160(c), the USA's 'omnibus labour relations and collective bargaining statute.' In the Act, affirmative action 'denoted an employer's duty to take positive measures to undo the effects of past unfair labour practices against unions and to prevent them from recurring in the future.' In the civil rights context, the origin of contemporary affirmative action policy is commonly traced to President John F. Kennedy's Executive Order, issued on 16th March 1961. Executive Order 10,925 required government contractors to take affirmative action, establishing sanctions for noncompliance, including termination of contracts (R.A. Johnson, 1990: 78).

This was followed up by President Lyndon B. Johnson in 1965 with Executive Order 11,246 which barred discrimination on the basis of race, colour, religion or national origin by federal contractors and subcontractors. This Order created the Office of Federal Contract Compliance within the Department of Labor to superintend enforcement. Revised Order No. 4, issued by the Department of Labor, required that 'goals' and 'timetables' be set for the employment of minority group members in job categories where they are presently 'under-utilized'. 'Under-utilization' is defined as having fewer members of the group in the category actually employed than would reasonably be expected from their availability (Goldman, 1976: 180). 'Minority groups' referred to 'Blacks, Spanish-surnamed Americans, American Indians, and Orientals' (Cahn, 1993: 1). Federal courts have at times imposed mandatory targets or quotas upon employers found guilty of discrimination, though this is not a common occurrence (Sawer, 1985: 6).

Since these early initiatives, many, many words have been written in defence of and against the proposals. To an extent, the same arguments are repeated over and over again, and one gets the feeling that the debate will never go away. Proponents and opponents sometimes shift ground. 'Public' opinion is solicited and the results are used both by those against and for 'affirmative action'. Lawrence Becker (1993: 93) bemoans the repetition in the political debates, that there is 'so little evidence of progress toward consensus and political closure.' However, he admits with some perspicacity, '[S]ome of the repetitive quality of arguments about affirmative action may be due to the fact that they are being used as set pieces in larger projects.'

It is too simple to say there are two contending positions because there is no agreement about what affirmative action involves. In fact, understandings of affirmative action have been affected by the ongoing debate. The battle then has been waged around *meanings* of affirmative action. The dominant current understanding, even among supporters of the reform, is that affirmative action means 'preferential' treatment to assist 'disadvantaged' people to move into better jobs. As Margaret Radin (1991: 134–6) says, 'the dominant ordinary language view is that affirmative action gives benefits to people who are less qualified or less deserving than white men or indeed are wholly unqualified or undeserving.'[3] At issue is whether or not such 'assistance' is justifiable or fair.

What is most interesting is how this dominant understanding has emerged. It certainly was not the only understanding canvassed in the early years of the debate. Serious theoretical contributions drew attention to the fact that such an approach assumed that appointment procedures as currently implemented were objective and that the merit of candidates was an easily measured quantum (see for example Thalberg, 1973, 1980; Sher, 1975; Wasserstrom, 1976; Heins, 1987; and, more recently, Young, 1990). Contrary to this view, these theorists insisted that outgroups remained outgroups because ingroups assessed them by their own standards. Hence, affirmative action was not 'preferential' treatment but an acknowledgement that power and bias were at work in appointments. John Livingston put the case in 1979 that 'In the modern meritocracy, the process of selection is not made by nature or by Adam Smith's Invisible Hand, but by admissions and personnel officers who apply cultural standards to applicants for admissions, appointment and promotion' (Livingston, 1979: 132).

The fact that even supporters of the reform today accept a characterization of affirmative action as *preferential* treatment raises important questions about the evolution of the debate. For it will be argued that, once this case is accepted, a good deal has been given away. While the term 'to prefer' on its own carries no judgement regarding desert and means simply 'to choose or esteem above another' (*Webster's Seventh New Collegiate Dictionary*, 1967: 670), the implication behind 'preferential' hiring or promotion policies is that the selected candidate has been advanced above others who are better qualified. Such an understanding leaves proponents on the defensive. More significantly, it leaves untouched and unchallenged practices which exclude certain groups from positions of influence and authority.

Hence the central debate today is about what forms of 'preferential' treatment are acceptable, not about what factors are responsible for precluding 'women', 'Blacks' and other 'others' from power. And in this debate the swing of opinion and influence is decidedly against what are called strong forms of such treatment.[4] In a recent collection of philosophical speculations on the appropriateness of affirmative action in universities (Cahn, 1993), the clear majority decided that strategies like quotas or targeted hiring went too far. There is, of course, a kind of logic leading to this end point. For once one accepts the language of 'preferential' treatment one is immediately involved in the need to justify 'preference'. The flipside is the need to justify limiting the 'opportunities' of others. The fact that one of the most serious and radical contributors to the collection mentioned above (Becker, 1993) concentrated upon finding some way of giving 'preference' *without* affecting others is testament to the strength of these structuring arguments.

So how did affirmative action become 'preference'? The first stage in this process, I argue, is the way in which affirmative action has been branded (and I use this term deliberately) 'equal results' within an equal opportunity/equal results dichotomy.

The major theoretical focus in the first decades of the reform was whether affirmative action was congruent with the dominant American credo of equal opportunity. Equal results, as everyone 'knew', was associated with the kind of equalizing performed by communist regimes (see, for example, Nagel, 1979: 104). Americans by contrast 'believed' in offering opportunity for talent and reward for merit. They did not believe that people should all be the 'same' in terms of status or wealth. All they insisted upon was that everyone have a 'fair go' on a 'level playing field' – that procedures be fair.

Affirmative action was then portrayed as subverting these processes, interfering in fair competition and, even worse, *guaranteeing outcomes* for certain people. Affirmative action meant 'equal results' and hence was un-American.

The widespread conviction that these beliefs are entrenched in the American psyche has meant that theorists who support the reform feel the need to find a space for affirmative action by making it fit some notion of 'equal opportunity'. They attempt to find a way to make affirmative action legitimate. As an obvious example, supporters of affirmative action commonly make the disclaimer that the affirmative action they support does not involve quotas (see for example Davis, 1993: 1). It is about making opportunities *really* equal or fair. To this end, it is necessary to bring those who face or who have faced discrimination 'up to' the 'starting gate' of the 'race'. Affirmative action was defended in just these terms by Lyndon Johnson in 1965 (quoted in Davis, 1993: 5): '[Y]ou do not take a person who for years has been hobbled by chains and liberate him [*sic*] and then say, "You are free to compete with all the others", and still believe (that you are) being fair.'

Iris Young (1990: Chapter 7) argues that the antidiscrimination doctrine, which stresses that equal treatment is all that American citizens are entitled to, frames the affirmative action discussion in ways which limit the impact of the reform. However, many proponents, including Lyndon Johnson, make the point that treating unequals equally will simply perpetuate inequality. The structuring discourse which delimits the meaning of affirmative action is not then an inflexible commitment to 'equal treatment' but one which says that 'unequal' treatment is 'permitted' only to 'remedy' 'disadvantage'.[5]

The repercussions of trying to fit affirmative action to equal opportunity illustrate the intrinsic problem with taking principles and then fitting your reform to them (see Fox-Genovese, 1986). In the process, you constrain your vision of what is possible and what is at stake. You also leave yourself open to interminable debates within the terms of the framework you have accepted. Hence, the key issue becomes just how much 'preference' is 'compatible' with equal opportunity.

The point here is that *attempting to make affirmative action congruent with equal opportunity produces an understanding of affirmative action as assistance to the needy*. And as outlined in the preceding chapter, this has all sorts of consequences. In summary, it means that notions of merit go unquestioned. It also accepts a broad vision of society as open to opportunities, except in a few instances. Additionally, it opens the door to other opportunity-creating models, such as managing diversity, as will be seen later in the chapter. Hence it leaves in place existing relations of domination (see Thompson, 1987) with a nod to the needs of the 'disadvantaged'.

'Political' culture and 'public' opinion

Elsewhere (Bacchi, 1992a) I have suggested the need to develop a heightened sensitivity to the political origins and effects of political concepts and categories. My target was the notion of political culture and, in particular, the proposal that 'Americans' and 'equal opportunity' are coterminous.

This view appears in numerous places (see, for example, Douglas Rae et al., 1981: 64). Here I borrow from the well-known political scientists Verba and Orren. They state that 'Americans have a distinctive set of beliefs about equality.' In particular, they have a 'stronger taste for political than for economic equality' and 'these beliefs have deep cultural roots.' These 'shared values' set the 'rules of play' for both the market and the political arena, and are 'instrumental' in 'shaping the public policies that give practical effect to political belief' (Verba and Orren, 1985: 2). Their study, not surprisingly, concludes that most Americans support 'equality of opportunity', not 'equality of result', which is equated with affirmative action.

Similar to Verba and Orren, Kluegel and Smith conclude that the 'white American public' is more likely to support 'equal opportunity policy' if it is formulated to 'be consistent with prevailing values of individualism', and that programmes that change Blacks to fit into the 'current stratification order' are more likely to succeed than those which call for changes 'in the stratification order itself' (Kluegel and Smith, 1983: 819; Kluegel, 1985: 762). As an extension of this argument, we are told that the major explanation for opposition to affirmative action derives not from simple anti-Black views but from a belief that, because Blacks are receiving 'preferential' treatment, they pose a serious challenge to 'cherished values' such as individualism and self-reliance (Kluegel and Smith 1983: 798; see also Dovidio, Mann and Gaertner 1989: 86–7). This explanation has been called the 'new racism'.

The idea that Americans put 'right' rules ahead of individual notions of what is 'good' has become pivotal in contemporary American political philosophy. John Rawls is only the best example. Rawls (1971), as Michael Sandel explains, objects to a utilitarian vision of society because the idea of the greatest good of the greatest number implies that the good of some minority members must be sacrificed (Sandel, 1982: 3, 140). A way to overcome this infringement of individual liberty emerges in the idea that freely contracting rational actors, hypothetically unaware of their future status and beliefs, could agree upon fundamental rules for governing society (Rawls, 1971). Justice then becomes equated with a set of principles which stands outside of individual needs and desires, but which simultaneously delimits the consequences of conflicting values. In effect, justice is represented as a procedure for reconciling disputes.

It is important, I argue, to uncover the historical roots of this idea of a distinctive, univocal American political culture. Ross (1991) locates the 'discovery' of 'political culture' in the turbulent 1920s, a period of ethnic unrest and industrial violence. The challenge these conditions posed to America's future was met, says Ross (1991: 454), by social scientists like Dewey and Merriam who felt that it had to be demonstrated that the United States could cope with dramatic value conflicts. The idea emerged that 'consensus' in the United States rested not on a consensus of *particular* values but upon an agreed method of *adjusting* conflicting values. This vision of the American way of life as depending upon 'fair rules of play' became American 'political culture'. Here is a clear example of the point made in Chapter 1 about the way in which conceptual categories serve political purposes. Seyla Benhabib calls this the 'meta-politics of dialogue', ways of setting the agenda for what is considered 'appropriate or inappropriate matters of public debate' (Benhabib, 1989: 155–6).

A sensitivity to the politics which produced the understanding that Americans place greater importance on right rules than right results or effects makes it possible to question the assumption that this understanding represents some unfractured consensus. And, following from this arises the possibility that the 'new racism' may not be all that different from 'old' racism. Here I am suggesting that opposition to affirmative action for Blacks may have more to do with racist attitudes than with a commitment to some notion of procedural justice, as is claimed by Kluegel and Smith (see above). I would argue that the 'procedural justice' cart *follows* rather than precedes the racist horse.

Johannes Fabian (1983: 156) identifies the way in which the kind of 'panculturalism' I've been describing homogenizes dissent. He explains: 'Practically everybody agrees that we can make sense of another society only to the extent that we grasp it as a whole, an organism, a configuration, a system.' At the same time, however, 'by insisting that culture is a system (ethos, model, blueprint, and so forth) which "informs" or "regulates" action, holistic social science fails to provide a theory of praxis.' Culture becomes a *predictor* rather than a *result* of behaviour.

In many accounts 'political culture' is conflated with 'ideology' which is presented similarly as unitary and seamless. In contrast to this view, social psychologists Billig et al. (1988: 128, 140; see also Wagner) contend that there are tensions *within* ideologies which mean that individuals are often caught in dilemmas when choosing a political stance. They point out, for example, that formal liberal theories emphasize *both* the value of full individual development *and* interdependence. There is also a coincidence of beliefs 'in *both* a fundamental human equality and an infinite human variety' which means that the extent of similarity or difference between persons always constitutes a 'potentially contestable issue' (italics in original). Notions about 'individual difference' and 'human equality' can therefore be used to support different ends, as becomes clear in almost every ethical debate.

My survey of attitudes to affirmative action among university staff and students (Bacchi, 1991a, 1991b, 1991c) found a clear ambivalence in respondents about how to achieve social justice. The vast majority moderately supported proposals that resources ought to be distributed according to effort, achievements *and* need. This is no simple endorsement of commonly accepted notions of equal opportunity.

Bron Taylor (1991) in an impressive study of American reactions to affirmative action supports my contention that political views in the United States are less homogeneous than the way they are presented in much political science literature, and the way they are talked about in public debate. He found '[B]oth strong endorsement of and ambivalence about the equal opportunity principle coexist in the attitudes of many of the respondents' (1991: 174), and concluded that 'this ambivalence reflects tensions among competing values in U.S. culture'. He notes that 'quite a few respondents expressed substantive principles of equality but did not have a language or context for expressing or even understanding the importance of their moral sentiment' (1991: 178). He finally concludes (1991: 193) that 'distributive outcomes by and large are perceived to be legitimate.'

Taylor, however, feels the need to explain these results as congruent with 'equal opportunity' instead of suggesting quite simply that some Americans feel it acceptable to redistribute wealth. He distinguishes between what he calls *pure equality of opportunity* which views equal opportunity as 'equal legal access' combined with an 'uncompromising adherence to the idea that the "best qualified" ought always to be hired', and the *equal opportunity principle* or *merit principle*, which stresses that 'all persons should have equal access to whatever goods are needed to develop their natural talents so that persons with equal natural talents have equal opportunities and resources to develop their talents and compete in the market economy' (B. Taylor, 1991: 11). Affirmative action finds its rationale within the latter understanding of equal opportunity, according to Taylor, since it is about providing equal access to equal opportunities.

Not surprisingly, then, Taylor also works within an understanding of affirmative action as 'preference'. Taylor's model includes two kinds of affirmative action, protective and preferential, though he feels that there are 'preferential aspects even to the forms of affirmative action that, on the affirmative action spectrum, are close to the protective forms described above'. He considers the challenge posed by those who claim that the term 'preferential' is misleading since 'all that such treatment really does is counteract the massive preferential treatment the culture imparts to white men' (B. Taylor, 1991: 12), but dismisses the claim as 'disingenuous and obscurantist'. Taylor explains:

> my experience leads me to conclude that the attempt by proponents of affirmative action to excise the term *preferential* from the conceptualization of affirmative action . . . seems disingenuous because such proponents usually favor not only protective affirmative action but also forms of affirmative action that ensure minimum qualifications are met and then (at least relative to the affirmative action continuum) wish to promote rapid progress toward specific numerical goals. It seems obscurantist because attempts to define affirmative action only in protective terms underplays the various ways affirmative action programs usually do lead to preferential treatment . . . . (1991: 130; italics in original)

Taylor has inadequately sorted through some of the debates here. Later, in a footnote (233, fn. 4), he acknowledges the importance of the argument that 'one way discrimination is perpetuated is by the domi-nance of elite white men over the means of production – which includes the production of the idea of what counts as *merit*' (note he refers to Wasserstrom as developing this argument). But he fails to see that taking this idea seriously means challenging an understanding of affirmative action as 'preference'. Hence he cannot see that those who question the meaning of 'merit' see claims that affirmative action *is* 'preference' as themselves being obscurantist, since they obscure the power relations which constitute recipients of affirmative action as 'supplicants'.

As I indicated above, once one accepts that affirmative action means 'preference', the next logical step is to consider whether and when 'preference' is justified. Taylor takes this step (1991: 14). He says the most crucial question is 'whether preferential treatment for women and nonwhites can ever be morally justified.' His answer is that 'some short-term compromise of pure equality of opportunity is needed to promote actual equality of opportunity overall and over the long term' (1991: 177).

Taylor's analysis of American attitudes is far more sophisticated than that offered by Verba and Orren. His sample deliberately includes rep-resentatives of groups excluded in the main from positions of political influence, an important oversight in the latter study (see Bacchi, 1992a: 24). Beyond this he acknowledges the need to 'privilege' the views of oppressed groups (B. Taylor, 1991: 186–97). He also illustrates con-vincingly that some of the common assumptions regarding affirmative action have little support. For example, he found that very few, even among those who disapproved of affirmative action, perceived of it as 'having the insidious purpose or consequences of excluding and depriving white men of their fundamental liberties' (1991: 188–9). Nor did he find evidence that women or nonwhites in his sample felt stig-matized by affirmative action, a constant warning from those opposed to the reform (1991: 194).

Taylor concludes that affirmative action is grounded in liberalism, that in fact it functions as one important contemporary legitimating strategy for liberalism's market society (1991: 9): '[T]his strategy suggests that through reforms such as affirmative action, market competition can be made increasingly fair.' And here he is doubtless correct. What he does not see is that it is only *his* understanding of affirmative action as 'preference' which is congruent with liberalism in this way. So he has created a self-fulfilling prophecy and does not realize how he has arrived there.

Michel Rosenfeld (1991) does much the same thing. He takes as his starting point liberal political and social theory and accepts the assump-tion that qualifications can be fairly judged. His project is to justify affirmative action within these constraints. This he does by arguing for 'fair means-regarding equal opportunity', a term borrowed from *Equalities* (Rae et al., 1981), which says that people must be compensated for conditions which deprive them of the means to compete. His affirmative action has as its goal 'making whole' the 'victims' of these conditions.

Rosenfeld (1991: 335) states quite correctly that within his terms of reference affirmative action is conservative 'insofar as it is designed to eradicate the effects of first-order discrimination without undermining any overall education or employment scheme that operates in accordance with the principle of equal opportunity.' And, it follows that the kinds of affirmative action his model permits are limited. So, in cases where it is difficult or impossible to prove past discrimination, only voluntary affirmative action is justified.

Now, Rosenfeld is doubtless a progressive; and the model of equal opportunity he defends is an unconventional one. For example, he believes that there is nothing which affirms that talent should be rewarded, and he feels that power and wealth ought to be more evenly distributed. Still, his desire to make affirmative action legitimate within the terms of liberalism has imposed limitations on understandings of what affirmative action could mean. Rosenfeld's model also produces very different outcomes for 'Blacks' and 'women', about which more will be said shortly.

The point of this discussion has been to illustrate how some political theorists have delegitimized and delimited affirmative action through invoking an idea of political culture. In these studies conceptual categories, here 'equal opportunity' and 'equal results', are used to generate the impression of a homogeneous value community with no place for affirmative action. Here I draw attention to Moore's (1988) warning that an overemphasis on 'culture' can homogenize societies, eliminating the tensions and conflicts within them.

Going further, I have shown that the prominence of this concern leads theorists sympathetic to affirmative action to rework it in order to make it fit American 'culture'. This has produced the consensus view that affirmative action is indeed 'handouts' to the 'disadvantaged' and therefore must be kept within reasonable limits.

Looking specifically at the situation of women, Joan Eveline (1994a, 1994b) has argued that the effects of a 'disadvantage' discourse are serious indeed. Not only do the 'disadvantaged' become the problem, but the fact that those in power are the ones deciding just who is disadvantaged, what is the nature of their disadvantage, and the range of appropriate solutions, remains hidden. Eveline calls for a discursive shift to challenge the advantage of those in power. This, she explains, exposes the politics shaping current discursive constructions of affirmative action.

Affirmative action and the invisible 'women'

The major claim in this book is that the category 'women' has little political standing in the countries studied. 'Women' is positioned among the 'disadvantaged' and suffers from all the effects of this location. But, within this discourse, 'women' is positioned as less 'needy' than other claimant groups. This is illustrated both in the theory and in the practice of affirmative action in the United States.

In this study I do not try to measure 'effects' of affirmative action *per se*; instead I concentrate on what the legislation says, how the courts have interpreted it, and how theorists have represented 'women' within the debates surrounding it. In fact, I would suggest that attempts to measure effects reinforce a view that any advances made by 'women' and other outgroups are due to affirmative action. Attributing any increase in 'women's' workforce participation rate generally and in specific jobs and positions to affirmative action makes every woman appointed a *de facto* affirmative action appointee. It is exactly this, I suggest, which makes some women and some members of other outgroups, dislike it.

The extent to which 'women' is an addendum rather than a starting place for policy formulation in this area is illustrated in the history of antidiscrimination and civil rights. Post-independence American history has been dominated by race issues. A civil war erupted in 1861, sparked in many accounts by a call to end slavery. Since that time, civil rights and affirmative action have been couched in the language of justified compensation to Blacks.

'Women's' status seldom came up in the debates surrounding the 1964 Civil Rights Act, surprisingly since equal pay for women was being discussed concurrently. Interest in and the advent of equal pay for 'women' prior to addressing issues of discrimination for 'women' occurred also in Canada and Australia, as we shall see. Though I do not explore this phenomenon in this work, I think it indicates that political interest in 'women' was prompted primarily by concerns for workforce growth and the need to protect men workers from 'cheap' women competitors. In the event, the amendment to include 'women' among the other groups against whom discrimination would not be permitted was introduced by a southerner who hoped the inclusion would lead to the bill's *defeat* (Burstein, 1985: 23; Davis, 1993: 12). Since 1941, Executive Orders have forbidden race, creed and national origin discrimination by federal contractors. Sex was not included as a forbidden ground of discrimination until 1967 (Davis, 1993: 7).

As we have already seen, affirmative action for 'minorities' can be traced to Executive Orders 10,925, issued by Kennedy in 1961 and 11,246, issued by Johnson in 1965. Two years later (13 October, 1967) the latter was amended by Executive Order 11,375 to expand its coverage to include 'women' (R.A. Johnson, 1990: 78).

Initially the Office of Federal Contract Compliance focused on Black workers in the construction industry. According to Roberta Johnson (1990: 79), this was because the Assistant Secretary of Labor for Employment Standards, Arthur Fletcher, a former football player, chose construction for the establishing of guidelines. 'Women' was initially excluded from the Guidelines. In fact, the Secretary of Labor Hodgson publicly remarked in 1970 that he had 'no intention of applying literally exactly the same approach for women' as was applied to eliminate discrimination against minorities (in R.A. Johnson, 1990: 79). 'Women' became full beneficiaries in April 1973.

However, there is no guarantee that 'women' will be included in the affirmative action pools, which are up to each employer to define (R.A. Johnson, 1990: 84). This helps to explain why, in the long history of court judgments relating to affirmative action, only once has the case for 'women' been considered. This was in *Johnson* v. *Transportation Agency, Santa Clara County* (March 1987) which was decided in the claimant's favour. In this case, as Marjorie Heins (1987: 191) reports, the press almost uniformly trumpeted it as approval of the hiring of a 'less qualified woman' over a 'more qualified man'.

As in practice, so in theory there has been a distinct lack of interest in 'women'. A quick perusal of the major theoretical analyses of affirmative action in the United States illustrates how often 'women' is relegated to a footnote. The common explanation is that the arguments concerning affirmative action are most clearly developed using the example of race and that gender raises somewhat different, less 'pressing' issues. Frederick Lynch (1989) justifies his lack of attention to gender issues in his study of affirmative action in these words: 'I am somewhat less concerned with affirmative action in the form of gender preferences; for the cutting edge in rhetoric and effort appears to have been with regard to racial/ethnic matters.' John Edwards (1987: 201) has written a comparative analysis of 'positive discrimination' in the United States and in Britain, in which the 'position of women' is described as 'different and in some respects more complicated [than the position of minorities] – although not, I think, more pressing' (see also Fullinwider, 1980).

More interesting still for this study are those theorists who state forthrightly that 'women' are not as 'disadvantaged' as Blacks or other ethnic minorities, and that the justification for affirmative action for 'women' is hence considerably less. A common conclusion is that 'women's' situation is not so serious, and that, given a trade-off due to limited resources, the problem of race will justifiably receive prior attention. According to Alan Goldman (1976: 193), 'competition among groups covered by the affirmative action goals policy – for example, between women and blacks – will amount to preferential treatment of those least harmed by prior discrimination and thus least deserving in terms of the policy's own rationale', implying that 'women' will get places that should go to Blacks (see also Rosenfeld, 1991: 154, 300).

Let me emphasize here that I do not wish to dispute this claim but that I wish to challenge the shape it takes. That is, I do not intend to engage in some sort of comparison of poverty rates between 'women' and 'Blacks'. Rather I wish to challenge the suggestion that it is appropriate and meaningful to make these sorts of comparisons. It is clear, for example, as Elizabeth Spelman (1988: 120) insists, that '[I]f the terms of one's theory require that a person is either female or Black . . . there is no room to describe someone who is both.' The way in which comparisons between racism and sexism make Black women disappear is a critical shortcoming in any such analysis.

I also want to argue that it is important to explore the processes by which the category 'women' is discounted and the effects this has. Those engaged in theorizing affirmative action generally offer different kinds of explanations for affirmative action for 'women' and for 'Blacks'. This is not to say that I think the situations of 'women' and 'Blacks' are the same, but again that it is important to see the *kinds of differences* these theorists highlight and where they leave 'women'.

As mentioned in the previous chapter, it is fairly common to suggest that 'women' cannot claim the historical legacy of slavery. And since this legacy and the guilt it carries in its wake are most often mentioned as a rationale for some kind of 'compensation', it is not surprising that 'women's' situation is deemed less worthy of 'redress'.

So, attitudes toward affirmative action for 'women' are linked to the *kinds* of explanations deemed compelling for the reform. While compensation is certainly the weakest rationale for affirmative action – here I agree with Bron Taylor (1991: 176–7) – it is commonly invoked. It is also the explanation which most obviously designates recipients as 'wanting' and as needing 'assistance'. For example, in George Sher's (1975) explanatory model, past discrimination is seen to produce 'privations' which affect the 'ability to compete'. He is most concerned with economic privations and sees affirmative action as needed to counteract these. But, Sher argues, since most women had two parents, they would not have faced this kind of privation, even if the mother had experienced discrimination. Hence, in his view, Blacks are 'the group most deserving.'

Where 'women' are deemed to face 'disadvantage', it is explained that the causes are more complex and that no one is to 'blame'. This is because 'women' are presumed to make job 'choices' which fit in with 'their' family responsibilities or their beliefs about what are appropriate occupations for 'women'. So, Michel Rosenfeld (1991: 201) seems to accept, the major problem 'women' face is 'stereotypical social attitudes' and hence it is inappropriate to see affirmative action for 'women' as compensatory. Although he concludes that affirmative action plans for 'women' can still be given legal and constitutional justification, the different causes of the 'problem' have effects. For 'women', he argues, 'it seems unfair to impose a duty of compensation on a select number of employers who are no more responsible for perpetuating gender-based stereotypes than anyone else.' Hence, only voluntary affirmative action plans are justified.

Rosenfeld (1991: 154) is disturbed that 'preferential treatment of blacks' is subjected to 'strict' judicial scrutiny, in comparison to the 'intermediate scrutiny' applied to gender classifications:

> This means that preferential treatment of blacks should survive constitutional attack only if 'necessary' to achieve a 'compelling' state purpose, whereas preferential treatment of women would be constitutionally permissible even if only 'substantially related' to an 'important' state purpose.

Whereas I have argued that subjecting affirmative action to either test is inappropriate since affirmative action should not be seen as an exemption from antidiscrimination laws (see Chapter 2), Rosenberg's concern means that he misses the point that, in general, discrimination against 'women' receives *less 'scrutiny'*. As Mark Tushnett suggests in a passing reference (1991: 164, fn. 41), the different levels of scrutiny indicate that some classifications 'are normatively a bit troubling, but not so troubling as racial classifications; gender-based statutes are the best example.'

Rosenfeld would probably claim that he makes a strong case for affirmative action for 'women'. But he fails to see how his representation of the 'problem' for 'women' as different in character from the 'problem' for 'Blacks' buys into the very stereotypes he claims to want to challenge. In his view (1991: 200), '[T]o the extent that women themselves may not desire certain kinds of jobs, job segregation according to gender does indeed seem to be different than its racially based counterpart.' From this follows his summation that for Blacks the problem has been 'racial discrimination, segregation, and the projection of demeaning stereotypes'; for women, 'it is the pervasive dissemination of social attitudes that portray women as ill suited to carry out various kinds of responsible jobs' (1991: 204).

Not only is this an overly simple contrast, but there is a distinct implication that one of these experiences is worse than the other. So, it is not surprising that, when Rosenfeld (1991: 327) later considers a hypothetical scenario in which a priority has to be established among claimants, 'Blacks' win out over 'women'.

The assumption that 'women' do not want certain kinds of jobs, either because they have absorbed stereotypical attitudes or because of domestic responsibilities, is often used to challenge claims that 'women' face discrimination. In his well-publicized report on 'antibias regulation' to the Carnegie Commisson on Higher Education (Lester, 1974), Richard Lester states explicitly that the lower numbers of women in the higher ranks of academe is due to the fact that 'female faculty devote less time and energy to professional development than men and more to home responsibilities' (see also Lynch, 1989: 179). Vicki Schultz (1992: 311) calls this the 'pre-labor market view' which assumes that 'women's' work interests are fixed before they enter paid work. This position is clearly illustrated in an important sex discrimination case, *EEOC* v. *Sears Roebuck & Co* (1985). The argument put by Sears was that 'women' did not want higher paying commission sales jobs because 'women' were less aggressive than 'men' and had family duties which made it difficult for them to travel. In a previous work (Bacchi, 1990: Chapter 10), I explain how this argument, which was successful, displaced responsibility for reasonable working conditions *from* the company *to* parents and their personal 'choices' about the division of domestic labour. Here I am emphasizing how 'women's' 'disadvantage' is tied to 'their' domestic obligations in a way that seems to make affirmative action, *as presently understood*, totally inappropriate.

The *Sears* case is not an aberration. Schultz (1992: 298) notes that employers have raised what she calls the 'lack of interest' argument in at least 54 sex discrimination claims, spanning from 1972 to 1989. And, as Schultz reports, 'in almost half the cases (23, or 42.6%), courts accepted the employer's argument and interpreted sex discrimination as the expression of women's own lack of interest in higher-paying nontraditional jobs.' Usefully for the argument being developed here, Schultz contrasts the presumptions in race discrimination cases. Here, courts generally acknowledge that human choices are never formed in a vacuum and that Blacks might well be disinclined to apply for jobs when they had little reason to expect they would be hired. I say generally because of the following comment by Justice Sandra Day O'Connor in *City of Richmond* v. *J.A. Croson Company* (1989): 'Blacks may be disproportionately attracted to industries other than construction' (quoted in R.A. Johnson, 1990: 83). I would suggest that this is the exception that proves the rule, which is that 'lack of interest' explanations appear commonsensical when applied to 'women'. This contrast in presumption illustrates, as Schultz (1992: 300) says, 'the degree to which judges have accepted the dominant cultural image of women as marginal workers.'

Schultz (1992: 309) goes on to show that liberal judges also constitute the category 'women' in ways which see 'women' and 'workers' as a contradiction in terms. In these cases, the focus is upon the 'exceptional woman' who escapes the characteristics generally attributed to the group, and the goal is to ensure that no obstacles are placed in *her* pursuit of better job opportunities.

Affirmative action is often seen as a cause of conflict *between* these 'exceptional' women and 'traditional' women, called by Rosenfeld 'female assimilationists' and 'female traditionalists'. Lynch (1989: 75) refers in passing to a 'latent conflict' between career women and homemaker wives 'generated by affirmative action'. Rosenfeld describes the conflict as one 'between groups that subscribe to different ideologies' (1991: 317). According to Rosenfeld, this kind of conflict has 'no apparent counterpart in the case of blacks', because 'female proponents of traditional sex roles may genuinely assert that these spheres should be spheres of differentiation when it comes to gender'. This is in contrast to Black opponents of affirmative action, like Thomas Sowell, whose arguments Rosenfeld dismisses as 'strategic'.[6] Rosenfeld's position (1991: 319) is that 'traditional women' have a 'legitimate' objection to affirmative action because if, through it, 'a large number of women obtain desirable positions that otherwise would have gone to men, female traditionalists, who depend on the earnings of male relatives to sustain their way of life, risk becoming worse off'.

Again, 'women' are seen to be 'different' from 'Blacks' because some women might 'legitimately' 'choose' a different sphere of life. As in the 'lack of interest' cases described above, this 'choice' is seen to operate independently of political constraints. 'Women' are either 'traditional' or 'assimilationist'. This is a version of the sameness/difference dichotomy which suggests that 'women' are either like 'men', or are different from them. Elsewhere (Bacchi, 1990) I have shown that this kind of comparison ignores the way in which social conditions produce constraints on 'choices'. It also enshrines a notion of 'woman' from which some women are 'allowed' to deviate.

Rosenfeld (1991: 320) goes on to elevate the claims of 'assimilationist women' over those of 'traditional women' on the grounds that support of the former for affirmative action is 'more weighty relative to their life plans': 'affirmative action is tied in with the opportunity to compete on an equal footing, with the equality of respect and dignity associated with not being discriminated [sic] on the basis of gender, with the satisfaction to be derived from holding an enriching and fulfilling job'. Therefore, for 'female assimilationists', affirmative action 'may affect both self-respect and security', while for 'female traditionalists' it 'only seems to reduce security'.

Instead of problematizing a system which devalues nurturing and care of children, Rosenberg sets out 'assimilation' into existing work relations as the key to self-respect. So, while in his schema, the notion of 'woman' is not used to undermine affirmative action for 'women', 'woman' and the responsibilities associated with this designation are denigrated. Here, affirmative action for 'women' means being allowed to become like 'men'. This form of incorporation of 'women' is the dominant theme explored in Chapter 5.

Some opponents of strong affirmative action draw attention to the 'problem' of family responsibilities, but in a perverse fashion. Alan Goldman (1976: 194), for example, is prepared to endorse child care as a 'remedial' form of affirmative action for 'women'. Richard Lester (1974: 40) states that '[F]emale faculty especially need those provisions for periods when pregnancy and child-rearing may make part-time employment necessary and desirable.' Now, few feminists today would deny the need to address the unequal division of domestic labour and many, myself included, would like to see a kind of affirmative action which trained men for such duties. But Goldman and Lester have no such agenda. Rather the 'problem' is seen to be 'women's' family responsibilities – and the solution, to facilitate the combining of paid work and family responsibilities by *women*, not to disrupt the assumed gender distribution of these roles. In this way 'women's' 'difference' is used to explain their 'disadvantage', while the notion that they are 'different' is maintained. And this very 'difference' is used to delegitimize strong affirmative action for 'women'.

In these examples, the traditional characterization of 'woman' is used to undermine strong affirmative action for 'women'. Domestic responsibilities are 'women's' responsibilities and, since 'women' 'choose' them, strong affirmative action is considered inappropriate. Among supporters of some 'preferential' treatment, such as Rosenfeld, some women are allowed to become like 'men'. In these cases, domestic responsibilities simply disappear from the analysis.

The 'problem' of domestic responsibilities, as Paul Burstein (1985: 175) suggests, may be one reason affirmative action for 'women' is more controversial or more resisted than other kinds of affirmative action. Theorized differently, it threatens the lifestyles of more men more directly by undermining the public/private split which allows many men to leave domestic responsibilities to women. It may also help to explain why Black opponents of affirmative action tend to be men.[7]

'Women' and invisible Black women

The point of the above analysis is not that it is inappropriate to consider differences in the kinds of oppression linked to race or gender, but to see how comparisons between 'Blacks' and 'women' have been used to undermine affirmative action for 'women' or to limit the impact it could have. The flipside of the politics of race and affirmative action in the United States is that many feminist theorists have felt impelled to argue that 'women' are indeed *as oppressed as* 'Blacks'.

Classic feminist texts, including William Thompson's *Appeal* (1825 [1983]), Mary Wollstonecraft's *Vindication of the Rights of Women* (1792 [1978]), and John Stuart Mill's *Subjection of Women* (1869 [1983]) all 'exploit the power of the slavery analogy', to borrow Vron Ware's words (1992: 109), to interpret 'women's' 'servitude'. Historically the women's movement in the United States has ridden on the coat-tails of the nineteenth-century anti-slavery and late twentieth-century black liberation movements. As Vron Ware (1992: 31) puts it: 'feminism owed its analysis of oppression, its reliance on autonomy and separatism, its understanding of equality, to the emergence of black politics throughout the sixties.'

Women in both periods, who have tried to find some space to debate 'women's' situation, have often employed a race/sex analogy (LaRue, 1976). Margaret Simons (1979) examines this strategy in the work of Simone de Beauvoir, Kate Millett, Shulamith Firestone, and Mary Daly (see also H. Hacker, 1951; Weisstein, 1970). The coining of the term 'sexism' from 'racism' is only the most obvious example of attempts to define 'women's' oppression as *like* 'Black' oppression.

Black feminist theorists (for example, LaRue, 1976; Simons, 1979; King, 1989; Williams, 1991) have drawn attention to problems with the analogy. They have made two major points. First, that the women who drew these comparisons represented a distinct subgroup of women. They were mainly white and hence the kinds of problems they saw as important were not necessarily the problems some Black women would identify as important. A related point is that the race/sex analogy makes Black women disappear. As Deborah King (1989) explains, 'The experience of black women is apparently assumed, though never explicitly stated, to be synonymous with that of either black males or white females'. King insists that the 'substantive differences' in forms of oppression 'need to be identified and to inform conceptualizations.'

A key point in this book is the need to pay attention to the consequences of feminist attempts to find a political space for 'women'. Where this has involved claiming that '*women*' are like other outgroups, it has meant of necessity denying the differences among women. Within the context of antidiscrimination and affirmative action law, it has also meant that 'women' are set in competition with 'other minorities' (Bacchi, 1990: 170; Davis, 1993: 35, 45).

As Kimberle Crenshaw (1989: 145–52) explains, the end result is that, in this framework, 'efforts to restructure the distribution of opportunity' are defeated, and change is limited to 'minor adjustments within an established hierarchy'. This is not surprising in her view as antidiscrimination law is 'not grounded in a bottom-up commitment to improve the substantive conditions for those who are victimized by the interplay of numerous factors.' She challenges the whole process-based definition of discrimination which views 'that the wrong which antidiscrimination law addresses is the use of race or gender factors to interfere with decisions that would otherwise be fair or neutral.' This point is touched on in Chapter 2.

Crenshaw (1989: 151) criticizes what she calls the 'but for' model in antidiscrimination law. Nitya Duclos (1993) calls it the 'only one thing wrong at a time' antidiscrimination doctrine. In this model, 'sex and race discrimination comes to be defined in terms of the experiences of those who are privileged *but for* their racial or sexual characteristics [my italics].' For Black women, this model has meant trying to fit their experiences to categories which are inappropriate, as Crenshaw (1989: 151) explains: 'the racial context in which Black women find themselves makes the creation of a political consciousness that is oppositional to Black men difficult. Yet . . . the assertion of racial community sometimes supports defensive priorities that marginalize Black women.' The problem is more than the creation of separate categories of 'disadvantage', however. As Nitya Duclos (1993: 26) explains, the problem is a concept of discrimination which 'conceives of difference as an inherent characteristic of the nondominant group rather than a feature arising out of the relationship between groups.' Because of this, as Kimberle Crenshaw (1989: 151) insists, 'the *privileging* of whiteness or maleness is implicit [italics in original].' Iris Young (1990) and Martha Minow (1990) draw similar conclusions.

Looking for possible ways forward, Nitya Duclos (1993: 50) makes several important points. First, she insists that the solution is *not* to eliminate categories, even if this were possible: 'We can continue to use the categories we have, in this case the grounds of discrimination, but we should strive to make them flexible, dynamic, and relational.'[8] Going further, she (here as Nitya Iyer, 1993: 204–5) suggests finding ways to expose the limitations of the categorical approach to equality. This means displacing 'the dominant group's hold on the centre'. To this end, '[W]e need to generate a self-consciousness about the location of the dominant group, to make visible the invisible norms against which claimants are measured.'

Chapters 1 and 2 develop a very similar argument. There the case is made that drawing attention to the invisible norm means highlighting the place and power of the categorizers, those who create the categories of antidiscrimination and affirmative action law, and who then demand that women and Blacks fit themselves to them. I contend further that drawing attention to the particular constellation of power relations which has impelled women activists to campaign for 'women' *or* 'Blacks' frees up their political options and releases them from the interminable debates about who 'women' and 'Blacks' are. The political task becomes exposing the ways in which 'women' and other categories are deployed, and contesting deployments which delimit progressive change.

Here, we need to point out that setting 'women' against other outgroups minimizes change in at least two ways. First, the 'spoils' are to be divvied up. And second, only those who can manage to fit their case to established categories of 'disadvantage' get heard.

'Women', 'class' and 'culture'

Given the limitations on current understandings of affirmative action, it is not surprising that it has been attacked by many on the left (Nagel, 1979; Sher, 1975; Young, 1990). Common criticisms are that it benefits only some women and some Blacks – those who need 'help' least – and that it is assimilationist, compelling outgroups to adopt the standards of ingroups. Marilyn Frye (1992: 787) describes it as 'a quite selective strategy of assimilation, co-optation, and tokenism.' We have also seen that the reform positions outgroups as the problem and, despite the focus on groups, is ultimately individualistic since the goal is to remove obstacles to individual advancement (see Chapter 2).

Some of these criticisms are also endorsed by opponents who align themselves with conservative politics. The argument that the reform is overinclusive is particularly popular (Edwards, 1987; Lynch, 1989). This position is commonly linked to an analysis which insists that poverty is the 'real' cause of 'disadvantage' (Wilson, 1987). To quote William Julius Wilson, 'the race-specific policies emanating from the civil rights revolution, although beneficial to more advantaged blacks . . . do little for those who are truly disadvantaged' (1987: 110, 153). Affirmative action is also blamed for the increasing fragmentation of the population. The prophecy that it would reinforce racial and other categories, when the goal should have been to render these unimportant, is held to have come to pass (see Lynch, 1989 for example).

Given these conditions it is not surprising that some reformers are in retreat, and reforms aimed at 'class' seem like a good place to retreat to. According to Paul Starr (1992), due to the fallout accompanying affirmative action, 'Americans concerned about reducing racial inequalities' ought to shift their focus to 'the reconstruction of civil society in minority communities' and 'broad policies for economic opportunity and security that benefit low- and middle-income Americans, black and white alike.' Barbara Ehrenreich (1989) makes the point that at particular junctures in American history a focus on poverty has been considered safer than a focus on race. This is so because analysts create the 'poor' to suit their analysis. This is particularly relevant to the recent invention of an 'underclass'.

Starr (1992) refers consistently to affirmative action as 'preferential policies', confirming the dominant common understanding described at the outset of this chapter. He also takes on board the argument that affirmative action has perpetuated racism, by accentuating rather than annulling racial divisions. His rationale for affirmative action is 'reparations' and hence the 'most deserving recipients' are 'Blacks': 'I believe obligations of the United States to black Americans are historically singular.' 'Women' receives little attention, and then only in the context of family. As we shall see, 'women' is commonly subsumed by and in 'family'. So, Starr (1992: 13) highlights as useful, 'child support assurance', which 'would have a progressive impact on women's economic circumstances after divorce and sharply cut back the existing welfare system', and 'family leave policies' that 'help parents, *usually mothers*, spend more time at home [my italics]'.

As in the discussion above, it is noteworthy that the implication here is that 'women's' problems stem from the domestic division of labour and that the solution is to make it easier for 'women' to balance paid work and family responsibilities. While Starr would see himself as a progressive, he notes that conservatives ought to recognize how his proposals advance their goals. In his words, '[T]here ought to be no disagreement . . . on the principle that social policy should aim to support and instill family responsibility.' The turn to 'class' then has serious implications for many women, reinforcing in some interpretations a vision of 'women' as society's carers.

Other reformers, disillusioned with affirmative action and the fallout it attracts, have found a commitment to 'diversity' promising. The language of 'diversity' has an obvious appeal. It heralds a different kind of 'Great Society', one in which 'differences' will be valued. To Marilyn Frye (1992: 788–9), for example, '"[M]ulticulturalism" has a sweeter sound . . . than "affirmative action"'. It also provides an opening to supporters of affirmative action for staff and students to claim that being able to represent the knowledges and values of particular groups and communities constitutes a part of merit.

The diversity debate has to a degree transformed the discourses surrounding affirmative action (see, for example, the articles in *Change: The Magazine of Higher Learning*, 1991). Marilyn Frye (1992: 789, fn. 13) notes that in the university at which she works, the term affirmative action has become *lingua non grata* among those who are institutionally responsible for promoting 'diversity' and that the term multiculturalism is preferred. On university campuses, debates about diversity have become entangled in political disputes about the appropriate shape of a liberal arts curriculum. Liberals have taken up the mantle of 'diversity'; social conservatives talk about its dangers. Frye (1992: 781) refers to the 'recent national tempest about "diversity" and the canonical curriculum.' Lynch (1989) berates the 'radical language' of 'diversity' (see also Alan Bloom, 1987).

Paradoxically the diversity discourse has been taken up in management literature as a defence of the 'free' market. In brief, managers are being told that in the next century they will have to 'manage diverse workforces' and that they had better become familiar with ways to do this. Much is made of the fact that in the near future the majority of new job entrants will come from minorities or will be women. Attention is also drawn to the benefits of having a diverse workforce when wishing to capture an increasingly diverse (ethnic) market.

R. Roosevelt Thomas (Solomon, 1991: 92), the guru of 'diversity management' in the United States,[9] sees this approach to change as a step forward from affirmative action because affirmative action forces companies to take on newcomers and to make them fit. This, it is argued, generates an us–them mentality, causes conflict, and reduces the productivity of the enterprise (see also Caudron, 1993; Jackson et al., 1992; Castelli, 1990). The aim of learning to 'manage diversity', according to Thomas, is to identify all of the organization's activities as a 'positive-sum' game in which 'all employees can gain from the enhanced productivity of people who are currently underachieving.' The underlying philosophy, as in much human resource management, is creating conditions to get 'satisfactory performance' from the new diverse workforce.

Thomas (1990: 112) is blunt: '[I]t means getting from employees, first, everything we have a right to expect, and second – if we do it well – everything they have to give.'

The language of economic rationalism frames managing diversity programmes. The argument runs that 'deregulation' will enhance competitiveness and this will generate commercial incentives to 'reward merit regardless of other factors' (Niland and Champion, 1990: 5). A basic assumption is, as Thomas says, that 'prejudice is almost gone'. Productivity, we are told, is the employers' primary concern and hence they will grasp the logic of 'creating a work setting geared to the upward mobility of all kinds of people, including white males' (Thomas, 1990: 108).

Much has been made of the fact that, when affirmative action came under attack from the Reagan administration, American employers rallied to its defence (*Harvard Law Review*, 1989). This attracted attention largely because of the initial hostility in the business community to the reform when it was first introduced. The turnabout on the part of employers is a result of the way in which affirmative action has been translated into policy. We have seen how it has come to be understood primarily as removing obstacles to opportunity. Since these obstacles are located in employment systems, it is argued that it is appropriate to have employers perform the required analysis of these systems. Most often, human resource departments are assigned responsibility for this analysis.

Managing diversity takes this understanding to its logical conclusion. Repeating that affirmative action is 'good business practice', the argument comes full circle and employers insist that they can do it best themselves. 'Managing diversity' is used to describe this 'new' regime of self-regulation.[10] In this way a scenario is constructed in which employers become the ones responsible for what affirmative action means and how it is implemented. Hence, it is not surprising that overt employer resistance to affirmative action has become modest praise. Legislated affirmative action has not, as feared, undermined management prerogative; it has confirmed it. This is to be expected in an era marked by resurgence of a belief in market forces and the virtues of privatization and deregulation (Taylor-Gooby, 1994: 388, 401).

It is interesting to note how, perversely, a conceptual development in understandings of discrimination could be used to support this interpretation. As discussed in the last chapter, the notion of structural discrimination evolved as a response to the inadequacies of a model of discrimination as due to individual evil intent. The focus shifted to the way in which institutional practices which appear neutral can have discriminatory outcomes (Bacchi, 1990: 162–5). Locating the 'problem' in an organization's systems, however, provides the necessary rationale for turning over the design of affirmative action to those who know those systems best – employers. Hence, what started as an attempt to confront employers with the depth of the discrimination 'problem' has produced a management approach which leaves employers in control of employer–employee relations.

The emphasis in much of the managing diversity literature is that diversity must be valued – people must be allowed to be 'different'. A good deal of this sounds positive. Thomas (1990: 112) appears almost postmodern in his rejection of the 'melting pot', and in his insistence that companies come to terms with *unassimilated diversity*' (italics in original). In managing diversity our 'differences' are such that efforts at change bypass the group and look to the individual. According to Thomas, managing diversity 'is a vision which sidesteps the questions of equality, ignores the tensions of co-existence, plays down the uncomfortable realities of differences and focuses instead on individual enablement.'

Managing diversity looks to a cultural awareness model of change which starts from the premise that sensitivity to people's 'differences' will remove hostility (Kagod, 1991: 8). There is an implication in much of the literature that *talking* about differences will reduce racial, sexual and other kinds of hostility and discrimination.

This model, as several critics point out, understates the power politics at work in discrimination (Stasiulis, 1991: 246). Clare Burton (1992) highlights the dangers in this analysis: 'it hides structural inequality which becomes invisible when the problem is individualised and broadly dispersed in this way, to cover all differences'. Put more tersely, '[S]ex and race-based power relations and control strategies are denied.' In effect, the managing diversity exponents studied here undermine the starting premise of antidiscrimination law, that groups like 'women', Blacks and those with disabilities, among others, are the targets of discriminatory practices and hence ought to be the targets of reform.

It is possible to see diversity management as consistent with the dominant understanding of affirmative action since it emphasizes removing obstacles to opportunity. However, the managing diversity discourse makes groups disappear completely. There is thus also a shift away from any sense that specified groups in the United States experience 'disadvantage'.

I have noted the limitations of a 'disadvantage' discourse and the problems with homogeneous target groups elsewhere. However, here we see that attempts to smooth over categorical distinctions can also be regressive. The lesson is salutary for those wishing to acknowledge 'difference'. The way in which the apparently progressive notions of 'diversity' and 'structural discrimination' can be co-opted also suggests the limitations of conceptual revision as a reform strategy. Instead more emphasis needs to be placed on *the ways in which concepts are deployed to serve particular political ends*.

Managing diversity has particular implications for 'women'. In a sense it simply highlights a point made previously – that 'women' as a category is an afterthought in American politics and political theory. It is clear in the managing diversity literature that 'diversity' is about racial or ethnic diversity. It is difficult even to find a place for 'women' in diversity management programmes. 'Women' is, if anything, an embarrassment, since it is assumed that different cultures have different attitudes to 'women' and their role, and these attitudes must be accommodated. 'Women' becomes one of the 'differences' that can be talked about and sorted out.

There is also little attention given to domestic responsibilities in much managing diversity literature. Given the conviction that the goal is to get from employees 'everything they have to give', this is not surprising. When the subject is raised, it is within the framework discussed earlier – that something should be done to assist 'women' with 'their' domestic obligations. 'Women' continues to be the problem, and 'men's' relationship to home and family goes unanalysed.

Conclusion

The American example illustrates forcefully the ways in which structuring discourses set limits on change. Notions of 'disadvantage' currently exist alongside a new emphasis on 'individual enablement' and 'creating a work setting geared to the upward mobility of all kinds people, including white males' (Thomas, 1990: 108).

Both conceptualizations of inequality have serious limitations. The former allows ingroups to decide upon the extent of their beneficence. The latter leaves unequal power relations unexamined and in place. Within the former, groups are impelled to ignore their internal complexity. Within the latter, internal complexity displaces the group. The lesson in all this is the need to become sensitive *to the ways in which categories feature in political debates, either as objects to be reified or as distinctions to be blurred.*

In the affirmative action debate in the United States, 'women' as a category is ignored, or subsumed within understandings developed for other social categories. When 'women' is considered, a particular notion of 'woman' is applied – one which associates all women with domestic responsibilities and which assumes that this allocation is both natural and just. In some cases, as we have seen, this understanding is used to challenge the *raison d'être* of strong affirmative action for 'women'.

Unpacking these understandings highlights the politics of theory and compels participation in that politics. It is clearly necessary to insist upon a recognition of the differential location of women based upon their class, race, sexual preference, and so on. At the same time, it is dangerous in the extreme to abandon the category 'women'. Rather there is a continuing need to contest its meanings and the political uses to which these are put.

Notes

1 Mary Jane Mossman (1989: 207) uses the notion of women as an afterthought but in a different way from the way I use it. She suggests that theories of the individual or of the community 'address the experiences of women as an afterthought rather than using women's experiences as central to the construction of a framework of analysis.' Though I agree with the implication that theories like individualism and collectivism reflect the interests of those who generate them, I would be reluctant to take on a notion of 'women's experiences' in such an unproblematized form. On this point see Scott, 1992. Rather I am emphasizing that little theoretical attention is paid to 'women' as a category. I would also stress the political uses of notions like 'individualism' and 'collectivism' rather than suggesting that they have some commonly understood meaning.

2 Currently volunteers in California are collecting over six hundred thousand signatures on a petition to force a referendum on the issue in 1996. The 'Civil Rights Initiative', backed by the State's Republican Party, would ban State institutions from using 'race, sex, color, ethnicity, or national origin as a criterion for discrimination against, or granting preferential treatment to, any individual or group.' One of its supporters, Professor Glynn Custred, who teaches at California State University, and who is a self-proclaimed conservative, marshals liberal political ideals to defend his case, illustrating the kind of political uses of conceptual categories which this volume hopes to highlight. To quote Professor Custred, 'This initiative is designed to make sure we have a color-blind society with individual rights rather than group entitlements' (quoted in *The Adelaide Advertiser*, 14 January, 1995, p. 15). Two recent Supreme Court decisions, one increasing the level of scrutiny applied to granting contracts to minority firms and another holding that 'test scores and achievements by minority students could be considered only as they related directly to past discrimination' (*Guardian Weekly*, 18 June, 1995), suggest that the conservative attack on affirmative action is having results.

3 As support for this conclusion, a recent review of books on affirmative action by a sympathizer, Andrew Hacker (1992: 30), distinguishes between affirmative action and equal opportunity in this way: 'it [affirmative action] usually calls for hiring or promoting persons who either have not met the customary criteria, or are lower down on the list of those deemed to be qualified.' Another supporter, Gertrude Ezorsky (quoted in Hacker) agrees that 'a typical affirmative action case' is one in which 'a basically qualified black is selected over a more qualified white.' Similarly, Catharine Stimpson (1993: 4) draws a distinction between two affirmative action strategies, the first 'to reach out and encourage historically disadvantaged groups', the second, 'to permit race and/or gender to become a preference in hiring, admissions, and financial aid – in the belief that preference will remedy past discrimination.'

4 See Chapter 2 for clarification of the constructed difference between 'hard' or 'strong', and 'soft' affirmative action.

5 Young (1990: 195) says that '[S]upporters of affirmative action would be less on the defensive . . . if they positively acknowledged that these policies discriminate, instead of trying to argue that they are an extension of or compatible with a principle of non-discrimination.' While I take the point that Young might be using the term 'to discriminate' simply to mean 'to differentiate', at other places in her text (158, 212) she uses the language of 'special treatment' and 'disadvantage' without noting that such language positions recipients of affirmative action as 'beneficiaries' and as the 'problem'. This is unfortunate as she does a superb job of challenging the apparent neutrality of appointments procedures and criteria.

6 Rosenfeld (1991: 319 and *passim*) attempts to develop a model for reconciling differing positions on affirmative action through a notion of justice as reversible reciprocity based on Habermas's idea of communicative ethics. In this model, only views which are 'genuine', and hence not strategic, are considered as acceptable in the dialogic process: 'one of the

fundamental tenets of such an ethics is the commitment to remain open to nonstrategic attempts at dialogic persuasion'. See also Sowell, 1984.

7 Julianne Malveaux (1991: 60) makes the point that all Black conservatives are men in her discussion of Thomas Sowell, Walter Williams, Glenn Loury, and Shelby Steele. She suggests that '[T]hese black men tend to be high achievers who may feel diminished by the notion that they got where they are because of affirmative action.'

8 Australia's recent Law Reform Commission Report (1994: 65–8) addressed this problem and suggested that in Australia, where there are separate federal laws for sex discrimination and race discrimination, a possible option is 'to allow the complainant under each head to be joined and make provision for them to be heard together.' The argument advanced was that '[T]he joining of complaints should enable the tribunal to assess properly the true loss, damage or injury suffered by the complainant.'

9 Thomas is the executive director of the American Institute for Managing Diversity at Atlanta's Morehouse College. In 1990 he wrote a key article, followed by a book (1991) endorsing 'diversity management'.

10 It should be noted that some defenders of a managing diversity approach insist that government regulation of industry initiatives is crucial (Agocs, Burr and Somerset, 1992).

4

The Politics of Displacement

The existence of affirmative action policies for women in the countries considered in this volume shows that at particular times, in some places, 'women' has been accorded recognition as a category deserving political attention. This book examines how this has been achieved and details a variety of strategies implemented to delimit the extent and nature of this attention. One of the most insidious of these is the politics of displacement. This is a shorthand phrase which describes the identification of 'women' as one among a number of what are seen as interest groups competing for affirmative action 'favours'. The strategy finds a place in all the countries under study but nowhere is it better exemplified than in Canada.

The way in which Canadian Employment Equity[1] legislation targets four designated groups – 'women', Aboriginal peoples, the disabled and visible minorities – has deleterious consequences for all the groups concerned and these will be discussed. But, it will be argued, women suffer most from the design of this policy.

It should be made clear at the outset that there is no implication in this analysis that groups other than women do not face discrimination, nor that 'women' is a homogeneous group. Nor is it implied that categories are not required in order to address discrimination, though the point has been made several times that current understandings of discrimination effectively disaggregate targeted groups into competing individuals. The point here is to highlight how identity categories are manipulated for political ends and in particular to demonstrate how this manoeuvre displaces 'women'.

A good deal has been written recently on the social construction of political identities (Gunew and Yeatman, 1993; Donald and Rattansi, 1992; Pettman, 1992b). This chapter supplements this literature and highlights the dangers involved in engaging in identity politics without examining the effects of category construction. It also illustrates the importance of paying attention to specificities of time and place in the deployment of identity categories. Finally, it shows the close connection between identity categories and conceptual categories in debates around the relationship between claims by women to individual rights and the claims of groups, including groups of women activists, to collective rights.

Canadian history revolves around efforts to create a nation and a sense of nation. The chief impediments to these efforts have been the vast geographical area, which encompasses diverse bases of production, and the historical legacy of the British conquest of French inhabitants in 1763. The first has produced identity claims tied to region; the second, claims tied to language, national origin and founding people status. Sometimes, as in Quebec, the two kinds of claims coincide (Van Loon and Whittington, 1981: 70). Attempts to forge a nation and to hold it together have had to find ways to accommodate these claims. The 1841 Act of Union sought a *modus vivendi* between the new English and the conquered French settlements. The British North America Act (1867) was bought at the price of a continental railway system linking West to East, a Senate based on proportional representation of the provinces, a constitution which gave the federal government 'a comprehensive power to make law' but which exempted from this general grant 'certain carefully specified powers' to be held by the provinces, and guarantees of separate school rights for religious minorities (Van Loon and Whittington, 1981: 244–5).

As Jane Jenson (1991: 214) describes, there have been times when a national identity seemed more fragile and times when it achieved some semblance of permanency. The latter occurred during the Second World War, for example, when in her words, 'the two problematic couplets (Canada–US; English–French) were interpreted through a lens that could view the whole and that privileged that whole, a lens that fitted with the regulatory patterns established after 1945 for both the economy and politics.' Significantly for this study, Jenson argues that in this nationwide conception of citizenship, little attention was paid to the 'special needs of particular groups' – 'only individuals could be endowed with rights'.[2]

In the last 20 years, however, identity claims based upon attachment to collectivities have proliferated. The most publicized of these are associated with the resurgence of demands for separatism in Quebec, the emergence of Canada's First Nations as a lobby, the politicization of ethnic minorities, and the emergence of equality-seeking groups attached to new social movements. This last category includes groups of women activists. Jenson (1991: 221) notes that Canadian feminists have sought 'not only the right to strive for equality with men but also the acknowledgement that achievement of that goal could involve, at times, recognition that women are a collectivity distinct in many ways from men.' She identifies affirmative action as an indication of this demand for 'categorical equity'. As Jenson notes, the demand for 'fairer representation for all categories of the population' means that 'the terms "Canada" and "Canadians", as well as "citizen" and "fairness", are again hotly contested.' Jenson (1991: 222) feels that '[O]nly if this conflict is again resolved and some consensus is reached about fairly assigned citizenship rights, will the next "Canadian identity" acquire meaning and practical content'.

This chapter is about this contestation. More precisely, it argues that 'women' is not faring well in this contestation and suggests reasons why this is so.

Employment equity at work

In 1986 the Federal Conservative Party introduced the Legislated Employment Equity Program (LEEP) which became the Employment Equity Act (EEA), and the Federal Contractors' Program (FCP) which together encompass Canada's approach to labour market affirmative action (or employment equity). EEA covers approximately 370 federally-regulated employers primarily in the banking, communications and transportation industries. FCP targets another 1350 companies.

Under EEA, companies have to submit an annual report. In this report they provide a 'workforce census', showing where designated groups are located in their companies, and setting targets which compare with availability data, about which more will be said shortly. Under the FCP, which is a policy not a legislated programme, companies who wish to do business with the government sign a certificate of commitment to introduce employment equity. There is no reporting requirement. Companies are subjected to compliance reviews which evaluate their programmes. Those which fall short are disbarred from competition for future contracts until they get their 'house in order' (Agocs, Burr and Somerset, 1992: 1–5).

The many critics of EEA focus on the overconcentration on numbers reporting and the lack of attention to qualitative measures (Canadian Congress for Learning Opportunities for Women, 1992: 2; National Action Committee on the Status of Women, 1992b: 1; Canadian Advisory Council on the Status of Women, 1992: 23–4). Put bluntly, this legislation requires only that employers report statistics; there is not even a requirement that they institute an employment equity programme. The 1992 Redway Review (Canada, 1992) acknowledged these weaknesses in the legislation but to date no attempt has been made to alter reporting mechanisms.

There are also problems with the implementation of FCP. Companies are warned when a review is impending and it is difficult to see any reason for them to take any action before this warning. The former Director of FCP, Neil Gavigan (interviewed 17 May, 1994), confirmed that very few employers had a programme in place when they were first contacted for review. There is then a desk audit, time to comply, an in-person audit, more time to comply, a possible appeal mechanism, and a final recourse to ministerial intervention. In the words of Marnie Clark, former Director General, Employment Equity Branch, 'There are a lot of steps along the way' (Sullivan, 1988: 18). As early as 1985 the Canadian Labour Congress foresaw problems with what they described as 'a never-ending appeal procedure' (Canadian Labour Congress (CLC),

1985: 10). And again, employers have little impetus to implement change until compelled to. In addition, Gavigan explained, there is a tendency for review officers, who are taken in hand by company executives, to feel sympathy for employers. In the event, compliance reviews are secret documents and to date only four employers have been sanctioned. At the stage of sanction a company has only to introduce a programme to regain access to bidding. Monetary sanctions of up to $50 000 can be applied but, up to and including 1990, no sanction exceeded $3000 (Canadian Congress for Learning Opportunities for Women, 1992: 9).

As in the United States, affirmative action/employment equity is seen to be part of business and management planning. One is struck by the extent to which programme design is left in the hands of employers, and monitoring is perfunctory (Canada, 1992). EEA stipulates the need to consult with unions or bargaining agents, and with other employee representatives where no union exists. But it is clear that this con-sultation is not taking place (Canada, 1992: 15–16). Moreover, employers are free to set their own targets and objectives, and to modify these according to what is considered reasonable given the economic climate (Abella, 1987: 9). Monitoring has been left to the Canadian Human Rights Commission (CHRC), which has caused endless confusion about roles and responsibilities.[3]

As in the United States, numbers of employers, initially hostile to the proposal of legislated affirmative action, are today lavishing praise on the government for supporting what is described as just 'good busi-ness practice' (Employment and Immigration Canada, 1992b). There are annual award ceremonies for examples of 'best practice' (Employment and Immigration Canada, 1992a: 4). There is also evidence that a new discourse of managing diversity threatens to displace employment equity, in ways similar to those traced in the United States in Chapter 3 (Public Service Commission of Canada, 1993).[4]

Meanings of affirmative action

Canada's antidiscrimination policy is lodged within and handled through its human rights commissions. The idea of a human rights policy emerged after the Second World War, stimulated by the international struggle against fascism and the 'surge of egalitarian idealism which the war had generated' (Howe, 1991: 787). A new concept of state responsibility to provide for the social right to equal opportunity developed.

The conceptual evolution of understandings of antidiscrimination in Canada broadly followed the pattern established in the United States and discernible in most Western industrialized countries. An initial focus on intent was replaced by attention to structural or systemic discrimination, and this was accompanied by endorsement of proactive measures such as affirmative action (Howe, 1991: 794, 798). R. Brian Howe shows how antidiscrimination could be and was supported both by reform liberals and by conservatives. Many of the latter were themselves members of minorities who claimed first-hand experience of discrimination. This they denounced as a practice 'at odds with the individual freedom of its victims' and 'as a contradiction of Canadian liberal values' (Howe, 1991: 786). However, they trod and still tread an uneasy line between their opposition to discrimination and their hesitation to turn to the state to do something about it.

Echoing the analysis of equal opportunity rhetoric in the United States (see Chapter 3), Howe suggests that in Canada 'a continuum of positions exists between reformers and conservative liberals, a continuum which shifts over time' (Howe, 1991: 787). As I have already argued, it is both more accurate and more useful to think about the debates surrounding antidiscrimination and affirmative action in this way instead of constructing opposed camps of thought and presenting them as irreconcilable. In fact, as argued in the preceding chapter, the tendency to construct sharply opposed ways of thinking about the issue is itself a political manoeuvre, intended to paint one option as wholly foreign and undesirable. So, we find debates about 'equal opportunity' versus 'equal results', and the condemnation of affirmative action as 'reverse discrimination' and 'social engineering', which we have seen in the United States, replicated in Canada (Howe, 1991: 798; Knopff, 1989).[5]

In Canada, however, there has been much greater willingness to use the language of 'equal results'. This willingness appeared as early as 1982 when the Public Service Commission announced that Canadian affirmative action is a 'results-oriented approach' intended to redress 'systemic discrimination in employment practices' (quoted in Winn, 1985). In the Commission Report (Abella, 1984) which led to the introduction of employment equity, Rhys Phillips, one of the architects of employment equity in Canada, describes affirmative action as 'a comprehensive planning process designed to bring about not only equality of opportunity but also equality of results' (Phillips, 1984: 22). Some of this rhetoric is ambiguous, however. Rosalie Abella, who headed the Commission on Equality in Employment, made it plain that 'Employment equity is access to the fullest *opportunity* to exercise individual potential' (Abella, 1987: 2; my italics). Her main concern was to challenge notions of formal equality which specified that equality meant treating likes alike:

> There is a difference between treating people equally as we do in civil rights and treating people as equals as we do in human rights. For purposes of the former, we treat everyone the same; for purposes of the latter, we treat them according to their differences.

This is an argument which has still to be accepted in many jurisdictions (Bacchi, 1990: 112 and *passim*).

The acceptance of 'differences' and the acceptance of the place of 'different' treatment in achieving equality is thus prominent in the design of Canadian employment equity legislation. The Employment Equity Act (1986, Section 2) specifies that 'employment equity means more than treating persons in the same way but also requires special measures and the accommodation of differences.'

There is explicit affirmation that 'disadvantaged' groups require a range of 'special measures' and 'reasonable accommodation' in order to achieve equality in employment prospects. According to Employment Equity Branch's *Guide for Employers* (Canada, 1991: 11–12), special measures, which include such things as targeted recruitment or special training initiatives, are 'designed to accelerate the entry, development and promotion of designated group members from among the interested and qualified work force.' 'Reasonable accommodation' takes up the requirement in Canadian Human Rights codes which places employers under a duty to demonstrate a degree of flexibility in meeting the reasonable needs of employees. Reasonable accommodation can include things such as flexible work schedules to facilitate the balancing of work and family commitments. Most often, it refers to the need to redesign job duties and provide technical and human support services for the disabled.

The other indication of a commitment to move beyond formal equality and towards 'equal results' appears in references to a 'representative workforce'. The Abella Report forecast that employers would be required to compare their workforce census figures with 'currently available relevant external labour supply' (Abella, 1984: 206, fn. 43). The Employment Equity Act (1986, Section 4) stipulates that 'An employer shall . . . ensure that persons in designated groups achieve a degree of representation . . . that is at least proportionate to their representation (i) in the work force, or (ii) in those segments of the work force that are identifiable by qualification, eligibility, or geography.' This is the rationale behind the use of availability data (see Employment and Immigration Canada, 1991b: 20). As in the United States, Canadian companies are required to compare the percentages of designated groups in their companies, in promotions, in new hires and so on against a measure of their availability in the population. Statistics Canada plays an important role in providing companies with the required statistical information. However, there are disputes about the usefulness of this procedure. The statistics usually indicate workforce figures and, as critics point out, these reflect established patterns of discrimination (see for example Canadian Advisory Council on the Status of Women (CAC), 1992: 19; Harvey and Blakely, 1993; National Employment Equity Network, 1990: 7).

Nonetheless, the example of special measures and talk about a 'representative workforce' indicate that at one level some Canadian policy makers have developed an understanding of affirmative action broader than simply opening up opportunities (see C. Williams, 1986: 124–5). And it is interesting to speculate upon just what in the Canadian experience has made such moves possible. Here, as in the listing of four designated groups (discussion to follow), I would suggest that the debate around the introduction of a Charter of Rights, part of the process of patriating the constitution in 1981–82, created the space for these discursive shifts.

Leslie Pal (1993: 259) describes the discourses of the 'equality seeking groups', including those representing 'women', Aboriginal peoples and ethnic minorities, who campaigned to entrench the rights of these groups in the Charter. They demanded 'equality of status', 'equal rights to survival and prosperity' and, ultimately, 'equal outcomes and results'. As Pal says, this agenda goes 'well beyond the traditional or classical liberal vision of equal legal rights', and in his view shifted the political discourse leftward. These shifts, however, have been contained within an understanding of affirmative action, similar to that in the United States, which imposes serious limitations on the meaning of the reform.

In both the United States and in Canada, affirmative action is understood as a means of *assisting* those who are 'disadvantaged' to gain entry to existing positions and to promotions once in those positions. Even Canada's landmark *Andrews* decision, which dislodges the 'similarly situated' test for discrimination, is based upon a need to recognize 'disadvantage' (Bacchi and Marquis, 1994). This is to be accomplished through the removal of discriminatory barriers and with 'a little help along the way'. In both countries it is made explicit that any 'help' will stop short of 'undermining' existing standards of assessment.

There is an insistence that affirmative action does *not* contravene 'merit' and that those appointed would have to be 'qualified'. Government spokespeople repeatedly assert that Canada does not use quotas and that affirmative action does not transgress the merit principle (Winn, 1985: 28). Canada's Employment Equity Act (1986, Section 12) stipulates that the purpose of Employment Equity is 'To achieve equality in the workplace so that no person shall be denied employment opportunities or benefits for reasons *unrelated to ability*' (my italics). More recent literature distributed to employers (Employment and Immigration Canada, 1991b: 8) explains that the goal is 'full participation of *skilled individuals* from designated groups' (my italics). There is therefore an unquestioned assumption that the meaning of 'skill' is fairly straightforward. There is no questioning of existing means of ranking and assessment (see Colleen Sheppard, 1993).

As described in Chapter 2, the suggestion that 'disadvantaged' groups require some assistance to 'catch up', positions them as the problem, and leaves the characteristics and the advantages of those holding power unexamined (Eveline, 1994c; Bacchi, 1993). Moreover, this understanding means that decisions about the nature and size of the 'problem' reside with the dominant group (Razack, 1994: 68). At the same time, representing the reform as 'handouts to the needy' has led many members of targeted groups to disassociate themselves from the reform, undermining the base for political action.

Finally, the assumption that the goal is assimilation into existing work structures makes it difficult to criticize those structures. As Sherene Razack (1991: 49–50) points out, the focus in Canada may have shifted from 'abstract equality to equality measured in the pay and opportunities enjoyed by various groups'; however, this model continues to direct attention to 'how much of society's resources each possesses', inhibiting thinking about other forms of social organization.

The employment equity constituency

While, according to Howe (1991: 795), in the 1940s five groups were considered susceptible to discrimination and in need of protection – Japanese Canadians, Jews, Blacks, native peoples and women – it is notable that in the first instance, in Ontario in 1951, only discrimination based on race and religion in employment was prohibited. While legislation calling for equal pay for women was passed in the same year, it was not until the mid-1970s that protection against discrimination was extended to include sex and marital status, and not until 1986 did it extend to pregnancy. At the federal level, Cynthia Williams (1986: 108–9) confirms that in the 1950s discrimination was thought of largely with respect to race and religion: '[D]iscrimination against women was not a prominent issue on the civil liberties agenda'. As in the United States, it seems, 'women' was something of an afterthought in the antidiscrimination campaign.

As in the other Western industrialized countries examined in this book, 'women' marched onto the political agenda mainly because of economic considerations. These countries were experiencing a period of boom and a related labour shortage. Women were identified as available to fill this need (Prentice et al., 1988: 347). According to Cerise Morris (1980 in Toni Williams, 1990: 740), relative economic prosperity also created a space for development of humanitarian and civil rights claims. The resurgent women's movement was able to capitalize on this climate to register 'women' as claimants to political recognition. Their success in Canada is evidenced in the Royal Commission on the Status of Women (formed in 1968 and reported in 1970). Political factors, specifically that the Liberal government was a minority government and depended on the support of the more left-wing New Democratic Party, assisted these developments, as did the model of President Kennedy's Commission on the Status of Women (T. Williams, 1990: 740).

The particular reforms recommended by the Commission are not as important for the purposes of this study as is the fact that, in the words of Cerise Morris, '[B]y deciding to establish the RCSW [Royal

Commission on the Status of Women], the federal government clearly, and at one point in time, accepted and thus legitimized the social problem definition of the status of women' (Morris in Begin, 1992: 27). The essential point, confirmed by Monique Begin (1992: 26), is that before the Royal Commission 'women' did not represent 'a constituency in the political agenda of the Canadian state'.

It is also important that the stage of development of the women's movement at this time meant that there were important gaps in the Royal Commission's understanding of the varieties of women's experiences. Toni Williams demonstrates, for example, that 'the Report renders invisible the social and political realities of racialized Canadians.' Williams's argument, one which fits the analysis presented here, is that 'the law cannot centralize women's diversity because legal reform requires women to be just women' (T. Williams, 1990: 750, 739). 'Women' then was recognized in certain ways. The Report recommended, and the government proceeded to introduce in 1973, the Advisory Council on the Status of Women and in 1974 the Women's Programme in the Department of Secretary of State (Begin, 1992: 36). The Report also endorsed affirmative action for 'women', and in 1976 Cabinet adopted affirmative action for 'women' for hiring practices in Crown Corporations and in industries benefiting from government contracts (Burt, 1986: 150). Importantly, however, the Report was only ever endorsed in principle and the resources needed to implement it were not made available. This signalled to Sue Findlay, among others, the symbolic nature of the commitment to 'women'. And the gestures towards implementation established, as Findlay perceptively notes, a form of integration of 'women's' demands into established political discourse. Regarding 'women's' place on the Canadian political agenda, Findlay concludes: 'Responsiveness was limited to brief periods and was almost entirely due to converging political forces at a particular moment rather than reflecting any national commitment to women's equality' (Findlay, 1988: 32–42).

In the early 1970s there were clear indications of the mobilization of other political collectivities. The situation in French Canada played a significant role in the emergence of these identity claims. As Leslie Pal argues, in the early 1970s the federal government encouraged other ethnic groups to organize and to promote their interests as a way of diffusing any sense of Canada as two separate peoples and hence containing separatist stirrings in Quebec. The explicit recognition of multiculturalism and the provision of government funds to ethnic lobby groups played a part in the later emergence of claims by these groups to inclusion in employment equity (Pal, 1993: 14; see also Blishen, 1986: 19; Breton, 1986: 47). According to Jill Vickers (interview, 18 May, 1994), the women's movement at this time was also seen as a potentially unifying force in the country. Hence, the government made extra funds available to groups of women that endeavoured to become bilingual.

None of this is meant to imply that state representatives *created* ethnic groups or 'women' as political identities. As Carty and Brand (1993: 174, 179) explain, regarding the category 'visible minority women': 'The state could no longer ignore a constituency which was in the midst of its own politicization.' The more important point is to draw attention to the effects of government intervention on this mobilization and the effects on the shape of protest.

Lobbying around the introduction of a Charter of Rights in 1981 concentrated the efforts of women's groups, Aboriginal groups and multicultural groups, who campaigned for and won clauses protecting their rights (Bacchi and Marquis, 1994). Francis Abele (1991) refers appropriately to the emergence of 'Charter-induced identities' which challenged traditional regional loyalties. The disabled were also mobilizing at this time, supported in their claims by the reports of the Special Parliamentary Committee on the Disabled and the Handicapped into the discrimination they faced.

The political manoeuvring which took place around the Charter forecast the kinds of difficulties involved in staking a claim to group recognition for 'women'. The equality guarantees reside in sections 15 and 28. Section 15 replicates the antidiscrimination provisions of many Western nations. It is gender neutral and is based upon the rights of the individual. Section 15(1) reads:

> Every individual is equal before and under the law and has the right to the equal protection and equal benefit of the law without discrimination and, in particular, without discrimination based on race, national or ethnic origin, colour, religion, sex, age or mental or physical disability. (Brodsky and Day, 1989: iv)

Brodsky and Day (1989: 103, 117, 193) have shown that, to date, women have seldom launched appeals under the provision and in fact 'men's successes have been more than double those of women'. This experience led LEAF, the Women's Legal Education and Action Fund, to demand that a 'categorical determination' be made in discrimination cases making it clear that neither men in cases of sex discrimination nor whites in cases of racial discrimination need substantive equality.[6] Gender neutrality in antidiscrimination law has allowed 'women' to become invisible.

Subsection 2 of Section 15 is the affirmative action section. That is, as in most other antidiscrimination legislation, it is an explicit exemption which 'allows' legislative intervention on behalf of 'disadvantaged' groups. It reads:

> Subsection (1) does not preclude any law, program or activity that has as its object the amelioration of conditions of disadvantaged individuals or groups including those that are disadvantaged because of race, national or ethnic origin, colour, religion, sex, age or mental or physical disability. (Brodsky and Day, 1989: iv)

The fact that such an exemption is deemed to be necessary reveals the implicit understanding that such intervention would under normal circumstances be considered a kind of discrimination, albeit 'positive discrimination'. We have seen in Chapter 2 how this understanding of affirmative action makes it difficult to challenge the ways in which those in positions of power, mainly men, have achieved that power, while it leaves the impression that women, and other recipients of affirmative action, are receiving beneficent treatment.

The Charter included specific clauses protecting religious freedom, the rights of Aboriginal peoples and Canada's multicultural heritage.[7] Some Canadian women feared that under the last of these a cultural group might claim a custom which denigrated women as falling within its equality guarantee. To protect women against this eventuality, Canadian women's groups campaigned for and won the insertion of Section 28 which reads: 'Notwithstanding anything in this Charter, the rights and freedoms referred to in it are guaranteed equally to male and female persons.' This 'taking of 28', as it came to be known, was considered to be a great victory for the women's movement (Kome, 1983).

While Section 28 certainly seems to suggest that 'women' has achieved categorical recognition in the Charter, in fact the wording can be and is being read as gender neutral, or applying 'equally' to men and women (Brodsky and Day, 1989: 82). Moreover, the way in which the federal government proceeded to trade off the equality rights in Sections 15 and 28 as a concession to the provinces, provides a truer indication of the position of 'women' in Canadian category politics.

At a federal–provincial conference of First Ministers on November 2, 1981, the federal government introduced an override clause (Section 33 (1)) which gave the parliament or legislature of a province the power to override the rights in the Charter, including the equality rights in Sections 15 and 28. A massive mobilization among women, outraged at this proposal, resulted in the government removing Section 28 from the application of the override clause (Brodsky and Day, 1989: 17).

Individual and collective rights

The difficulties faced by Canadian women activists around Charter negotiations provide insights into some of the problems with two conceptual categories – individualism and collectivism – commonly used to explain social relations. Their experiences also highlight the anomalous position of 'women' in relationship to other identity categories.

Historically in Western countries, given that women constitute half the population, it has seemed to make sense to demand that rights won by men as individuals be extended to women as individuals. That is, no woman was to be excluded from civil, political or social rights, the three categories of rights identified by T.H. Marshall (1950), accorded a man.

However, a number of feminists have illustrated that a combination of characteristics affecting large numbers of women effectively excludes them from individual rights (see, for example, Pateman, 1988; Kingdom, 1991; and Tapper, 1986). For example, that many women have to regulate their behaviour to avoid male violence means they have less freedom of assembly and more constraints on their exercise of political agency (K. Jones, 1990: 787; Ware, 1992: 7). Again, because most women have a different relationship to paid labour due to their assuming primary responsibility for home and family, they fare less well than men in welfare regimes which attach social rights to employment (Lister, 1990). This means that, as Sherene Razack (1994: 66, 72) puts it, '[T]he idea of rights, turning as it does on notions of individual freedom and autonomy, helps to regulate what can be seen and acknowledged in women's lives.' She elaborates: 'the price of autonomy is the enslavement of others, notably women.'

But when groups of women have come to claim *collective* status for 'women', they have encountered other problems. Women activists have tended to use analogies with other groups as discursive openings to make claims for 'women'. While these analogies serve this purpose, they are always inexact and conditions affecting women are never at the forefront of analysis. In addition, women always seem to be making a claim belatedly, riding on the coat-tails of other 'obviously' oppressed groups. We have seen an example of this in the previous chapter where American women tried to draw parallels between 'women' and 'Blacks'. Similarly, socialist feminists in several countries have spoken of 'women' as a 'class'. In the Canadian case, logically given the history we have briefly sketched, the category 'women' is most often placed alongside groups which base their claims in cultural or national heritage. There is a whole literature debating the 'justice' of group rights for such minorities (see, for example, Kymlicka, 1989, 1992; Kukathas, 1992; Taylor and Gutmann, 1992; Baker, 1994). Particular problems arise, however, when women activists attempt to fit 'women's' claims to cultural categories.

Here, the most obvious problem is that, while some feminist theory suggests that 'women' constitutes a cultural identity, others are unhappy with this kind of claim.[8] Moreover, many women have attachments to other cultural/national collectivities; for example, Francophone feminists in Quebec who support Quebec nationalism and Aboriginal women who advocate sovereignty for the First Nations argue that 'women's individual rights and their nations' collective rights cannot be separated' (Vickers, Rankin and Appelle, 1993: 322). Some Aboriginal women have argued that collective rights, meaning in this instance the collective rights of the First Nations, must supersede individual rights (Vickers, Rankin and Appelle, 1993: 322; see also LaChapelle, 1982; Stasiulis, 1987; Simms, 1992; Turpel, 1993). The problem of 'other' collective affiliations is so serious in Canada that Vickers, Rankin and Appelle (1993: 324) have coined the term 'identity feminism' to refer to identities 'organized around minority women's differences from the women in the majority in the movement'.

The other major problem is that the notion of community lodged within cultural identity claims has been mobilized at times in ways that harm some women (Razack, 1994: 69; Bacchi, 1990). This is often achieved through appeals to conceptions of 'family', conceptions which effectively erase 'women'.[9] Appeals to culture, moreover, sometimes serve as a rationale for maintaining practices which harm some women. Some obvious cases here are cliterodectomy and infibulation, sati, and the 'honor defense' of wife slaying in Brazil (Slack, 1988; Thomas and Beasley, 1993). These more dramatic examples should not blind us to the ways in which most cultures fail to consider violence against women as a problem comparable in severity to violence against men, or the ways in which many cultures impose norms of appearance and behaviour on women which are constraining.

Avigail Eisenberg (1994) has attempted to bypass the suggestion that there is an inherent conflict in Western legislation and jurisprudence between individual and collective rights. She suggests that courts are in fact using a common standard which is based upon the extent to which a characteristic is held to be critical to a person's identity. While Eisenberg feels that this analysis captures the case of 'women' as well as other groups, the examples she uses are all based upon cultural affiliation. Hence, it nicely illustrates the problem discussed above – in order to 'fit' an analysis, academic or jurisprudential, which attaches rights to characteristics that determine identity, women activists have had to make claims about common identity which prove problematic. It is just such claims that have led to charges of false universalism and essentialism (Razack, 1994: 69).

This problem illustrates a dominant theme in this book – the ways in which being an outgroup and on the defensive seem to compel the adoption of strategies which produce their own dilemmas. It is because 'women' seems to need a defence as a collective identity that women activists are forced into homogenizing characterizations of 'women'. Men have the luxury to claim theoretical purity in this domain because they have no need to mount a claim to recognition for 'men'. As Martha Minow (1990) explores and Nitya Duclos (1993: 47) elaborates, what needs to be challenged is the power which allows one group to call another 'different' and to force upon it the task of justification of category status.[10] Exposing or calling 'men' a category is a tactic designed to reveal the effects that have followed from having to defend 'women' as a category.

In a response to Charles Taylor's essay on the politics of recognition, Susan Wolf notes that, when examining feminist and multicultural politics, '[T]he situation of women . . . is not fully parallel with that of members of unappreciated cultures' (in Taylor and Gutmann, 1992: 75).

She makes the point that '[T]he predominant problem for women as women is not that the larger or more powerful sector of the community fails to notice or be interested in preserving women's gendered identity, but that this identity is put to the service of oppression and exploitation.' I would have liked Wolf to pursue this analysis further but she had other targets for her critique. Still, it amazes me that so little comment is attracted by what seems to be an obvious problem – the ways in which 'women' and 'cultural communities' are different. Consider, as an example, the lack of inclusion of works by women authors and 'other' cultures in the academic curriculum. Wolf argues that as a population 'we', referring here to the United States, are more diverse than we used to be, and hence representations of cultures now a part of 'ours' need to be added to the 'canon'. In contrast, I would suggest that women have always been 'here'; and their works have not just failed to be added, they have been suppressed – because they were written by women.

Douglas Sanders (1991) appears to have made a useful distinction between 'group rights' and 'collective rights', placing women's claims in the former category. However, in his analysis, demands for group rights are transient and clearly lack the status of cultural claims. Women activists thus seem to be damned if they try to 'fit' their case to a cultural model, and damned if they opt out of this comparison.

On the one hand I would claim that 'women' needs to be placed outside available *kinds* of identity categories. However, making just this point suggests a general inadequacy with those categories. In particular it suggests the need to challenge the presumed binary opposition between individual and collective rights and to draw attention to the ways these notions operate in some political debates to foreclose particular kinds of claims.

One problem is that to press one's 'fundamental human dignity' it has been held to be necessary to suppress any sense of collective affiliation. For women, however, their human value has *never* been assessed *separately* from their 'womanness'. Being a woman has necessarily meant being seen as part of the collectivity 'women'. And yet, when groups of women draw attention to this, their claims are challenged, displaced or reshaped in ways that minimize meaningful change. While some recent Court decisions in the areas of pornography and abortion seem to suggest some willingness to listen to these claims (Mahoney, 1993: 124–7),[11] the discursive positioning of 'women' in employment equity and in recent constitutional debates suggests rather that 'women' is accorded a subordinate place in Canadian category politics.

'Women' and affirmative action

Initially, as we have seen, affirmative action plans in Canada identified 'women' as their target. But by the time of the Commission on Equality in Employment (1984), headed by Rosalie Abella, it was clear that Canadian employment equity would include four target groups: Aboriginal peoples, visible minorities, the disabled and 'women'. Indeed this was specified in the Commission terms of reference (Abella, 1984).

Officially, the characteristics which entitle a group to targeted category status include labour participation and unemployment rates, income levels, and occupational segregation.[12] Agocs, Burr and Somerset (1992: 38) note the importance of other factors such as how organized a group is, how strongly they share a common identity, public perceptions of who is 'deserving', and 'official definitions of the groups that constitute Canada's pluralistic society'. Francophones, gays and lesbians, and the elderly have campaigned on occasion for inclusion but to date they have been judged as not meeting the criteria. Some reformers in Canada felt that broadening the range of target populations would reduce the possibility of a backlash to affirmative action as faced in the United States. And for the four groups concerned, alliance seemed more promising than opposition. One of the initiators of the reform, Rhys Phillips (interviewed 10 May, 1994), explained that 'women' provided the numbers while the other groups provided 'sympathy value'.[13]

There has been endless discussion about the meaning of the category 'visible minorities' and just whom it includes. It seems no one knows where the term originated (Stasiulis, 1991: 235). It was clearly an attempt to bypass references to 'race' which were considered to be risky and potentially offensive. There are currently problems with the way in which the category operates. For example, it omits migrants from countries where skin colour does not make them 'visible'. And, as some witnesses to the Redway review of employment equity (Canada, 1992: 8; see also Stasiulis, 1991: 241) complained, 'not all visible minorities experience the same type or level of disadvantage in employment.'

Another problem is self-identification. That is, workforces are surveyed and workers are asked to specify if indeed they are a member of a visible minority. Clearly some people feel it is potentially stigmatizing to self-identity and hence fail to do so. Employers, however, are in a situation where they wish to make 'visible' every member of these groups in order to meet their targets – hence, they have attempted to argue that employers should be able to identify members of the designated categories. To date, issues of privacy are prevailing and it is unlikely that employers will be granted this power (Canada, 1992: 9).

The problem of self-identification applies to Aboriginal peoples and the disabled as well. It does not apply to 'women' because gender is assumed to be a social fact. As the literature from Employment and Immigration Canada (1991c: 4) makes plain, 'Some of the necessary information for employment equity planning will be available in existing personnel files, e.g. salary, sex . . .'.

The question of self-identification raises problems with establishing categories which tie people's oppression to separable identities, a theme touched on in the previous chapter. As several authors have noted, people's lives do not come neatly compartmentalized into gender, race or disability (Ng, 1990, 1993; Duclos, 1993). There is no way within this understanding to capture what Deborah King (1989: 78–80) has called the 'multiple jeopardy' of multiple oppressions. Nor does the application of a common employment equity approach allow recognition of the 'substantive differences' *among* forms of oppression and *within* forms of oppression, due to class distinctions for example. Finally, establishing four 'disadvantaged' groups has led to some tensions among them in the competition for scarce resources (Agocs, Burr, and Somerset, 1992: 196).

The targeting of four groups has particular negative effects for 'women'. Because 'women' constitutes a separate category in employment equity, the other categories are deemed to be constituted by men, unofficially of course and perhaps even unconsciously. Nicole Morgan (1988: 40) tells the story how at one public service conference on employment equity, 'one director said, "I think we should pay more attention to the disabled now". His remark was met with applause but one woman pointed out that 50% of "the disabled" were women. There was a silence.' No doubt, as Morgan remarks, 'the phrase "the disabled" had, in the minds of most people been synonymous with "disabled men"'.

The effect, as Sue Findlay (1993a: 156; 1993b: 212) and others (Duclos, 1993: 44; National Action Committee, 1992b: 3) have argued, is that women who are discriminated against on two or more grounds fall through the cracks in the system. Despite the lack of success of employment equity generally, it is clear that women in the other categories are making less headway than the men in those categories (Leck and Saunders, 1992; Christofides and Swidinsky, 1994; see also CAC, 1993: 79, fns. 35, 36, 37). This is not what the logic of employment equity would lead us to expect. Since employers can list 'doubly disadvantaged' people in more than one category, one would think that there would be distinct statistical advantages to taking on more of these people. This, of course, presumes that employers hire rationally, and that hiring and promotions are not affected by discriminatory attitudes. The statistical results coming out of Canada have put paid to that argument.

While the 'other' groups are deemed to be constituted by men, paradoxically and perversely 'women' becomes typecast as 'white women', or even 'white middle-class women' (National Action Committee on the Status of Women (NAC), 1992b: 4). Sue Findlay described the response to the use of affirmative action in the Ontario College of Art: 'John Grube, spokesperson for the anti-Equity faculty representatives on the Governing Council, recently referred to the policy as "this ugly piece of racism and homophobia" from "white middle-class feminist sponsors"' (Findlay, 1990: 32–3). This has the effect of undermining 'women's' status as 'disadvantaged', necessary to legitimize affirmative action in current understandings.

One of the grounds, you may recall, used to convince women activists to ally with other 'disadvantaged' groups was that this would give 'women' access to the sympathy value these other groups attracted. This has not happened. Instead, several of the submissions to the committees set up to look into employment equity have suggested that 'women' have had their day and that it is time to look to the other groups (who are, to repeat, almost *de facto*, seen to be constituted by men) (Canadian Alliance for Visible Minorities, 1992; see also Findlay, 1990: 35; Agocs, Burr and Somerset, 1992: 359, 387).

So, in Canadian employment equity, a demand that the specific conditions of 'women's' oppression be considered would now be extremely difficult to make. The workings of category politics have effectively displaced 'women' from the agenda. They have also had the effect of setting 'women' against the 'other' groups, undermining opportunities for political alliance. Canadian feminists have played a significant role in drawing attention to these failings in the legislation and their discoveries have had important and dramatic effects on both their theory and their practices. The existence of numerous lobby groups for disabled, immigrant and visible minority women, has meant that Canadian feminist theory is centrally concerned with theorizing 'differences among women' and the relationship between race, class, gender and other oppressions (see, for example, Gunew and Yeatman, 1993; Bannerji, 1993; Carty, 1993). Canadian feminists are far from alone in this project, but I would argue that they have been more directly confronted on this issue than feminists elsewhere, due largely to the history of negotiation and compromise between English and French-speaking feminists.

In addition, the discovery that women from other oppressed groups fall through the cracks in employment equity has highlighted the need to examine the effects on these groups of the way in which working with and through the government affects feminist practices. Sue Findlay (1993b: 218), who headed the Women's Programme in its early years, argues that the process of implementation has 'privileged the participation of white women who are articulate and well-educated, middle-class, able-bodied and most often heterosexual.'

Moving beyond theory, important Canadian feminist groups have instituted affirmative action within their own organizations for women in the other targeted categories (Vickers, Rankin, and Appelle, 1993: 294; Sheehy, 1991: 456). As an indication of a new awareness of the 'diversity of women', the CAC (1993: 109) recently insisted that '[T]he true measure of the fairness of any policy or practice is how it applies to the most disadvantaged among us.'[14] Almost perversely then, the fact that Canadian employment equity erases women in the other targeted categories has made doubly and trebly oppressed women increasingly visible to more advantaged women.

Where is 'women'?

As the Canadian Advisory Council on the Status of Women (1993: 3) states, the constitutional debate in Canada has framed the decade of the 1980s. In 1982 the constitution was patriated but Quebec refused to endorse the process. Since then efforts have concentrated upon reintegrating Quebec into the 'nation'.

To date the closest these efforts have come to success was in what has been called the Meech Lake Accord, worked out at Meech Lake, Quebec on 30 April, 1987 (Roberts, 1989: viii). This Accord met Quebec's demands for adhesion to the Constitution Act (1982) through the recognition that 'Quebec constitutes within Canada a distinct society'. There was also recognition that the existence of French-speaking Canadians in Quebec and elsewhere in Canada constituted a 'fundamental characteristic' of Canada, and a commitment to preserve that 'fundamental characteristic'.

The groups which had campaigned to have their rights protected in the 1982 Charter of Rights worked to ensure that this special status for Quebec did not undermine those rights. Hence in Section 16 of the Accord it was specified that nothing in it threatened the multicultural character of Canada nor the rights of Aboriginal peoples. 'Women' was the only category specifically mentioned in the Charter to go unacknowledged in this section. Section 16 of the Accord reads: 'Nothing in section 2 of the *Constitution Act, 1867* affects section 25 or 27 of the *Canadian Charter of Rights and Freedoms*, section 35 of the *Constitution Act, 1982* or class 24 of section 91 of the *Constitution Act, 1867.*' As Barbara Roberts (1989: 9) notes, 'these all refer to multicultural and aboriginal rights.' A number of submissions from women's groups pressed for recognition of 'women's' rights. Groups from French Canada were somewhat ambivalent about what was needed. From the time of the Charter negotiations, French-Canadian women's organizations had felt confident that their rights were better defended by the Quebec than by the Federal government. This explains their opposition to the new Charter. Similarly in 1986 these groups felt that the 'distinct society' clause did not threaten their rights as 'women'. Still, to achieve some consistency between the Charter and the Accord, they were happy to have Section 28 of the Charter included in Section 16 of the Accord (Roberts, 1989: 9).

The debate about whether women indeed needed to fear a 'distinct society' clause illustrates the problems, discussed earlier, with available identity and conceptual categories. The Quebec Advisory Council on the Status of Women claimed, and it seems that most politicians agreed, that

Aboriginal peoples and the multicultural community were specifically mentioned in Section 16 of the Accord because the notion of a 'distinct society' clearly referred to matters of culture and heritage. 'Women', it was assumed, would *not* be threatened by such a clause because they were 'protected' by individual rights. In the words of the Council,

> Multicultural and native rights might need protection because the concept of distinct society has a collective character including a cultural and linguistic component which could conflict with other collective cultural rights. However, the CSF (*Conseil du statut de la femme du Quebec*) does not believe that a parallel argument can be made in the case of equality between men and women, that is to say, individual rights. (In Roberts, 1989: 42)

However, as the National Action Committee on the Status of Women (NAC) explained, and LEAF agreed, the fact that specific identity Charter guarantees, other than those for 'women', were repeated in the Accord was disconcerting. The NAC Brief (in Roberts, 1989: 39) stated: 'the inclusion of some Charter rights and not others in clause 16 leads to the conclusion that other Charter rights, including women's equality rights, were purposefully excluded.'

Those who recognized the implicit tension for women between individual and cultural rights felt the need to argue that women's claims to identity were the *same in character* as those of these other groups. All five national women's organizations, reports Beverley Baines (1987: 811–12), said that 'far from being a special case, women were *just like* the groups already included in s. 16 and that was why their omission was indeed so egregious' (my italics). As argued above, the fit between 'women' and cultural groups is, in fact, inexact but the historical character of category politics in Canada gives women activists little option but to argue in these terms. This is made clear in Baines's elaboration that 'women' 'resemble' 'aboriginal peoples' and 'people who rely on the multicultural heritage provision' *when 'they litigate Charter-based equality rights cases'* (Baines, 1987: 812; my italics).

In the event, the demand to include 'women' in Section 16 was ignored. Despite the fact that women's groups across Canada agreed that including Section 28 of the Charter in the Accord was desirable, it was excluded. Barbara Roberts (1989: 19) reports that the government attempted to blame this outcome on disagreements between Francophone and Anglophone feminists, deliberately distorting the positions in the submissions they received.

In subsequent constitutional discussions 'women' has failed to achieve separate representation. As the Canadian Advisory Council on the Status of Women (1993: 32, fn. 30) records, in the lead up to the Charlottetown Accord (1992):

> [D]espite a Federal Court of Appeal ruling that the Native Women's Association of Canada had 'an equal right of participation in the constitutional review process', women *as a group* were excluded from the meetings [my italics]' . . . The Native Council of Canada gave representatives of the Native

Women's Association of Canada and other women's groups some of its places at the table. While women appreciated the gesture, it did not address their fundamental problem, i.e., their exclusion as a group from the final phase of the constitutional process.

In addition, as the NAC has argued, the Charlottetown Accord sets up a hierarchy of rights:

> The Canada clause required *Canadians and their governments* to be committed to the development of minority linguistic rights but *only Canadians* are committed to the rights of women and racial minorities. *No-one* is required to be committed to the rights of those left out of the Canada Clause. (NAC, 1992c; my italics)

In the event this particular vision of category politics failed to win public acceptance. Fifty-two per cent of those who voted in the referendum on the Charlottetown Accord voted 'No' (CAC, 1993: 27).

Where is 'women' then in contemporary Canadian category politics? Susan Phillips's recent examination (1991) of government funding provides an insight. Phillips's analysis of grants by the Secretary of State over the past 10 years shows that 'funding is relatively secure for groups – official language minority associations and multicultural groups – which support the symbolic order of Canadian identity, but has declined considerably for groups which promote rights of other collectivities, notably women and Aboriginal peoples.'

We need to be aware of clear political motivation in the funding of certain groups, and in the denying of funds to other groups. This is true also in cases where women's groups receive funds. Carty and Brand (1993: 179) note, for example, that the state's efforts in promoting the formation of the National Organization of Immigrant and Visible Minority Women were meant to 'create a containing women's network', which it did by signifying 'these women's "immigrantness" and "visible minorityness" as the organizing principle. Their "womaness" was secondary.' Vickers, Rankin and Appelle (1993: 165) also describe the efforts of the Mulroney Government to divide women by the 'courting of groups representing visible minorities and groups of organized rural women'. These examples illustrate that drawing attention to the 'differences among women' does not on its own guarantee a progressive outcome. The political purposes behind the deployment of 'women' or 'visible minority women' or 'Aboriginal women' need to be scrutinized in each case.

There appears to be a shift underway in Canadian government strategies to foster national integration. As Susan Phillips notes (1991: 206, 211), 'the new buzzword of the 1990s' is 'partnerships' which represent 'a move away from support for interest advocacy and policy criticism to an emphasis on service delivery and implementation.' This shift can be characterized as a move away from *fostering* particular identity categories to *changing their character*. Perhaps the experience with the first approach has proved more problematic than anticipated. It could be argued, for example, that the attempt to undermine the impact of Quebec nationalism by sponsoring other cultural communities, described earlier, has backfired. Most recent constitutional negotiations make it plain that the federal government will need to accommodate French Canada's demands. This has been complicated, however, by the claims of other ethnic groups, groups which owe something to government support. The hope may be that it is more difficult to be critical of government policy from within a 'partnership' (Phillips, 1991: 211).

The move to 'partnerships' illustrates the point made in Chapter 1 that category politics can take a number of forms, including attempts to *subdue* categorical distinctions as well as attempts to *foster* the emergence of categories. It should also be remembered that the strategies are not mutually exclusive and can be worked simultaneously. Regardless of approach, the evidence in Canada is that claims for 'women' are effectively displaced.

Notes

1 As explained in Chapter 2, Rosalie Abella, who headed the Commission on Equality in Employment (1984), coined the term 'employment equity' to avoid the bad press associated with the American experience of affirmative action. Federal initiatives provide the focus for this chapter.

2 I say 'significantly' because a theme developed throughout this volume is that 'individual rights' have been particularly problematic for women to access, primarily because individual rights have been conceptualized in ways which take little account of many women's lives. More will be said about this later in the chapter.

3 The Canadian Human Rights Commission (CHRC) oversees Canada's antidiscrimination legislation. Hence, it is set up essentially to receive and act upon complaints. In theory, affirmative action is meant to go beyond an antidiscrimination approach by being proactive instead of complaint-based. However, since annual employment equity reports are sent to the CHRC, it is unclear how the Commission can use them if there is no specific complaint of discrimination. There have been a number of efforts to suggest that the CHRC could itself initiate a complaint of indirect discrimination if the reported statistics indicated an inexplicable gap between a company's workforce figures and workforce availability data. To date (1994), these efforts have simply produced unresolved jurisdictional disputes (Stasiulis, 1991: 240–1).

4 Michael Palliga, Acting Director of FCP, noted in interview (13 May, 1994) that many employers are now offering 'managing diversity' courses as evidence of their efforts to implement employment equity. Treasury Board is going to change officially the name of its Equity Unit to 'Managing Diversity' (personal correspondence from Susan Phillips, December, 1994).

5 The work of Rainer Knopff (1989), one of the chief critics of affirmative action, shows that the argument that 'women' are differently placed in discussions of discrimination, because they 'choose' jobs to fit in with 'their' family role, an argument prominent in the United States (see Chapter 3), is also replicated in Canada.

6 LEAF was set up following the introduction of the Charter to develop a 'litigation strategy', sponsoring cases under the Charter, which would lead to a well-developed understanding of women's needs (Atcheson, Eberts and Symes, 1983: 2). See also Bacchi and Marquis, 1994.

7 Section 29 of the Charter protects certain aspects of religious freedom by declaring that 'nothing in this Charter' abrogates rights to denominational schools. Section 35

declares that the guarantee of 'certain rights and freedoms' in the Charter 'shall not be construed to abrogate or derogate from the rights of aboriginal peoples'. Section 27 specifies that the Charter is to be 'interpreted in a manner consistent with the preservation and enhancement of the multicultural heritage of Canadians' (Brodsky and Day, 1989: 17).

8 This involves us in the whole debate about essentialism, feminist standpoint and feminist postmodern theory. For useful analysis of these issues, see Fuss (1989) and Bryson (1992).

9 I offer the following quote from de Tocqueville's *Democracy in America* (1840 [1946]) (quoted in Dumont, 1972: 52) as an example of the way in which individualism is made compatible with, and even dependent upon the family, by subsuming women: 'Individualism is a mature and calm feeling, which disposes each member of the community to sever himself from the mass of his fellow-creatures; and to draw apart *with his family* and his friends; so that, after he has thus formed a little circle of his own, he willingly leaves society at large to itself' (my italics).

10 As an example, the focus on 'culture' has led to the proposition that the most important problem excluded groups face is 'recognition' (Taylor and Gutmann, 1992). The reason offered is that lack of recognition leads to a demeaned self-image which becomes 'one of the most potent instruments of their own oppression' (Taylor and Gutmann, 1992: 25). This kind of argument is similar in tenor to 'fear of success' explanations for 'women's' subordination and suffers from similar limitations, primarily the lack of attention to the variety of ways in which power is exercised to keep certain social groups suppressed.

11 I say 'seem to suggest' because, as Anne Orford (1994: 93–5) points out, criminalizing some pornography, as in the recent *Butler* decision (*R* v *Butler*, 1992, 1 SCR 452), means that '[H]arm to women simply replaces morals-based arguments as a justification for upholding conventional obscenity legislation.' It makes no attempt to empower women to make complaints and it makes it more difficult to provide regulated, legal and safe work environments for workers in the pornography industry. Orford's concerns are given credibility in recent court decisions which, under the rubric of 'obscenity', have targeted lesbian bookstores (Toobin, 1994).

12 It is interesting to note that the Abella Commission specified that pay equity be considered part of employment equity. However, pay equity is generally treated as a separate problem. Though the approaches differ across federal and provincial jurisdictions, Canadians have made moves to introduce comparable worth through job evaluation schemes. The success of these schemes has been limited to date by the inability to alter pay scales in female-dominated occupations where no male comparator is present. A serious ill effect which has resulted from the separation of pay and employment equity is that it is now possible for employers to suggest that designated group members are progressing in their industry or occupation simply by renaming some job classifications – that is, there may be no improvement in pay scales. This has meant that employers sometimes express the desire to hire members of the four designated groups because they are 'cheaper' and 'less likely to unionize' (McDermott, 1992: 26). It has also meant that it is possible to claim that employment equity is being implemented although wages in general are unaffected or even dragged down. Hence, in the case of pay equity, *not* targeting four groups has provided loopholes for employers which limit the impact of the reform. Again, we are alerted to the need to look at the effects of the ways categories are deployed in specific cases.

13 The fact that targeted groups are seen to be in need of 'sympathy' illustrates how the reform is perceived – even among its supporters – as more a matter of charity than justice.

14 Having drawn attention to the inadequacy of a 'disadvantage' discourse generally, the point ought to be made here that feminist theory needs to recognize the advantages accruing to some women because of racism, heterosexism, and class bias.

5

The Politics of Incorporation

C. Bacchi and J. Eveline

This book weaves two 'narratives' together. One examines political conceptualizations of affirmative action; the other focuses on the positioning of the category 'women' within these conceptualizations. It uses the notion of category politics to reflect upon the ways in which conceptual and identity categories have been deployed to limit change. In earlier chapters we have seen how strong or 'hard' affirmative action[1] has been delegitimized by representing it as an attack on fundamental democratic values. We have seen how in response to this attack affirmative action became discursively constituted as handouts to the needy.

In the cases studied so far, where members of the category 'women' have been considered deserving recipients of this 'beneficence', they have generally been considered less deserving than 'others'. A common rationale for this positioning is that the kind of discrimination 'women' face is not as invidious or indeed as harmful since 'women's' under-representation in well-paying jobs or positions of influence is due to choices they themselves make. The stereotype of 'women', as naturally domestic, functions here to explain, or rather to explain away, discrimination.

The category 'woman' operates in other ways to delegitimize or diminish claims on behalf of 'women'. Setting 'women' apart as a political category has the effect in some settings of allowing a range of issues to be labelled 'women's issues'. The result here can be a strategic isolating of 'women' from a broader political agenda. 'Women' can then be 'added' without disturbing this agenda. I call this the politics of incorporation.[2] A shorthand phrase capturing the essence of this approach, borrowed from Victoria Foster (1992), is 'adding women and not stirring'. Feminist theorists have for some time spoken about the limitations of an approach they labelled 'adding women and stirring', which suggested putting women into existing analyses without seeing how women's inclusion undermined key premises (see Okin, 1991: 72). Foster has coined this modification – adding women and *not* stirring – as a way of making this same point more forcefully.

The mechanics of this strategy are complex. In this chapter I consider three ways in which incorporation of the sort just described occurs: first, adding 'women' to established institutional regimes without considering that these might need to change; second, adding 'women' to established institutional regimes in order to stabilize those regimes; third, adding 'women' to established national images without considering that these may be inadequate. Australia provides an ideal setting for considering these examples.

'Women' in Australia

In some ways affirmative action policy in Australia stands in sharp contrast to employment equity policy in Canada, which we examined in the preceding chapter. Most importantly for this volume, the 1986 legislation, entitled The Affirmative Action (Equal Employment Opportunity for Women) Act, targets only 'women'.

'Women' came onto the political agenda at much the same time and for much the same reason as it did in Canada and in the United States. There was a labour shortage which women were invited to end. The key concern with labour market participation is indicated by the recognition of women's rights to 'equal pay for equal work' in Australia in 1969, before a resurgent women's movement had mobilized.[3] In all three countries examined to date, equal pay laws preceded feminist mobilization, suggesting the primary focus was on moving women into the labour force.

To date, in Australia, the recognition of 'women' has not been altered as it has been in Canada, through the listing of 'women' alongside what have become 'competing interest groups' – or, at least this has not happened to the same extent. In the Federal Public Service, and in much state equal opportunity legislation, the clientele has been extended to include Aborigines, the disabled and people of non-English speaking background (NESBs) (Ronalds, 1987: 86). There have also been some suggestions recently that the federal legislation ought to be similarly 'broadened'.

'Women' has retained its categorical legitimacy in Australia for a number of reasons. Politics in Australia has historically been more class than race inflected, especially when compared to the United States, and few people have suggested using labour market affirmative action to address class inequality. As we have seen, in the United States the intensity of racial conflict has meant that 'Blacks' are generally placed ahead of 'women' in the affirmative action queue. In contrast, in Australia Aborigines have not had the numbers, partly due to the genocide which accompanied European invasion, to press their claims. Moreover, the push towards multiculturalism, which created the opening for the expansion of the employment equity constituency in Canada, has not – at least not yet – seriously affected traditional political alignments in Australia.

Despite the retention of a focus on 'women', in other ways developments in the understanding of affirmative action in Australia follow closely those traced in the United States and Canada. This ought not to be surprising considering the close historical, trade and communication links among these countries.

Affirmative action in Australia

As in the United States and Canada, 'women' was a latecomer to the antidiscrimination agenda in Australia. Racial discrimination was prohibited in 1975. The Whitlam Labor Government announced its intention to follow up its 1975 Racial Discrimination Act with legislation prohibiting discrimination on the grounds of sex but the government changed before this could be done.

In 1981 the Shadow Minister on the Status of Women, Susan Ryan, introduced a private member's bill which would have outlawed sex discrimination and introduced a requirement for all Commonwealth Government employers and all private sector employers with a minimum of 100 employees to introduce an affirmative action management plan for women (Ronalds, 1987: 14). Another change of government in 1983 led to the introduction of the Sex Discrimination bill by Ryan which became the Sex Discrimination Act the following year.

The affirmative action proposal was separated off from sex discrimination and dealt with in a Green Paper, *Affirmative Action for Women (1984)*. The Green Paper detailed an eight-step model of affirmative action, a model which remains substantially the same today and which requires those in charge to analyse the company's or the institution's employment profile, and to set objectives and forward estimates. At the same time the then Prime Minister, Bob Hawke, announced the establishment of an Affirmative Action Pilot Programme. Under this programme, 28 private sector companies and three higher education institutions agreed to implement affirmative action voluntarily within their own organization.

In 1985 a Working Party on Affirmative Action recommended legislation along the lines of Ryan's initial proposal. This led to the 1986 legislation mentioned above. This legislation, much like the EEA in Canada, introduced a compulsory annual reporting mechanism. Its coverage is much broader than the EEA's which covers approximately 370 federally-regulated employers; Australia's Affirmative Action Act requires all employers who employ more than 100 staff to report annually, involving some 2500 reports in 1993–1994 (Affirmative Action Agency, 1994). However, unlike the EEA, availability data is not used, nor is there any financial penalty for failure to report. The only sanction to date is being named in Parliament. Recently there have been efforts to tighten up on the reporting mechanism and contract compliance has been introduced.

In the lead-up to the 1986 legislation, representative business associations, including the Business Council of Australia, tried to ward off legislation. It was argued that the kinds of analyses described as 'affirmative action' did not require 'prescriptive legislation' since they were already 'an important part of sound personnel practices'. Hence, they were just 'good business sense'.[4] In the popular press and in academic literature, the debate echoed that in the United States. There were dire warnings that the legislation meant the introduction of quotas, undermining merit.[5] The American experience was repeatedly raised as an object lesson of a path Australia should not follow. For example, *The Age* (9 October, 1986) praised the proposed legislation for 'learning from the United States in rejecting quotas.' In fact, as was noted in Chapter 2, quotas are seldom used in the United States and are usually imposed only when there has been a finding of discrimination.

The issue became whether Australia wanted 'equal opportunity' or 'equal results'. As in the United States and Canada, those who called it 'equal results' meant to tar the reform as 'foreign'. The *Sydney Morning Herald* (11 April, 1986) quoted Ian Cameron, National Party MP: 'What the National Party is about is giving women incentives to stay at home and bring up young Australians the way they should be brought up, and not in some socialised, rat-bag Russianized child-care centre set up at the factory door.' Cameron here equated affirmative action with forcing women into paid labour, from which these predicted consequences would follow.

The attack from business put feminists and other supporters of affirmative action on the defensive. In an attempt to make the reform more palatable, the government and many other proponents presented it as aligned with business goals of efficiency and productivity. 'Women' became a 'resource' to be tapped. In the words of the then Prime Minister, Bob Hawke (19 October, 1986, *The Canberra Times*), 'the logic behind affirmative action [for women] is compellingly simple – no country could afford to neglect half its human resources.'[6] The legislation was carefully called The Affirmative Action (Equal Employment Opportunity for Women) Act to distance it from the controversial American model and its association with quotas. The legislation states explicitly that nothing in it contravenes 'merit' (Ronalds, 1987: 63–4).

Positioning affirmative action as congruent with economic imperatives sets limits on understandings of the reform. Public pronouncements stressed that a reform which called for 'results' would impose unfair economic constraints on industry. In 1977 Peter Wilenski, one of the architects of affirmative action in New South Wales, insisted that 'affirmative action plans which require quotas . . . can be regarded as inconsistent with the principle of open competition and can result in the *hiring of less efficient workers*' (Wilenski, 1977: 233; my italics). In 1984 the NSW Department of Premier and Cabinet issued a statement that:

> The imposition of quotas would have a negative effect for organisations in general and for women employees in particular. It would create a 'second stream' of jobs which are only to meet the quota requirements. Such an

approach would do nothing to raise women's labour market participation in an effective and long term way, and *would impose unreasonable and uneconomic requirements on organisations*. (Quoted in Kramar, 1987: 175–6; my italics)

In this understanding, 'results' implicitly means hiring 'unqualified' women, foreclosing discussion of what 'qualified' means.

Linking affirmative action to economic efficiency has other effects. It leaves the reform susceptible to economic fluctuations and to 'what the market will bear'. It leaves little room for demanding that industry accept social responsibility for its activities. In this situation, it is not surprising that the 'managing diversity' discourse, discussed at some length in Chapter 3, is finding fertile soil in Australia (see, for example, Niland and Champion, 1990).

'Soft' affirmative action is permitted on the grounds that some groups in society need limited 'assistance' in order to compete. The first serious defence of affirmative action, a 1974 piece by Gareth Evans (1974: 26–8), a Labor Senator in 1995, defined 'benign discrimination' as 'the singling out by the state of a designated group for more favourable treatment than is accorded the others.' The rationale is that 'groups suffering special disabilities' need to be 'specially helped'. The 'central problem', in Evans's view, 'is how such [benign] discrimination can be reconciled with the principle of equality.'

Hence, as in the United States and in Canada, so in Australia 'women' have been constituted as 'disadvantaged', as 'needy', as needing 'preferential treatment' in order to 'succeed'. As Pringle and Watson (1992: 61) describe, they are offered a 'social justice strategy' which 'effectively entrenches them in a position of disadvantage.' They are identified as needing and being given 'protection', a justification which mystifies the state's role in reproducing the current gender order. As Anne Orford (1994: 94) says, 'The myth that the liberal state exists to "protect" citizens distracts attention from the failure of the state to take action to address the material and ideological conditions contributing to the insecurity of many women.'

Moreover, as Eveline (1993, 1994a) points out, this categorizing of the problem as 'women's disadvantage' leaves no room for reference to, or accounts of, 'men's advantage'. The fact that 'men's advantage' is contingent on 'women's disadvantage', then, is obscured by liberal notions of equal opportunity.

'Women' as 'potential men'[7]

Because the Australian Affirmative Action legislation targets only 'women', it provides the ideal case to examine just whom 'women' represents, what 'they' are expected to want. Within the efficiency discourse just described, 'women' is seen to be constituted by those who wish to be *included* within the structures and institutions geared for 'efficiency'. 'They' are not all women. 'They' are the 'exceptional women' in Rosenfeld's model (see Chapter 3). 'They' are the ones who 'choose' to 'opt' for the 'challenge' of a career. Though governments have become wary of explicitly denigrating the homemaker/mother, there remains the implication that women who take advantage of new job 'opportunities' will be 'moving up'.

Within this 'inclusionary' or incorporation model, affirmative action programmes concentrate on 'training' for 'women', and/or on the integration of 'women' into so-called 'nontraditional areas'. Treating 'women' as the problem that must be fixed (Eveline, 1993, 1994a) obscures the way in which women are actively and structurally excluded from nontraditional and other workplaces by some men (see Cockburn, 1991). Moreover, as Jane Kenway and Jill Blackmore (1988) note, the strategy of encouraging girls to take up nontraditional areas of study (for example, mathematics, science and technology), endorsed in the government's *Draft National Plan of Action for Women in Tertiary Education*, is 'more a reflection of the Federal Government's enthusiasm for attracting people to these fields than for gender equity as such.' Despite the claim that affirmative action goes beyond the antidiscrimination approach because affirmative action is proactive, the focus remains on 'removing barriers' for those who wish to 'succeed'. Within this liberal model policies remain silent about redistributing advantages from those who have already 'succeeded'. The model precludes questions about how 'success' is linked to the limiting of competition, from which only the few can take advantage.

'Family responsibilities' are being taken up within affirmative action guidelines (Harris, 1994: 3). However, to date, these responses stop at the level of 'assisting' 'women' to gain access to employment, or to facilitate *their* balancing of domestic and paid work responsibilities. It is classic in Australian discourses of gender equality to view structural change as needing to occur so that 'women' can more easily manage work and family responsibilities. It is rare to see the issue addressed by focusing on how 'men' might better manage the two. Hence the assumption is that 'women' will go on being responsible for both. Child care and maternity leave become add-ons for 'women', and pose no real challenge to the careerist ethic. This exemplifies one understanding of what I mean by 'adding "women" and not stirring'.

In addition, the commitment to 'family-friendly' workplaces in Australia to date is minimal. The Affirmative Action Agency's reporting data indicate that only 7.5 per cent of organizations covered by the Act report work and family measures (Affirmative Action Agency, 1992b: 50). Val Braithwaite's (1992: 31) study of employer compliance with the Affirmative Action Act confirms that most employers see attempts to address the needs of workers with family responsibilites through career break schemes, child care facilities, paternity leave, and job sharing as 'marginally desirable but impractical.' A recent study shows that Australia's finance industry maintains unofficial 'career track' and 'job track' streams, colloquially called 'mommy track' streams overseas, by limiting job share arrangements to the latter (Junor et al., 1993: 108).

'Equal opportunity' guidelines require employers to remove 'inappropriate' questions from interview schedules. For example, it is considered unacceptable to ask job applicants (for example women) about child care arrangements or lack thereof. In this model, 'women' are admitted as 'potential men'. As I argue in *Same Difference* (Bacchi, 1990), we will have moved somewhere in our understanding of these issues when applicants *are asked* about their family commitments so that something can be done to meet them.

One would have expected more attention to be paid to work conditions in Australia given the relative strength of the Australian union movement and the common ground between the agendas of 'equal employment opportunity' and trade unionism around conditions of employment, including parental leave, part-time work, work-based child care, and flexible working arrangements. Management, however, has responded by locating 'equal opportunity' within their personnel function and employing a number of other strategies to keep the issue away from unions. Sylvia Winters (1987: 168) describes how some employers sought 'to compromise single-channel, union management negotiations by having non-unionists participate in EEO Consultative Committees'. As in Canada, management has resisted and continues to resist the step in the affirmative action programme which calls for consultation with unions (Affirmative Action Agency, 1992b: 111, 115). Affirmative action is represented as a 'non-industrial issue' and simply as part of good human resource management.[8]

Treating 'women' as 'potential men' clearly fits the agenda of some employers who wish to minimize disruption of traditional work regimes. Others, who claim to recognize the need to respond to employees' family commitments, continue to have difficulty envisioning measures which go beyond efforts to meet 'women' 'halfway'. The fact that 'equal opportunity' has been transformed into a human resource issue indicates, moreover, that decisions in this area will be left in the hands of managers. Cynthia Cockburn describes the kind of shift in thinking which is needed to institute meaningful change:

> For women to escape subordination to men the relationship of home to work has to change beyond anything yet envisaged in the name of equality policy. Men have to be domesticated and in the workplace (to use Joan Acker's phrase) the rhythm and timing of work must be adapted to the rhythms outside. (Cockburn 1991, 12; see also Acker, 1987)

The European Parliament recently produced a report which offers a useful summary of the kinds of changes in attitudes and policies this implies:

> Even if child care facilities, social services according to need, etc. are expanded as far as possible, that still leaves a significant number of basic social activities

which are essential for individual well-being and for the socio-cultural development of society and *which cannot be organized on a market basis.* Both sexes, regardless of marital status, must be in a position to engage in such activities. *This requires legislation and also positive action to motivate men to participate in basic social activities.* (European Parliament, 1993: 18; my italics)

Other practical suggestions include the introduction of 'a general and radical shortening of working time', career break schemes, an expansion of social services in terms of quality, child benefit payments, individual taxation, and 'recognition of basic social activity skills in connection with recruitment and promotions.'

In both Cockburn and the European Parliament report, attention is directed to the need for 'men' to change. Their recommendations, including affirmative action to get 'men' to assume domestic and other social responsibilities, move beyond an incorporationist model.

In Australia, as in the United States and in Canada, the relationship between paid work and family responsibilities has been managed through the constructed categories of 'public' and 'private'. With a myriad of meanings, the general impact has been to suggest that areas of our lives deemed 'private' need to be sequestered off from 'public' intervention and scrutiny (Pateman, 1983; Okin, 1991). Val Plumwood (1995: 107) identifies these as '"the private economy", and the area excised in the household or domestic sphere'. Frances Olsen (1985) shows that the categories 'public' and 'private' mystify relationships between individuals and institutions. She notes perceptively that the state is intervening in the lives of citizens all the time, even when it does nothing – not providing public child care or not addressing domestic violence for example.

A rethinking of the relationship between 'public' and 'private' spheres provides a necessary backdrop to the sorts of proposals raised by Cockburn and the European Parliament report. Kate Soper offers a radical redefinition of these spheres such that the 'public' 'would no longer designate the domain of national chauvinism and individual careerism, but become associated with the extension of political space for the renegotiation of "public" interests, standards of success and existing divisions of labour' (1990: 204–6). Renegotiation, she argues, would reveal the narrowness of a 'public' life that 'down-played all other interests and attachments than those of work and career.' Such a revaluing of roles and relations she considers a necessary condition of meaningful institutional restructuring.

Proposals to allow 'private' enterprise to 'manage diversity' outside the purview of 'public' supervision undermine efforts to bring a degree of accountability to employment policy which would allow the space for the renegotiation Soper endorses. Hence, they must be resisted. Failure to do so ensures that, for the time being at least, the bifurcation of lives into 'public' and 'private' parts, with the first assuming prior value, will continue. Plumwood (1995: 115) argues convincingly that what is needed is democratization of both areas designated 'private', the economy and the household.

Invisible women

One of the chief insights of the current poststructuralist wave of feminist theorizing is that the categories 'women' and 'women's interests' remain susceptible to uses which undermine feminist goals (Pringle and Watson, 1992: 57). Unfortunately, insisting that 'women' be recognized has no necessary effect on the ways this recognition takes place. So, it ought not to be surprising that explicit legislative targeting of 'women' can be used to pay *less* attention to 'women'.

For example, an important Green Paper (Dawkins, 1987) on reform of Australia's higher educational institutions made only one mention of 'women', and this was a reference to the Affirmative Action Act under consideration here. It was 'as if', by mentioning affirmative action, all that needed to be said about 'women' had been said. Blackmore and Kenway (1988) tried to argue that, rather, affirmative action needed to be built into institutional profiles. Kenway (1989: 128) notes that the White Paper (Dawkins, 1988) which followed the Green Paper picked up and responded to some of the critiques about the lack of attention to equity but that:

> [I]n developing its equity policies for women, the government has been careful to select only those aspects of the feminist agenda . . . which either support or do not threaten the tolerance limits of its plans for restructuring and redirecting the higher education sector along economistic lines.

Usefully, Kenway (1989: 131–2) builds upon Mary O'Brien's (1984) notion of 'commatization', the listing of 'women' alongside other 'disadvantaged' groups – Blacks comma, gays comma, women comma, disabled comma, aged comma – to consider the ways in which men adjust to the impact of feminism. Among these Kenway includes: men's location of gender at the margins of their social theory, an approach to the formation of committees which says 'and we must have a woman', an approach to course design which says 'and we'd better have something on gender', and the creation of EEO (Equal Employment Opportunity) committees which invariably are the least prestigious and least powerful committees.

A recent report (J. Taylor, 1992) from the Women's Adviser in South Australia illustrates again how the creation of government units dedicated to 'women' can become a rationale for neglecting numbers of women. In this report, Aboriginal women, women from non-English speaking backgrounds and women with disabilities noted that the agencies set up to deal with the subgroups to which they belonged (Office of Multicultural and Ethnic Affairs, Disability Adviser, and State Aboriginal Affairs) did not feel responsible for 'women'. Instead everything to do with 'women' was being handed over to the Women's Advisory Unit. A comment from the Office of Multicultural and Ethnic Affairs bears out their view: 'it would be advantageous if responsibility for NESB and immigrant women's issues be assigned to a specific project officer within the WAU [Women's Advisory Unit]'. The Women's Adviser noted appropriately, in reply:

> The Women's Advisory Unit has a very broad mandate, that is, to over half the population of South Australia. One of the continuing difficulties is establishing resource priorities where there is already an agency servicing a target population of people who suffer a double oppression (i.e. NESB women, disabled women, Aboriginal women). (Taylor, 1992: 28)

This case illustrates how the creation of 'women's' units can provide rationalization for limiting the resources committed to women.

Even more disturbing is the finding by Aileen Moreton-Robinson (1992) that, within the Commonwealth Aboriginal and Torres Strait Islander Commission (known as ATSIC), despite a commitment to equal opportunity for Aboriginals and Torres Strait Islanders, 'women', people from non-English speaking backgrounds and people with disabilities, '[E]qual Employment Opportunity seems to favor indigenous men over indigenous women and over some non-indigenous women.' The problem, as Moreton-Robinson explains, is that within the Commission, 'race' has become the 'marker' for identifying discriminatory practices in employment. This is because ATSIC is 'designed' to address 'race' questions; questions affecting 'women' are assumed to be dealt with elsewhere, in specialist units for 'women', like the Affirmative Action Agency. Hence, the EEO programmes at ATSIC make explicit the separation between indigenous people as a racial group and others, but not the separation between indigenous women and indigenous men. This lack of separation, as Moreton-Robinson notes, 'has direct implications for their equal employment opportunities.'[9]

So in Australia, as in Canada, the design of affirmative action and equal opportunity policies, despite their differences, allows some women – specifically women who are members of other outgroups – to fall through the cracks. Despite representations by several groups to change the federal affirmative action legislation to meet the needs of particular groups of women and to implement specific measures for women members of other EEO target groups, *Next Steps* (Affirmative Action Agency, 1992b), the recent review of Australia's affirmative action legislation, made no such recommendation. Moreton-Robinson (1992: 9) makes the disturbing revelation that the Affirmative Action Agency does not even keep labour market statistics on indigenous women.

Perversely, directing attention to the needs of 'other' women is no guarantee of needed reform. We have already observed this happening in Canada (Chapter 4). Kenway (1989: 132–3) notes in her discussion of the White Paper on Higher Education that the government directed attention to 'disadvantaged women', overlooking that 'women in higher education as a group are subject to shared forms of discrimination even if these may have different dimensions and may be experienced somewhat differently by different sub-groups of women.' Just as drawing attention to 'women' can be a way of narrowing an agenda, so too can drawing attention to 'disadvantaged women'. Category politics in Australia has proved ultimately flexible in diverting initiatives for change.

'Women' as civilizers

A study by Joan Eveline and Michael Booth of the introduction of affirmative action at Australia's Argyle Diamond Mine provides another example of how 'women' has been incorporated into Australian institutions without serious alterations to these institutions. In fact, the Argyle study shows how affirmative action for 'women' was seen by managers as a way of stabilizing rather than challenging the status quo. In this instance, the 'women' envisioned by managers retain markers of the archetypical 'woman'; they are seen as caretakers and nurturers, representatives of peace and civility. It was the employers' hope that 'women's' presence would reduce the chances of industrial unrest and 'keep the boys happy' (Eveline et al., 1989; Eveline, 1994a, 1995a, 1995b).

During the early 1980s, the developing tripartite system of the Accord, discussed in the next section, was portrayed as a triumph for corporate consensus. That display of mutual goodwill between government and industry, aided by some of Australia's largest enterprises, spilled over into the Affirmative Action initiative. Among these companies was CRA, the parent company of the Argyle Diamond Mine (ADM) venture. On promising an involvement in the Voluntary Affirmative Action Pilot Program, the directors of CRA passed this on to the rather reluctant directors of its infant Argyle Diamonds.

Yet the mine's planners had good reasons for introducing women miners into this new venture at a remote north-west mine site. Since stoppages and slowdowns had proved costly to past mining enterprises, the aim was to avoid the hard-bitten 'Pilbara mentality' of the seasoned miner: the propensity for industrial action (H.M. Thompson, 1984). One way to do this, planners decided, was to introduce a new type of mine worker: Argyle miners would be untrained in mining, socially malleable, politically open to working cooperatively, and industrially non-combative. Company literature is liberally sprinkled with terms like 'greenfields', 'industrially naive', 'virgin workforce', 'adaptable', 'highly educated', 'quick learners', as descriptors of the type of employee characteristics wanted. For the 'New Age' management of ADM, these characteristics fitted with computerized technology, on-site and ongoing training of workers new to mining, and a workforce which spent only two weeks out of every four at the mine.

Since workers resided in Perth and were flown back and forth to the mine for fortnightly relays, the costly family infrastructure usually associated with mining towns could now be done without. However, with no family town provided there would be few women as the symbolic servicers of men. From earlier ventures, CRA's planners had deduced that 'women' represent a 'civilizing influence' in mining communities. In the usual mining town, wives and daughters were said to ensure that standards of dress and behaviour are kept up. Moreover, in the company's trial alluvial plant (where women had sorted the diamonds and comprised 28 per cent of workers) management found that better care was taken of the equipment than was usual among miners, there was less antagonism between men and the overall safety record improved.

In the event the planners of ADM made good use of the discourse that affirmative action will benefit employers, the dominant representation of the reform as discussed above. Invited to comment on what was important about the company's affirmative action strategy, one of the senior planners said:

> We need to see just what affirmative action and equal employment opportunity is about in terms of importance. . . . having a large number of females has helped Site because it has improved the behaviour of males. I mean they're just your average peacock and it's amazing how they dress better, stay cleaner, behave more appropriately, when there are females around than when they are not. [We] talked about it beforehand. We argued that . . . there were some very pragmatic reasons for it. (Eveline, 1995a: 96)

For the management team the introduction of women as miners was a way of 'normalizing' ADM's workforce. Gender specificity, not gender neutrality, was the determining principle here. The results were deeply gendered in other ways. Few of the women at ADM had children under 18, whereas many of the men did.

Yet it was not simply assumed that the enterprise should and did benefit from the stability accorded by women's employment. At shop-floor level, the group represented as gaining the most from affirmative action for 'women' was male miners. Among shift bosses and workers, managerial control was not portrayed as the most significant feature of affirmative action for women. Rather, what was stressed was how male employees gained additional comforts and services. Male miners interviewed in the Argyle study were almost unanimous that the employment of women made the remote mining life more 'like home' for them. With women around, men said, the place was cleaner, and there was always someone to talk to or discuss family problems with. Moreover, women took orders better, and, because they could often be given the mundane jobs, there were fewer fights between men (Eveline et al., 1989). The men were responding to a set of ground rules in which men's comfort, men's self-image, men's quality of life, men's position of primacy, were represented as primarily important here. As a matter of course, affirmative action for 'women' was coded as quite properly advantaging 'men', a form of representation akin to what Burton (1991) calls a 'masculinity protection strategy'.

So, while 'normalization' may increase the proportion of women to men, it also rehearses a discourse of 'women' as subordinate or subsidiary – not equal – to 'men'. When a woman goes to work at the mine, she is expected to carry her share of paid work. However, she is also implicitly situated as the locus of affectivity, which places her as responsible for care and nurture of her male colleagues. In this understanding, affirmative action offers 'women' to service men.

Such an understanding creates serious implementation problems. This is illustrated in the dispute generated by the attempt by management to remove workplace pin-ups which had offended some women workers. Throughout the dispute, the mechanical fitters, all men, threatened to strike if the pin-ups were removed. Most of the fitters protested that removal of the pin-ups interfered with their rights as the original occupiers of the workplace. One of the men spelt it out this way: 'If the women want to come into our workforce they can bloody well put up with it. And if they don't like it they can bloody leave' (Eveline, 1995a: 98). The dilemma for management here is that they wanted 'women' in order to tame the workforce, not to *cause* industrial disputation. They had also sold affirmative action as a reform which would benefit men and 'keep them happy'. It was difficult to maintain this argument in the face of the fitters' rage.

One of the chief problems with traditional studies of compliance is that there is a tendency to bypass the processes of implementation. Compliance is usually treated as a property of a discrete design procedure. The law emphasizes the relation between regulator and managerial response and leaves the relation between implementor (management) and beneficiary (women workers) out of the regulative picture. Absent from the design, also, are procedures for handling a group from which resistance can be expected – male employees and bosses.

When these factors are considered, a more nuanced understanding of the effects of affirmative action becomes available. The Argyle study reveals a depth of antagonism toward women who chose to enter the mines, an antagonism which sat uneasily alongside an acceptance of women in *certain* roles. Women were 'welcomed' in this case as 'women' but the clear message was that they were on *'men's'* terrain.

'Women' as 'citizens'

We saw in the previous chapter that political discourses about 'women' are often also discourses about 'nation'.[10] This is because those who hold political power are vitally concerned about the nature of the constituency which underpins their legitimacy. The relationship between

govenment and this constituency, as I have suggested in other places in
the text, is a blend of response and fabrication.

The relationship between 'women' and 'citizenship' is a contested
one.[11] The traditional markers of 'citizens', such as the ability to defend
the 'nation', are historically masculine. I mentioned earlier (see Chapter
4) that the rights of citizenship, civil, political and social, have been
constituted historically in ways which make them less accessible to
many women. And yet in this post-women's suffrage era,[12] there is a
taken-for-grantedness about 'women's' citizenship status. In Australia
the form this has taken is congruent with the attempts there to bring
'women' into the labour market – that is, 'women' are offered incorporation into existing definitions of what it means to be a citizen, and
these definitions privilege 'economic man' (Johnson, 1994). There is little
reflection upon the gendered character of those definitions.

Here, as elsewhere, we are talking about 'images' of nation and of
'citizen', and the way these discuss 'women'. There is no implication
that any of this *necessarily* translates into meaningful conditions of life.
Commitments to *kinds* of nations and *kinds* of citizens, as with the other
conceptual categories examined, operate at a discursive level, have
political uses and political effects.

Anne Summers's (1975) classic portrayal of images of Australian
womanhood offered Australian women a familiar dichotomy – 'damned
whores' or 'God's police'. The country's convict background produced a
concern among colonial administrators to provide women to service
men's sexual needs, lest men be lured into 'perverse' sexualities, and for
women to temper the frontier environment. The sharp division between
the *kinds* of women – the whore and the madonna/civilizer – who
would be expected to fill these needs disguises the common grounding
in a belief that 'women's' purpose is to serve 'men'. Not coincidentally
then, Australia's national character type is prototypically male. Feminist
historians have ably demonstrated the 'blurred vision' which produced
the 'independent, free-wheeling Bushman' (Lake, 1986: 122) as
archetype, a vision which ignored both the heavy urban concentration
of the population and the roles of women in the community. Early
twentieth-century modifications, while adding a dimension of 'responsible breadwinning' to the masculine model, did not displace 'man' as
the measure of the true Australian. Amanda Sinclair (1994: 13), for
example, notes the correspondence between the characteristics associated
with this icon, 'solitary toughness', 'not admitting vulnerability' and
'strength under stress', and Australia's executive culture.

In the recent Republican debate,[13] Jill Ker Conway (1993/1994: 80) has
observed that the most vocal leaders of the Australian Republican
Movement seem unable 'to consider civic virtue in any but the old male
tradition.' She refers to the attempts by the Movement's leader, Thomas
Keneally, to 'communicate the ideals' of the Australian Republican
Movement (ARM) by exalting the sporting ritual of Australian Rules

football. Conway notes pointedly: 'if the ARM wants to exalt ritualized male combat watched by beery and raucous male crowds as the core of a new national identity, it is not surprising that some Australian feminists greet it coolly.' Conway explores the inadequacy of the models of Australian national character, illustrated in the emphasis on outlaw heroes like Ned Kelly, the Wild Colonial Boy, and the 'long retinue of anti-social male wanderers in the outback'. She describes these as poor models for civic virtue, 'because they are uncommitted and unable to form viable connections to settled society.' The problem here is not simply the content of the image but that it, consistent with historical constructions of Australian character, positions 'women' as onlookers or outsiders.

Recently, as Carol Johnson (1993a, 1993b) describes, both of Australia's major national parties, the Australian Liberal and the Australian Labor Parties, have been engaged in efforts to reconstruct 'the Australian citizen of the 21st century'. Johnson stresses the politics behind the constructing of identity in a way which resonates with the position developed in this book. She (1992: 16) emphasizes that analyses of the politics of identity – both the 'more obviously public ones such as appeals to nationalism' but also 'intensely personal ones' – can make for our understanding of political regimes. This is because governments, political parties and political leaders '. . . utilise appeals to popular conceptions of identity in order to increase their electoral appeal', and because, to an extent, 'how people vote partly depends on how they "see themselves"'. She also notes that the citizenship debate has focused upon images of *masculinity*.

For the former Labor Prime Minister, Paul Keating, the main motivation was the creation of a national identity which would drive his economic vision for Australia. In his view, the Australian 'yob' is considered inadequate as an overseas ambassador. Nothing is said, however, about how this identity marginalizes 'women', nor about its implications for many women: 'He [Keating] is not, for example, suggesting that yobs should become less sexist or that either yobs or artistes should do more housework' (Johnson, 1993b: 5).

'Women', Johnson (1993b: 6–7) points out, has not been ignored in Keating's speculations about twentieth-century Australia, but has not found a way into reconceptualizations of who is an Australian. 'Women' come onto the agenda through Labor's continuing commitment to the Affirmative Action policy and for the same reason outlined earlier, as 'resources' crucial to the country's economic future. Keating reminds us: 'Neither individual employers nor the nation can afford to waste the valuable contributions which women can, and do, make to our economy' (*Australian Parliamentary Debates*, Representatives, 19 February 1986, p. 862 in Johnson, 1993b: 7).

Within this vision, 'women' is positioned ambiguously. On the one hand, 'women' is targeted for 'special programs' to meet 'special needs' (Johnson, 1993b: 4). On the other, women are told that some of their needs, the case in point here being child care, go beyond 'women's issues'. In an important speech launching the *New National Agenda for Women* (10 February, 1993), Keating noted that he had included child care in his earlier (the previous day) policy statement, *Investing in the Nation*, because

> [C]hild care should be treated with the same seriousness as education or aged care. The time is long past, as far as I am concerned, where child care was tagged as a 'women's issue' or a 'welfare issue' and only attracted the crumbs from the table where the budget banquet was enjoyed. I know how paramount an issue child care is for women. (quoted in Johnson, 1993b: 7)

The ambiguity is made complete with the statement that child care is an issue 'paramount' for 'women'.

As Johnson summarizes, 'women' tend to be depicted as having a 'double identity' in the 'new Australian nation', 'as employees and as people with particular family responsibilities' (Johnson, 1993b: 8). While their 'difference' is inscribed, they are 'offered' the opportunity to join the new economic future.

Johnson (1993b) elaborates a comparison between the social conceptions of the Australian Labor Party and the Australian Liberal Party. She notes that the former expressly commits itself to a vision of cooperation and consensus between social groups while the latter 'tends to view people as fragmented individuals'.

Labor government rhetoric, says Johnson (1993a: 82), has 'traditionally seen citizens as members of economically and socially defined groups, such as business and labour, that should work together for the common good.' This image has been maintained in recent years despite the 'greater emphasis on deregulation and the role of market forces.' The groups which forge Labor's 'consensus' (Johnson, 1990) are the same groups which ground Sweden's corporatist culture (see Chapter 6) – government, business and unions. 'Women' is 'granted' group status, but only on the sidelines.

The move to corporatist politics in Australia is exemplified in the Prices and Incomes Accord established between labour and the government in the lead-up to the 1983 election. Under the Accord unions, the majority of which continue to be heavily male-dominated, agreed to wage restraint in exchange for promised price constraint and a gradual increase in the social wage. As Danny Blackman (1984: 17) argues, while employers were not directly involved in the negotiations, the Accord is 'essentially a document aimed at business, at gaining the confidence of the private sector in Australia.' It was meant to illustrate that the ALP was capable of steering the economy out of the recession.

The Accord had little to say about 'women'. Reminiscent of the Green Paper on Higher Education discussed above, there is only one reference, in the section on education, to equal opportunity policy, where 'women' is listed as a target group alongside 'rural women' and 'Aborigines'. As noted at the outset of this chapter, while Australia's Affirmative Action Act continues to target only 'women', much discussion of equal opportunity assumes a list of 'disadvantaged' groups. There is room, within Labor's stated commitment to a group-based social vision, for these categories.

The appeal to a group-based social vision provided the opening for women in the ALP to demand, as women have done elsewhere, when the discourse allows such claims, a minimum percentage of women as party representatives. This has resulted recently in the ALP accepting a 35 per cent 'quota' of women in winnable seats. This significant development does not, however, address the kinds of changes in Parliament which would make life as a representative possible for women who assume domestic responsibilities. Nor does it explain why 35 per cent is considered 'equality' or guarantees a change in practice. In a recent South Australian preselection battle, as Carol Altmann (1995) reports, '[T]he factional deal stitched up by the State Executive and endorsed by the National Executive . . . saw four men and one woman on the five-member ticket.'

In contrast to the Labor focus on social groups, the Liberals speak about people as 'fragmented individuals' (Johnson, 1993b: 13). For 'women', as Johnson describes, the approach is to 'try to incorporate exceptional women into the image of the tough, self-reliant individual beloved of traditional laissez-faire individualism.' In 1992, John Hewson, then Liberal leader of the Opposition, stated that 'the greatest compliment we can pay the women of Australia – is to treat them exactly the same way as everyone else.' In this spirit the Liberal Party has endorsed 'equal opportunity'. The declared support for 'equal opportunity' for 'women' sits uncomfortably, however, alongside the Liberal Party's continued evocation of the 'family' as the key unit of citizenship. A recent Liberal policy statement (Liberal/National, 1994: 28, 7) states: 'Expanding opportunities and choices for women throughout the Australian community is a core objective of the Coalition.' The same document asserts that 'Families are the foundation of a stable society.' Johnson (1994: 5–6) points out that, while there is no necessary inconsistency here, since the Liberals talk about 'family-friendly workplaces', they also wish to encourage the idea of families in which one parent stays home. Gender-neutral language only disguises the implication that, in most cases, this will be a woman. It is unclear at this stage how this inconsistency will be overcome but, as C. Johnson (1990: 85) argues, the only way to reconcile an appeal to individualism with an endorsement of family is to think of the family as represented by the 'breadwinner', who is most often seen to be a man.

The options for women, Labor's 'special-needs' group or Liberals' individuals 'like men', should by now be familiar. 'Women' in both cases is deployed in ways which fit political agendas designed for other purposes. In neither case is 'women' the starting point for rethinking policy or national image. As in Canada and the United States, references to 'women' appear *ad hoc* and opportunistic. The lack of substantive analysis suggests political motivation in attempting to appeal to groups of women voters (Pringle and Watson, 1992: 57), while enunciating goals congruent with other, 'more important' political objectives.

In direct contradiction of the 'multifarious, pluralistic identities' heralded by postmodern theorizing (Johnson, 1993b: 16), Australian politics, and in this there are doubtless replicas, offers narrow, gender-inflected visions of citizenship. The discussion concentrates on positing national characteristics needed for the economy. Characteristics which touch on other parts of life go unexamined or are confined to an ill-defined 'family' or 'private' sphere. While 'women' is now acknowledged in limited ways, little rethinking of fundamental social relations is occurring.

Postscript: adding 'men'

There is a new twist to the strategies being employed within the politics of incorporation. I call it 'adding "men" while subtracting "women" and still not stirring'. It has shown its face in at least two cases, which are related in certain ways, in Australia – the debates about 'men's' health and the education of 'boys'.

As a result of lengthy campaigning by the Australian women's movement, some funding at the federal and state (Australian Capital Territory, ACT) levels was set aside to establish women's health services in 1990. Shortly after this decision, an adviser in the Department of Health, Dr Alex Proudfoot, challenged the funding decision as discriminatory against 'men'. His complaint to the Human Rights and Equal Opportunity Commission was initially dismissed by Commissioner Quentin Bryce but was handed back to the Commissioner through a decision of the Federal Court. After a protracted and much publicized hearing procedure, Dr Proudfoot's claims were dismissed.

The case is interesting for a number of reasons. First, it illustrates how existing gender-neutral sex discrimination laws allow men to invoke them against women. Second, it reveals how, discursively, attempts to deal with 'women's' inequality are sometimes positioned as 'in opposition' to 'men'. Third, the resolution in favour of 'women' owed something to the existence of the affirmative action exemption to sex discrimination, Section 33, which allows that it is not unlawful to do an act, if its purpose is to provide 'equal opportunities' for specified groups (Ronalds, 1987: 153). The decision handed down by the President of the Human Rights and Equal Opportunity Commission, Sir Ronald Wilson, on 17 March 1992[14] was indeed more complex than this implies and made reference to other sections of the Sex Discrimination Act. For my purposes, what is important is that Justice Wilson found women's health services discriminatory and looked to find a way to justify this 'discrimination'.

The point here, introduced in Chapter 2, is that existing under-standings of affirmative action, even as these are translated into legislation, portray affirmative action as discrimination, allowable in some circumstances. This understanding leaves the reform constantly open to threat of challenge, with no guarantee that in the next instance, the decision will not go the other way. At issue here, as Dorothy Broom (1992: 10–11) points out, is not just 'women's' health services, or affirmative action for 'women', but any legislation which targets any outgroup. While this is the case, formal equality, which ignores people's particular circumstances, remains essentially unchallenged.

While Proudfoot was defeated, concerns about 'men's' health have not gone away. A federal report in July 1992 announced that the death rate of working-aged men is 92 per cent higher than their female colleagues. The press caption (*The Weekend Australian*, 25–26 July, 1992, p. 3) heralded – 'Being a man is a health hazard'. A recent article in a publication produced by a large national insurance company (*In Touch*, NIB Health Funds, January, 1995, pp. 10–11) proclaimed, 'Men's health is becoming an issue of national concern.' It referred to acknowl-edgement of the Federal Minister for Health, Dr Carmen Lawrence, that men's health was 'one of the big problems in society'.

In the second of the two cases introduced above – recent education debate – there has been no explicit legal challenge to programmes, such as the National Agenda for Girls, that address questions to do with 'girls'' unequal educational experiences. Instead it is simply being sug-gested that 'boys' need more attention; that a National Agenda for Boys, or something very like it, is necessary. A 1994 inquiry into boys' education chaired by NSW MP, Mr Stephen O'Doherty, was followed by announcements that initiatives would soon be taken to improve 'boys'' level of self-esteem and participation in a wide range of academic and associated activities (*The Australian*, 2 February, 1995).[15]

The similarity between the health and education examples is that, in both, 'men' and 'boys' are portrayed as 'losing out' *because of* the attention paid to 'women' and 'girls'. The discourse has shifted from 'women's disadvantage' to 'men's disadvantage',[16] while, as Eveline (1994c) argues, there is still no talk of 'men's advantage'. Another similarity in the two cases is that some men are beginning to pay attention to the ways in which gender affects 'men's' health and the education of 'boys'. This is doubtless an important issue, and feminists have long been interested in and concerned about the fallout accompanying dominant masculine stereotypes. What is disturbing is that both cases are generally offered as win–lose scenarios. In order to *win* recognition of 'men's' health issues, Proudfoot wished to *remove* the newly gained recognition of 'women's' health issues. Similarly in the education debate, the assumption is that the battle for 'girls' has been won, and it is now time to turn attention, and resources, to 'boys'. We see here an example of the tendency for 'women' as a group to be blamed (Graham et al., 1988: 223) for the problems faced by 'men'.

There is the impression in the health and education debates, an impression found elsewhere in this study, that 'girls'/'women' have had their day and now it is 'boys'/'men's' turn. So, we are told that 'girls' at school are now achieving better than 'boys', though it is sometimes admitted that this scholastic success does not carry over into post-graduate study. In this approach, the *content* of the school curriculum goes unscrutinized. As Alison Jones (1993: 10) points out, in general, 'girls' are achieving an understanding of an 'alienated curriculum' – '[T]hey are learning that boys' and men's perspectives and achievements are better, more worth listening to, more authoritative. They are learning to undervalue women's work and authority and contribution to school knowledge.' They are offered an understanding of 'woman' as 'she' is currently positioned by men's discourses in our society.

These cases illustrate the ways in which category politics in Australia currently deflects attention from needed, but more deep-seated and more threatening change. As Bob Connell (reported in Legge, 1995: 21) has argued with respect to the education debate, what is required is 'a radical restructuring of schools involving sport, discipline systems, staffing policies and curriculum to emphasise participation over competition and the broader goal of social justice.' I have made a similar case (Bacchi, 1990) for the way in which debates about 'women's' sameness to or difference from 'men' detract attention from the need for an overhaul of work practices and social arrangements for care.

These recent manoeuvres are most interesting because they invoke the categories 'men'/'boys'. Throughout this study, I suggest that an important way to alter or to challenge the common uses/deployments of the category 'women' is to make 'men' visible. The health and education examples illustrate forcefully, however, that the problem is not simply making 'men' visible but keeping a focus on the ways in which different representations of relations between the sexes have varied political effects, and drawing attention to these. In this case, we need to show how the current turn to 'men' as disadvantaged is erasing not only 'women' as disadvantaged, but the very real advantages that accrue to those who best fit the category 'men' (see Eveline, 1994a). None of this implies that 'women' (or 'men' for that matter) ought to be dropped from feminist analysis and feminist campaigning. Rather it redirects attention to the political uses of categories.

Notes

1 See Chapter 2 for clarification of the constructed difference between 'hard' and 'soft' affirmative action.

2 I would like to acknowledge here my debt to Carol Johnson's (1990, 1992, 1993a,

1993b, 1994) work which draws attention to the way in which 'women' has been incorporated into the Australian Labor Party's (ALP) and the Liberal Party's political agendas. In this chapter I use the term 'incorporation' to refer to a wide range of strategies which marginalize 'women' by leaving 'men' situated as the unremarkable norm (see Chapter 1 for discussion).

3 In 1969 the Arbitration Commission called for equal pay for equal work. As Alina Holgate and Karen Milgrom (1985: 24) describe, '[T]he constrictiveness of the definition "equal pay for equal work" and the fact that fewer than 20% of the female workforce had gained any benefit at all from the 1969 equal pay case', led to a concerted campaign throughout the women's and trade union movements to gain recognition of 'equal pay for work of equal value'. Officially this was won in a 1972 Equal Pay Case and was phased in over three years.

4 See, for example, 'While Government and unions dither . . . Business Council primed for affirmative legislation', *Financial Review*, 22 April, 1985. Despite the caption, the BCA supported voluntary affirmative action programmes, not legislation. See also, 'Business groups go cold on affirmative action', *Financial Review*, 4 September, 1985.

5 A chief critic was Gabriel Moens of the Sydney University Law School who wrote a report originally commissioned by the Human Rights Commission under the Liberal Government. The report, repudiated by the Labor Government, was published with the support of the Centre for Independent Studies, a right-wing organization (Moens, 1985, 1989; Eisenstein, 1986: 20).

6 There are numerous examples of the 'women as resource' argument in press reports about affirmative action and in government documents targeting 'women'. See, for example, the government's *National Agenda for Women* (Office of the Status of Women, 1988) and the *Australian Women's Employment Strategy* (Department of Employment, Education and Training, 1988).

7 The term 'potential men' is borrowed from Irigaray, 1985: 8.

8 See, for example, 'Affirmative Action: Short Term Event or Long Term Process?', *Business Council Bulletin*, March 1989, p. 23. Margaret Thornton (1994) analyses the discourse of 'good management practice' in the publications of the Council for Equal Opportunity in Employment, a body set up by the Business Council of Australia. On the impact of managerial discourse on understandings of 'equal opportunity' see Yeatman 1990: 16 and *passim*. In moves by the Affirmative Action Agency since 1994 to tighten the reporting requirements of the Act, it is interesting to see the same discourse of 'best practice' being used to place higher demands on business for compliance (see Eveline, 1995a, 1995b).

9 However, some Aboriginal women have long argued that equal opportunity strategies are irrelevant to Aboriginal women since Aboriginal men are even more discriminated against than Aboriginal women when it comes to both employment and education. See O'Shane (1976); Burgmann (1984); Huggins (1994).

10 For a discussion of the ways in which 'nation-ness', as well as 'nationalism' are cultural artifacts, see Benedict Anderson (1983).

11 There is a vast literature on this subject. See, for example, Okin (1979), Pateman (1988). *Australian Feminist Studies* dedicated a recent issue (Autumn, 1994) to 'women' and 'citizenship'.

12 There is now to my knowledge no Western industrialized country which denies a vote to women.

13 There are moves afoot, mainly but not solely among members of the Australian Labor Party, to make Australia a republic. These moves ought to be seen as part of a larger agenda of constitutional reform which has been ongoing for the past five years. Among the issues touted is the introduction of a Bill of Rights. On this subject see Bacchi and Marquis, 1994.

14 Refer to Human Rights and Equal Opportunity Commission, Sex Discrimination Act, 1991–92 inquiry into complaint of Alexander Proudfoot against ACT Board of Health, ACT, Canberra Women's Health Centre Incorporated, Commonwealth of Australia.

15 See Foster (1992) for a critique of the precursors to this move of again overlooking girls' needs in favour of those of boys.

16 A recent article in *Campus Review* (Maslen, 1995: 1) carried the headline: 'Gender roles swapped: Report finds uni men "disadvantaged"'. The article condensed a report which heralded the increase in numbers of women in universities and in the labour force. While there are doubtless advances in these areas, the superficiality of a purely statistical summary of where women 'are' says little about their experiences, nor does it suggest how any of these changes can be said to 'disadvantage' men.

6

The Politics of Solidarity

There is no doubt that some political regimes attend more directly than others to the category 'women'. We have seen this already, with Australia formally committed to affirmative action for 'women' (see Chapter 5). We have also noted, however, that 'attention' does not always or necessarily mean that a commitment to 'women' ranks high on the political agenda. In fact, my research indicates that attention to 'women' can, almost perversely, serve to limit the resources spent on women.

The identity categories which 'drive' political agendas are not necessarily the same in every country/region, and these may shift over time. In some countries, as in the United States for example, it has to date been considered more legitimate to recognize 'race' than 'class' as constitutive of personhood. This does not mean that racial equality is either a goal or a consequence of policy. It means simply that the category 'race' has some political legitimacy. And, as we have seen, it has greater political legitimacy than 'women', creating problems for white and Black women. In other countries, 'class' is considered the primary identifying feature of 'citizens'. This chapter explores the kinds of problems this creates for women who try to claim categorical recognition for 'women' and to have claims on behalf of 'women' taken seriously. Sweden is the exemplar, though the ways in which class and class affiliations undermine the categorical legitimacy of 'women' has relevance in several of the countries examined in this work. This is most obviously so in Norway, the Netherlands and in Australia. In other countries, the problem may be less pronounced at the national level but may play a part within left-oriented organizations.

This chapter shows that in Sweden 'women' has been accorded a recognition of sorts, but that this recognition has been limited to reforms considered important by actors committed to other political agendas. Certain kinds of issues, specifically those designed to assist 'women' to combine labour force participation with motherhood, have been addressed and with positive results for many women. In addition, some policies, motivated by a desire to reduce the distance between classes, have benefited some women. But other issues, specifically those which constitute 'women' as in some way in competition with 'men' or in conflict with 'men', have had difficulty finding their way onto the political agenda or appear on the agenda in a transformed and nonthreatening way. Such is the case with positive action, the term generally used in Sweden to refer to the kinds of labour market policies called affirmative action in the United States and in Australia, and employment equity in Canada.

I call this chapter 'The Politics of Solidarity' because it argues that the rhetorical commitment to class solidarity by those in positions of political influence in Sweden has made it difficult for women activists to broach issues which set 'women' *against* 'men' and hence has limited the kinds of claims they have had success in raising. A solidaristic approach to class relations creates a presumption of solidarity between 'women' and 'men'. Hence a commitment to 'sexual harmony' determines the placement of 'women'. Joan Eveline (1994c: 68) uses the phrase 'sexual mutuality' to characterize the representation of gender relations in Sweden. As a recent government document makes clear, class solidarity sets the model: 'Under the Bill [referring to the 1988 Government Bill on the Equality Policy to the Mid-Nineties], a policy for equality between the sexes must be pursued along the same lines as the policy for equal opportunities for everybody in a wider sense (social class, race, religion, origin, etc.) (Ministry of Public Administration, 1990: 6). The positioning of 'social class' first in this list is, I would suggest, significant.

The chapter concentrates on relationships between 'women' and social democracy, with the Swedish Social-Democratic Party (SAP) a main actor. At times, it may even sound as if social democracy and Sweden are coterminous, which is understandable given that the SAP held power between 1932 and 1991, with the short exception of 1976–1982. However, the ways in which the bourgeois parties[1] engage with 'women' is also an important part of the story, especially with their return to power in 1991, and the impact this has had on the shape of politics generally in Sweden and on gender politics in particular.

There has been a serious, if brief, challenge to the class-based vision which characterized the earlier period, which has had important effects for 'women'. A new space opened up in which to press claims for 'women' *tout court*, and some women utilized this space, with some success in the 1994 elections which saw the Social Democrats return to power. The challenge to social democracy has also led some social democrats to herald 'working women' as the potential saviours of the movement. The possibilities and problems associated with these openings will be considered at the end of the chapter.

From the Swedish home to the Swedish model

Ideologies often build upon mythologies, and we need more studies of the ways in which both of these enter political discourse. The extent to which Scandinavians enjoy, and enjoy relating, the mythological origins of their commitment to social equality is striking. The Danish folk hero,

Grundtvig, who lived at the turn of the nineteenth century, is held up as exemplary. He introduced the Folk High Schools which continue to be regarded as key institutions contributing to the active creation of a national identity and social equality through promoting social mobility (Andersen, 1986). The goal, in Grundtvig's words, is clear – 'And yet in wealth far we have gone when few have too much, and poor are none'. The Social Democrat Prime Minister, Per Albin Hansson, captured both the romantic nationalism and the goal of equity in his depiction of the Swedish welfare state as a 'folk home', *folkhemmet*, in 1928 (Dahl, 1986: 107).

Much has been written about the Nordic 'passion for equality' (Graubard, 1986). There are disputes about whether this passion ought to be connected to socialism or to be seen simply as a cultural artifact from the days of agrarian radicalism in the late eighteenth and early nineteenth centuries. There is agreement, however, that, whatever the cause, it is fair to describe the population as *looking at* the world through the 'structural grid of classes' (Dahl, 1986).

The problem of class inequality has been considered the most significant one facing the country. The social groups accorded recognition have been those based upon economic status, unions representing wage-earners and employers. This is reflected in Sweden's corporatist approach to politics, the Swedish model. The Swedes, at least until recently, have been remarkably successful at creating workable arrangements for collective bargaining between employers and unions. Collective agreements have privileged status; and it is clear that the government understands when to stay out where it is not welcome (Rehn and Viklund, 1990).

Many studies attest to the fact that the Swedish model has produced real and important standard of living effects. The goal, to lessen the differentials between very wealthy and very poor, has to a degree been achieved. And few people face desperate poverty (Gustafsson and Uusitalo, 1988; Mitchell, 1991). One of the mechanisms introduced to achieve this goal, wage solidarity, has proved particularly beneficial for some women. Wage solidarity aimed to reduce the differentials between wage rates, particularly through raising the salaries of those at the bottom of the economic scale. Because women congregated at the bottom, they have often been the winners here. In fact, it has been suggested (Whitehouse, 1990: 368) that greater movement toward pay equity has been achieved through 'broadly egalitarian wage fixing arrangements and labour market policies' than through specific legislative provisions. Comparing Australia, Canada, Britain and Sweden, Whitehouse found that Sweden records the most equal pay structure among the four countries.

The strength of a class-equality discourse, however, has made it extremely difficult to bid for collective recognition for 'women' (see Eduards, 1989, 1991, 1992; Jenson and Mahon, 1993). Exacerbating this problem is the common characterization of Swedish politics as highly rational, consensual, deliberative and centralized (see Premfors, 1981). I am not saying that policy formulation is always conducted in these ways, only that it is often so characterized. This has produced what Maud Eduards (1992: 100) refers to as the 'non-conflictual rule' – a presumption that both 'men' and 'women' suffer from current 'gender relations' and that they will work *together* to change these relationships. The emphasis on consensus and social cohesion shaped the discourse which surrounded the early discussion of 'sexual inequality' in the 1960s. A 'sex roles' explanation of the problem dominated the literature. Admittedly sex role theory played a significant part in theorizing sexual inequality in all Western countries but the Swedes had, and still have, a particular passion for the concept.

In the Swedish 'sexual equality' discourse the argument advanced is that, due to socialization, 'women' and 'men' are trapped in constricting roles and that all will benefit when they are free to choose between spending time with their children or in paid labour. The impression is that 'men' and 'women' are equally constrained by sex roles and that a broadening of role options will benefit everyone. As one 1967 study put it, the 'more appropriate way' to view gender relations was 'in terms of sex roles', 'for we are not merely concerned with woman's role in respect to man, but with the role of men and women with respect to each other' (Linner, 1967: xv). The tone is conciliatory. There is no suggestion that men would have any reason to oppose change. There are no losers here. It is a 'win–win' situation. In the words of Olof Palme, the Social Democrat Prime Minister during these years, 'it is humankind that must be liberated' (Eduards et al., 1985: 158). The message is nicely captured in the title of a government publication, *Side by Side* (Gradin, 1985). Hence, a concern with 'women' and 'their' inequality appears on the Swedish political agenda as a concern with 'sexual equality'. And this is expressed consistently as a need to address 'inequality between men and women'. The language is gender neutral, as are the reforms. Nothing is to be 'given' to 'women' which is not offered to 'men'. As Anita Dahlberg (1984: 156) puts it, '[T]he one sex is thus not regarded as being in a less favourable position than the other in our society.'

There is some debate about whether women in Sweden have in fact demanded and fought for improvements in their status to the same extent as women elsewhere. Joyce Gelb (1990) feels that Swedish women have been compromised by their acceptance of the prevailing ideological commitment to class equality. Jane Jenson and Rianne Mahon (1993: 89) describe the problem more subtly. They explain that, in order to be heard, women activists have at times had to translate their demands into language which could be understood within the labour movement. This has usually meant replacing 'women' with terms like 'family' and 'work'.

Feminists face the unenviable task of simultaneously manoeuvring within and against dominant discourses. They manoeuvre *within* because, as members of a particular social setting, they are partly constituted by them. They manoeuvre *against*, in their attempts to carve out a new space for 'women's' claims. Dorothy Smith (1988: 55) describes how discourse – here she is referring to the discourse on femininity – is continually undergoing 'elaborations, contradiction, reworking at the local level among women actively participating in it.'

'Sexual equality' in Sweden

The People's Home, also known and referred to above as 'folk home', retained traditional notions of complementary spheres for 'men' and 'women'. The 'big' People's Home, public life, was simply intended to model the 'small life', domestic life, in which 'women' would remain (Eveline, 1994c: 108). In the words of Hansson, 'It is a matter of creating comfort and well-being there [meaning the big People's Home], making it good and warm, light and cheerful and free' (Hansson, in Hirdman, 1987: 29).

'Sexual equality' came onto the agenda for very practical reasons. Consistently, the goal has been to increase women's labour force participation (Hirdman, 1987), a motivation common to the countries studied in this volume. Sweden's situation was unique in some ways, however. The labour shortage which plagued many Western industrialized countries in the boom period of the 1960s occurred in Sweden from the turn of the century. There was also clear agreement among those in positions of political influence that 'native' women were preferable as employees to foreigners. At the same time, they expressed significant concern about the size of the population and a declining birth rate. Jenson and Mahon (1993: 83, fn. 26) note that '[I]n the first half of the 1900s, apparently 25 per cent of Swedish women of childbearing age chose not to have children.' This confluence of circumstances produced a commitment to provide means to encourage 'women' to reconcile maternity and labour force participation.

There have been several models advanced over the years to deal with this problem. The early Alva Myrdal recommended that 'women' and 'men' participate in the labour market and share the care work at home. But, as Jane Jenson and Rianne Mahon (1993: 82) describe, 'traditional understandings of gender relations' overwhelmed 'more imaginative thinking'. In response, Myrdal suggested that 'women's' labour force participation fit around and between their domestic commitments. She developed a life-style model wherein a woman would engage in paid labour for a spell, then take time off to have and raise her family, and return to paid labour later in life (Hirdman, 1987). The government responded with a number of 'family-friendly' measures – free maternity care, a maternity allowance, child allowances, a law (1939) 'enjoining employers from dismissing women on the grounds of marriage, pregnancy or childbearing' (Froman, 1994: 2). In the 1960s and early 1970s, there were more innovative reforms. The introduction of separate taxation for spouses in 1971 was meant to act as an incentive to lure more women into paid labour. Subsidized child care and parental insurance were also designed to facilitate women's movement into and out of the labour force (Persson, 1990: 228–9).

As in the other countries studied here, so too in Sweden, 'women's inequality' has been seen to be a labour market problem. But Sweden evolved innovative responses, sparked by a desire to keep women reproducing. It is 'women' as 'mothers' who are the focus of policy initiatives, and the family remains 'their' sphere primarily. In this understanding the 'problems' which have to be resolved become 'family' problems. There is little sense of 'women' opposing 'men' or competing with 'men'.

When 'women' are not mothers, they become individuals in the state's eyes. As Siv Gustafsson (1983: 3) states, 'The Swedish equality concept emphasizes the individual as opposed to the family'. This looks paradoxical given the progressive family policy just outlined. What is meant here is that individuals are encouraged to become self-sufficient so that they can move in and out of families with less need to call upon the state, though the state is perfectly willing to intervene to encourage self-sufficiency. This was one reason for the introduction of separate income taxation for wife and husband in 1971.

It is difficult to characterize social democratic ideology along any continuum which places individualism and collectivism at opposite poles (Esping-Andersen, 1990: 28). It is easier to identify the policy goals of those in power. As far as 'women' is concerned, the most important of these have been a desire to have more women in the labour force, to boost the birth rate, and a desire to encourage individual self-sufficiency. Maud Eduards (1989: 6) highlights the priority placed on the last of these: 'The most important thing is for each individual, woman or man, to be able to earn an independent livelihood through gainful employment.'

As Eduards goes on to argue, there are inherent conflicts in these goals. On the one hand, '[W]omen are to become independent, economically autonomous individuals, just like men.' On the other, 'society jealously safeguards women's ties with the family.' Hence, '[L]abour market policy and family policy are liable to pull in different directions.' While these sorts of tensions appear elsewhere – we have already noted such tensions in Australian Liberal Party policy for 'women' (see Chapter 5) and will discover the same in Sweden's bourgeois parties (discussion to follow) – it is perhaps more surprising to see them operating within social democratic policy and ideology. The way in which the positioning of 'women' reveals the ambiguities and inconsistencies in political ideologies serves only, in my view, to confirm that ideologies, like other conceptual categories, are more political than dogmatic in character.

There is no doubt that Swedish social democracy has produced policies which benefit many women. Parents are entitled to 450 days of paid parental leave, the first twelve months at 90 per cent of salary, and the remainder at a reduced amount.[2] A parliamentary decision in 1985 declared that all children over the age of one and a half have a right to municipal child care, and that that goal would soon be met (Widerberg, 1991; Statistics Sweden, 1990).

However, despite the existence of parental leave equally available to husband and wife, few men are using the benefit.[3] Recent research also suggests that there are serious problems with the way in which leave benefits are implemented. According to Karin Widerberg (1991), despite the legislation, pregnancy is only just tolerated and, while the legislation is formulated in such a way that it confers rights upon parents, there is no reciprocal obligation on employers to implement these rights in a fair and equitable manner. In addition, women, whether they engage in paid labour or not, are still doing the bulk of domestic labour (Calasanti and Bailey, 1991).

More recently, there has been a commitment to try to get 'men' to take up some share of family responsibilities. Within the last decade there has been increased attention to the 'role of the male' and in particular to the role of fathers. A publicity campaign in 1989–1990, called *Pappa Kom Hem* (Daddy Come Home) used posters, brochures and lapel buttons to exhort 'men' to spend more time with their children.[4] One month of parental leave has now been set aside for fathers; families will lose the month if fathers do not use it (Eveline, 1994c: 322 fn. 25). As Ingmarie Froman (1994: 2) points out, '[T]hese 30 days can, moreover, be taken any time up to the child's eighth birthday, so the father has plenty of time to select the timing of "his" month!'

Despite these efforts, it is clear that the primary focus has been on allowing *women* to combine family and labour market responsibilities (Eduards, 1989: 6). When parental leave was first taken up by Olof Palme, who was looking for a progressive initiative to announce at the 1969 International Labour Organization Convention, few, it seems, expected many fathers to use it. As Joan Eveline (1994c: 318) describes, child care was a more contentious issue since it threatened to encourage wives/mothers to leave 'their' families. Parental leave, by contrast, was seen as providing an 'ideological bridge between institutionalized care and mothering labour'. In fact, in some ways parental leave has reinforced the mothering role by redefining the 'good mother' as one who uses the available leave (Eveline, 1994c: 212). I am reminded here of Paul Starr's assurance that family leave policies advance conservative goals (1992; see Chapter 3).

Moreover, it can be argued that making it easier for women to blend mothering with paid labour has been indirectly reponsible for the high degree of sex segregation in Sweden's labour force.[5] The kinds of work women 'choose' will be affected by a vision of themselves as 'fitting in' around husbands' careers while being grateful for some respite from, and recognition of, their mothering role.

The emphasis in all these proposals remains on the shared problems of 'men' and 'women', and the need to resolve them together. Here I quote from the Ministry of Labour's Report, *The Changing Role of the Male* (1986: 3): '[T]he contemporary roles assigned to men and women are damaging to both. The consequences to the individuals who fail to live up to the accepted ideal are disastrous. *Particularly to men.'* (my italics). It is interesting to note here how a conciliatory approach to gender relations slides into one in which 'men' become the ones who suffer. One is reminded of the recent campaigns in Australia (see Chapter 5) to represent 'men' as 'disadvantaged'.

It is clear and important that Sweden has moved beyond a politics of incorporation, as we have seen it operating in Australia. To an extent, the Swedes have been adding 'women' *and* stirring. It is also important to see how 'public' is being redefined to include family issues, specifically those to do with child caring. However, the kind of problem 'sexual inequality' has been deemed to be, with the focus on gender complementarity and gender harmony, has placed severe constraints on attempts to make claims on behalf of 'women'. This is best illustrated in the understanding and implementation of positive action, and in the approach to issues which relate to sexuality. We will look at positive action first.

Positive action in Sweden

Sweden led the way in Europe, under Olof Palme in the early 1970s, in introducing 'positive actions' in the public sector. Several pilot schemes were also introduced to help break the sexual segregation of the labour market in the public and private sectors (Nielsen and Halvorsen, 1992: 31). One of the best known of these required firms which received government subsidies as a part of 'regional economic policy' to hire at least 40 per cent of the 'underrepresented sex' (Sundin, 1992: 105). Notably, however, Sweden's equality legislation, The Equality Between Men and Women at Work Act, passed in 1979 and enacted in 1980, came later than similar legislation in Norway and Denmark (Nielsen and Halvorsen, 1992: 9–10).[6]

The chief obstacle to the introduction of equal rights legislation came from employers, unions and social democrats who all agreed that they could best work out among themselves policies to improve 'women's' economic prospects. They agreed furthermore that the last thing they wanted was government interference in this area. The Delegation for Equality which existed from 1972 to 1976 argued that positive measures to promote equality were more important than a ban on sex discrimination. The view was expressed that such a ban could, in fact, hamper the 'positive action work' (Nielsen and Halvorsen, 1992: 41). To forestall or, in the event of its passage, to bypass legislative intervention, the main labour organizations in Sweden concluded a 'framework agreement' on equality in 1977 (Nielsen and Halvorsen, 1992: 31). It had been left to the bourgeois parties to impose antidiscrimination legislation, in the shape of the Equality Act, upon the 'social partners',[7] which they had done in 1976 when they came to power (Nielsen, 1983).

By and large the bourgeois parties share, with the social democrats, a commitment to equal status meaning individual self-sufficiency, and hence they support 'women's' involvement in gainful labour. The preamble to the equality legislation for which they were primarily responsible reads:

> Every individual irrespective of sex shall have the same practical opportunities not only for education or employment but also in principle the *same responsibility for his or her own maintenance* as well as shared responsibility for the upbringing of children and the home making. (In Gustafsson, 1983: 11; my italics)

It ought not to be surprising to find a commitment to sex equality in parties labelled ideological liberals. After all, as Juliet Mitchell (1984: 63) pointed out many years ago, 'Feminism as a conscious, that is self-conscious, protest movement, arose as part of a revolutionary bourgeois tradition that had equality of mankind (*sic*) as its highest goal.'[8]

However, there remains ambivalence about women's role in the family, an ambivalence similar to that noted among Australia's Liberals (see Chapter 5). When the bourgeois parties resumed power in 1991, the new Prime Minister, Carl Bildt, announced to Parliament the government's intention to provide a lump sum 'child care allowance, with the same amount for all children', to be spent on the kind of child care the family 'chose': 'child care of a high quality must be available for those who want it and increased financial opportunities for those who want to stay at home when their children are small' (Statement of Government Policy presented by the Prime Minister to the Swedish Parliament, 4 October, 1991; unofficial translation, p. 14). Such payment, many feminists argue, would simply reinforce existing sex roles, and leave many women in a low status, low paid occupation – 'housewife', though a gender-neutral label would probably be used (see Eveline, 1994c: 324–5). The language of 'choice' scarcely hides this intention.

While it is possible to see this ambivalence as a reflection of a continuing tension within liberalism between identification of the individual as the fundamental social unit and simultaneous support for the nuclear family (Bacchi, 1990: xii), it has also been suggested that the competing parties in the 1991 election simply needed to come up with distinctive packages to attract voters. The stated commitment to equality between the sexes by all the parties can be seen, to use Maud Eduards' words, as an 'ideological appendix', invoked primarily to achieve other political objectives (Eduards, 1991).

When the issue of 'sex equality' came onto the agenda in the 1970s, a clever stratagem was devised for giving it a particular stamp, a particular character which effectively removed it from what was considered the 'main business' of government, labour market policy.[9] Symbolically a new word – *jämställdhet* – was created to refer to the goal of 'equality between the sexes'. This was to distinguish it from *jämlikhet*, the term for general social equality. This move was explained as an indication of the government's *particular* commitment to the problem. At the same time, of course, it put gender issues into a separate category – one which was then more or less handed over to some women to work on. Separating gender equality from the general reform agenda, a tactic we have observed elsewhere, was also a way of reaffirming the government's prior commitment to class or, more precisely, to labour market issues.

The creation of *jämställdhet* followed the 'non-conflictual rule' (see above). According to Yvonne Hirdman, the broader meaning of equality, *jämlikhet*, was a more radical, individualistic and democratic concept, and hence the need to separate gender issues from it. In her understanding, *jämställdhet* was a 'calmer' term which suggested that 'women' and 'men' would work towards a common understanding of how best to deal with these difficult issues (Hirdman, 1987). *Jämställdhet* carries other messages. It has meant the introduction of the language of equal opportunity and an abandonment of the stated commitment to 'equal results' which lay behind the more general term. So, while it left behind the guarantee of individual recognition, it picked up the ideology of economic individualism.

So, in Sweden, *jämställdhet* or gender equality means that 'women' have an equal right to compete in the economic marketplace. Hence, the same kinds of arguments about whether positive action undermines merit and fair competition as have appeared, and as might be expected, in the United States also proliferate in Sweden.

The 1980 Equality Act was unique in its legislative approach. It was divided into two major parts: a ban on discrimination, and a *separate* statement regarding the duty of employers to pursue an active equality policy (Nielsen and Halvorsen, 1992: 10). This is an important innovation. The problems associated with incorporating a negative injunction against discrimination and a commitment to positive or affirmative action within the one legal instrument have been demonstrated repeatedly in this text. The most obvious of these is the way in which positive or affirmative action for 'women' is opened up to the charge of discrimination against 'men' (see the *Proudfoot* case in Chapter 5).

However, the apparent commitment to positive action in Sweden is severely compromised in two ways: first, its area of application is contained by provisions privileging collective agreements; and second, it, as with the rest of Sweden's equality rules, is gender neutral. There is extreme hostility to the idea that 'women' should be granted some form of 'advantage' not made equally available to 'men' (Silen, 1988; Persson-Tanimura, 1988; Eveline, 1994c: 98). Hence, men have had no need to claim that the legislation discriminates against them!

The most striking indication of the government's commitment to defending this representation of the state of affairs is the debate over the phrasing of the preamble to the 1980 Equality Act. The wording specifies that 'the aim of this Act is to promote equality between men and women in respect of employment, conditions of employment, and opportunities for development in employment (equality at work)' (Equal Opportunities Ombudsman, 1980). The women's movement at the time of the formulation of this legislation tried to have some gender-specific phrasing introduced. As Maud Eduards explains, 'the belief was that a gender-neutral ban on discriminatory practices would serve as a cover-up for the fact that it is women who are discriminated against' (Eduards et al., 1985: 149). In the event, gender neutrality prevailed. In the most recent amendments to the Swedish equality legislation the women's movement has scored a major symbolic victory – specific mention will be made of the fact that the chief purpose of the legislation is to address the 'disadvantages' faced by 'women'.

In the initial attempt to pass the Equality Act in 1978/79, a few individuals in the non-socialist camp voted against it and hence only the ban on discrimination was accepted. Later in 1979 a renewed attempt to get the whole Act through Parliament succeeded (Nielsen and Halvorsen, 1992: 9). The Act is understood to be a labour law and states clearly that its provisions are limited to 'working life' (Ministry of Public Administration, 1990: 14).

The 1978 draft had proposed active provisions binding upon individual employers and parties to collective agreements. As a concession to the bill's opponents, the confederation of trade unions (LO), the confederation of employers' organizations (SAF) and the social democratic party, Section 12 of the Act stipulates that in matters covered by the 'active part' of the legislation, referring to positive action, 'other rules may be laid down by a collective agreement concluded or approved by a central workers' organisation.' When such agreements exist, the Equality Ombudsman and Board, set up to administer the legislation, have nothing to do with enforcement (Nielsen and Halvorsen, 1992: 31, 36).

The 'social partners', as already noted, made a pre-emptive strike by negotiating just such an agreement before the legislation was enacted. Collective agreements specifying a commitment to gender equality, however, make vague references to the subject (Dahlberg, 1984). They are 'often framed in general terms and do not contain anything above what is stated in the Act.' Hence, not surprisingly, legal complaints of infringements of the rules are uncommon (Ministry of Public

Administration, 1990: 14). In 1990, the Equal Opportunity Ombudsman issued a report requesting that all employers be obliged to produce annually a scheme for equality work, and that the clause be made 'non-inter-changeable with collective agreements'. The recommendation was not accepted (Newman, 1990: 31). As with the other countries examined, we find that while employers are required to implement 'positive actions', they are left to define their content.[10]

This privileging of the 'bargaining parties' in deciding the content of equality measures[11] is particularly important given that union and employer bodies are heavily dominated by men. One study (Petersson, 1991: 67) has concluded that, if one considers all of the top positions in government, private enterprise, unions, science and the arts, women constitute 13 per cent. While Sweden is well ahead of the countries studied so far in terms of numbers of women in elected office,[12] there has been less success in getting women on government committees and boards, where most of the decision making takes place. And, while important changes have taken place in this arena,[13] there is no suggestion that positive action be used to change the gender composition of work councils or company boards. As Nielsen and Halvorsen make clear (1992: 42), 'The labour market organisations are at policy statement level in favour of equality, but they do not take positive action to counteract the hierarchical segregation by sex within their own structure.'

Paul Hirst (1990) has suggested that one way to improve upon democratic structures is through corporatism. He is clearly impressed by the Swedish model. His idea is that some form of decentralization of government authority through corporate representation would bring decision making in particular policy areas closer to the people. More precisely, it is assumed that people's economic interests, which are taken to be paramount, would be better represented in this model. However, for corporatism to improve upon democracy, some account must be taken of the different relationship of many women to the labour market. As the bulk of part-time workers and the bulk of those in low status jobs (status here measured by current standards), women are unlikely to improve their situation through the application of such a model. The way in which employers and unions in Sweden have neatly contrived to reduce positive action to empty promises, as illustrated above, is a case in point.

The gender-neutral character of approaches to positive action has also produced some odd effects. In the efforts to reduce sex segregation in the labour market, it is considered as important to get men into female-dominated occupations as it is to get women into male-dominated occupations. In some teachers' training colleges men applicants were accepted with an average mark below the limit set for women because 'it was not thought desirable that there should be a preponderance of women in the teaching profession as a whole' (Ministry of Education, 1984: 15). It was claimed that it is important to get more men into elementary education so that young children will not stereotype 'women' as the natural carers. The argument here is humanist and doubtless makes a good point. The limitation in this approach arises from the lack of attention to the fact that there are many more women than men in low status (measured by current standards), low paid jobs. In addition, it has been pointed out that, with the shift from heavy industry to service occupations, a large number of men will be looking for jobs in areas traditionally dominated by women. It is difficult to see how desegregation here will assist many women; it will probably only put some of them out of work (Skard and Haavio-Mannila, 1986).

There is also evidence that efforts to move men into 'women's' jobs are proving more successful than attempts to move women into 'men's' jobs. Elizabeth Fürst has found that men, carrying their sexual capital with them, have been made more welcome in traditional 'women's' work than women were when the situation was reversed (Fürst, 1985). Moreover, she (1988) found that many men used the move 'as a stepping stone to elsewhere' (see Eveline, 1994c: 102).

The early effort (1970s) to get companies which received subsidies for regional development to implement a quota of 40 per cent for the 'underrepresented sex', mentioned earlier, has undoubtedly increased the numbers of women employed. Here, however, it is important to note that these women are often segregated from the men in women-only work areas, and seldom become 'foremen'. Elisabeth Sundin (1992), who conducted an extensive study of this policy, also reports that the policy was so controversial that provision for exemptions was made. In half the cases where aid was approved, exemptions were granted. As Sundin concludes, 'Gender quotas are very often discussed but almost never used in Sweden'.

Nor should the motivation for the regional development quota be ignored. The problem, it seems, was that 'more young women than young men moved away from the Swedish periphery' (Sundin, 1992: 106). The concern then was to 'create the prerequisites for a balanced population development in the different parts of the country' (*Proposition 1981/82*: 113. Quoted in Sundin, 1992: 107–8). Employers, it seems, also held out hopes that 'women' would humanize the working climate. Here, we see a situation not unlike that described by Eveline in the Argyle study (Chapter 5) in which 'women' are targeted for positive action because it is assumed that they will improve 'men's' lives.

Joan Eveline (1994c: 112, fn. 19) relates an incident which nicely illustrates the way in which Sweden's gender-neutral positive action law operates, and the problems it poses for women activists. At the concluding Swedish conference of the four-year Nordiska BRYT Project, started in an attempt to redress sex segregation in Sweden's labour force, a report was offered on one initiative which had placed girls and boys studying science in separate classes for one year. The girls, it seems, performed much better and the boys considerably worse. When asked if they wanted the project to continue, most girls answered 'Yes' and most boys 'No'. The project ceased, however, because the educational assessment by a male psychologist held that it contravened Sweden's Equality Act: 'it provided advantages for girls which boys did not get.'

Eveline reports that, while numbers of the women at the Conference were upset at this decision, none challenged it openly. After all, this was the law and open confrontation between 'men' and 'women' would have been deemed inappropriate. This example, which in some ways echoes the education debate currently being conducted in Australia (see Chapter 5), shows that – regardless of whether the relational dynamic between 'men' and 'women' is conflictual, win–lose, as in Australia in this case, or consensual, win–win as in Sweden – claims for 'women' are denigrated.

Sexuality in a 'progressive' state

The Swedish approach to sexuality was part of the approach to 'sexual equality', or perhaps it is more correct to see it the other way around. As in the challenge to sex roles in the care of children, sexual liberation was interpreted to mean removing outmoded and constricting stereotyped behaviours. Hence, the search for 'true sexual democracy' meant that the double standard had to go. The focus was on individual development and this was meant to be equally accessible to 'women' and to 'men'. Sexual democracy was seen as part and parcel of social democracy, in the eyes of the author of *Sex and Society in Sweden*:

> During the time Sweden was developing its social democracy, Swedes were also attaining a degree of equality between the sexes to an extent perhaps unmatched anywhere in the world. Swedes have begun to accept sex as a basic part of life and its exercise – like any other form of human activity – as within the realm of individual freedom. (Linner, 1967: xv)

According to this author, the successes in the extension of equality into relations between men and women made the feminist movement 'outmoded' – and this in 1967!

A decade later a National Swedish Board of Education publication was slightly more guarded about the benefits of sexual emancipation which was now called a 'mixed blessing'. 'Negative consequences' were identified – 'the commercial exploitation of the sexual instinct through prostitution and pornography and through sexualized advertising' which, it is admitted, 'would never have attained their present scope without the weakening of the taboo on sexuality' (National Swedish Board of Education, 1977: 31). The overall impression, however, remained that in the trade-off between negative and positive consequences, positives were weighted more heavily – 'It has become easier for persons whose views are not distorted by sexism to integrate their sexuality harmoniously with their conscious personality' (National Swedish Board of Education, 1977).

But trade-offs there were, and these surfaced most clearly in a controversial Government Commission Report which proposed a number of changes to the penal code on sexual misconduct. One suggestion was to introduce different categories of sexual assault for the crime of rape. Similar proposals were being made elsewhere, but the Swedish Commission had one unusual innovation – that the severity of a sexual offence be judged with reference to the behaviour of the victim. Birgitta Wistrand (1981: 64) sees this 'way of thinking' as a 'continuation of the liberalization of sexual attitudes that began in the 1960s.' The assumption was that the woman is often an 'accomplice in rape', and hence her actions ought to be taken into account when considering the seriousness of the offence. If the woman had followed the man home, for example, according to the proposed law, 'she was partially to blame for what happened, and the rape would be viewed as of a less serious character.'

The Report caused an uproar among Swedish feminists. It flew directly in the face of the growing insistence by the women's movement that men should be held responsible for their behaviour and that neither a woman's previous sexual history, nor the cut of her clothing – nor indeed whether she went home with a man – legitimated to any degree his sexual abuse of her. A second commission was established and the original proposal removed (Almbladh, 1983).

Swedish feminists have faced similar kinds of problems with challenging pornography, problems which can also be seen as due in part to the 'new frankness toward sex' which characterized the decade of the 1960s (Wistrand, 1981: 80). To this should be added the strong Swedish opposition to censorship, again highlighting a distinctively individualist tinge to the 'Swedish model' (Groll, 1980). Pornography was debated in terms of freedom of the press rather than the effects upon 'women' or 'men'.

The emphasis on consensus and cooperation, together with a belief that 'women' and 'men' have equal access to exploring their sexual identities, has also created an environment where it has been difficult to broach the subject of sexual harassment. The kinds of views expressed about the subject, and these often come from women, are that there is no harm in sexual flirtation or that *our* men wouldn't do such a thing. Unfortunately, the evidence which is being collected is that they would and they do. A 1987 survey of 2000 women employed in both public and private sectors found that 17 per cent of women have 'been exposed to unwelcome sexual attention at work' (Ministry of Public Administration, 1990: 76).

Statements about the 'achievement' of 'sexual equality', and the reluctance of powerful political actors to admit conflict between 'women' and 'men' have also made it difficult to have domestic violence recognized as a serious social problem. Wife-beating, says Wistrand, was considered a 'very touchy issue' because the 'sanctity of private life' is a 'basic principle in our society' (Wistrand, 1981: 73). Some would find the identification of privacy as an essential part of Swedish political attitudes unexpected, especially given the way in which 'public' space in Sweden has been enlarged to include child caring. However, this still leaves untouched a 'private' sphere of intimate relations between 'women' and 'men'. Here, the explicit limiting of equality legislation to 'working life' is significant. The public/private dichotomy continues to function to sequester off areas deemed to be unimportant politically.

The attitude toward sexual crimes and crimes of violence against women is complicated further by the Swedes' general position on punishment and deterrence. The 'scales of punishment' for different crimes have been mitigated throughout. The desire has been to introduce shorter terms of imprisonment and more fines as sanctions (Engstrom, 1976). There is no doubt that Sweden has one of the most humane and progressive prison systems in the world. However, a combination of attitudes which privileges openness in sexual matters and castigates punishment as anachronistic has made it difficult for women activists to make certain claims without appearing punitive, moralistic, and 'un-Swedish'. In a recent study of battered wives, one victim complained:

> There is chaos in Sweden when it comes to justice. Men who batter may get a few months [in jail]. Men who kill a year or so. Men who rape get fines. . . . The women live with the memories all their lives. (Eduards and Elman, 1994)

A new space for 'women'

There are several indications that the tone of the debate around 'sexual equality' is changing. A new anger and sense of confrontation is being expressed by numbers of women activists. This is best illustrated by recent proposals for a 'women's party'.[14]

The 1991 election created the conditions for this change in tone. For the first time since 1928, the proportion of women in parliament, the Riksdag, declined, from 38 per cent to 33.5 per cent (Eduards, 1992: 86). Women party politicians across the political spectrum were distressed at this development. In both the Centre and Social Democratic parties, they were successful at electing more women to important posts in parliamentary standing committees. Other women activists were meeting in secret across the country and forming networks. In January 1992 the Greens announced that they would support Maria-Pia Boethius as leader of a new women's party.

The proposal attracted a range of reactions. None of the political parties ignored the move. Women in most of the parties backed away from the proposal but took the opening to reassert the importance of women's groups within their own parties. The National Federation of

Social Democratic Women announced intentions to launch a separate women's list for the next parliamentary election. They would present their own political platform, though it would conform with social democratic ideology. The women's federations of the four non-socialist parties in the new coalition rejected the women's party but noted that they actively monitored 'women's issues' within their parties (Eduards, 1992: 87–8). In the event, in the 1994 elections, several parties presented electoral lists in which every other candidate was a woman. As a result women's representation was boosted in the Riksdag, county councils and local authorities. A gesture has also been made to increase the status of equal opportunity issues. Responsibility in this area has been transferred from the Ministry of Social Affairs to the Cabinet Office (Froman, 1994: 3).

Issues to do with violence against 'women' have also gained a new respectability in recent years. A 1985 Ministry of Labour report on equal opportunities in Sweden reported that 'the ultimate and most dramatic expression of the lack of equal status between women and men is the incidence of battering, sexual assault, pornography and prostitution' (quoted in Eduards, 1992: 92). In 1988 laws came into effect providing restraining orders to persecuted women, and legal aid to those who had suffered severe sexual assault. Some film censorship and restrictions on violent videos are now in place (Swedish Institute, 1990). The most recent amendments to the Equality Act specify that sexual harassment is illegal. The non-socialist coalition which came to power in 1991 granted threatened women, 'who meet the requirements that must be fulfilled before a change of identity is permitted, the right to protection by bodyguards' (Eduards, 1992: 94).

While, as Maud Eduards says, these initiatives 'tend to address symptoms rather than the problem at the heart of the matter', they are needed reforms. They also link violence, sex and power 'in a way that is taboo in traditional Swedish equal status policies' (Eduards, 1991: 178). These changes are due in part to the unrelenting hard work of a dedicated core of women researchers and women activists in groups like Sweden's National Organization of Emergency Shelters (ROKS). They are also related to the threatened dethronement of social democracy with its class-based analysis. As mentioned earlier, historically it has been easier in Sweden for women activists to make claims on behalf of 'women' when the bourgeois parties are on the ascendant or in power.

This, however, does not mean that bourgeois party policies offer more to 'women'. I mentioned earlier their problematic position on lump-sum payments for child care. Nor do most women see them as offering more. In the 1991 election, a significant gender gap appeared, with women disproportionately favouring the Social Democrats or the Greens. This outcome was the end result of a decade during which there was an increased tendency for women (and a decreased tendency for men) to support the left (Eduards, 1992: 86, fn. 10).

This trend has created an opening for 'women' *within* social democracy. Jane Jenson and Rianne Mahon (1993) describe the recent courting of 'working women' as the potential saviours of social democracy. It is felt that a new 'wage earner' identity is needed to counter the creation by employers of a worker-identity category, the *medarbetare* ('cross-collar worker'), which fosters identification with one's employer and weakens links to national unions. Since the individualistic *medarbetare* in the private sector 'might support retrenchment in the public sector in order to restore the competitiveness of "their" firms and to increase disposable income', women, as both the majority in the public-sector workforce and major clients of the welfare state, are being talked about as 'the last defence' of the 'beleaguered People's Home.'

A new recognition of 'women' within social democracy is, as Jenson and Mahon (1993: 98) describe, only one possible scenario, however. There are strong indications that the SAP is moving towards social liberalism and this 'may come to mean the replacement of the Swedish model of universal social rights with programmes funded and run by the labour-market partners themselves', creating problems for wage-earning women. Moreover, the suggestion that 'solidaristic work' could advance gender as well as class equality leaves some tough issues unaddressed. These include how to integrate revaluation of 'women's work' with 'solidaristic work for solidaristic wages', and how to resolve 'tensions between full-time male wage-earners and women whose participation in the labour force shifts between full- and part-time work in accordance with the demands of their unpaid care work' (Jenson and Mahon, 1993: 97–9).

Conclusion

The Swedish case illustrates that it is too easy an assumption that a country with a more progressive political ideology, committed to greater social equality, will necessarily deal successfully with gender inequality (compare Forbes, 1989). In fact, we have seen how a commitment to the former can undermine the latter. The conviction that the most important social groups are classes makes it difficult to articulate claims for 'women'. Moreover, the belief that social equality means only a redistribution of wealth privileges economic issues over issues of bodily safety and integrity and over the importance of caring responsibilities.

Showing that commitments to 'class' pre-empt recognition of 'women' as an important political category does not mean that class is irrelevant in many women's lives. The point rather is to show that the politics of class and class-based organizations, in particular unions and employers, limits the space accorded 'women' and determines how 'women' gets taken up in policy debates. The containment of positive action through the priority assigned to collective agreements illustrates this point nicely.

The category 'men' appears in Swedish political discourse and has done so for some time. In Australia, where 'men' is a more recent player in category politics – at least to the extent that 'men' functions as a category in political debate – 'women' and 'men' are often set in competition, in win–lose scenarios (see Chapter 5). In Sweden, by contrast, the relationship between 'men' and 'women' is generally described as complementary and consensual. The particular positioning of these categories reflects historically-specific conditions. The conclusion emerging from this study, however, is that one condition at least overrides these variations. 'Women' constitutes an 'ideological appendix', to borrow Maud Eduards' (1991) phrase, to other political agendas. It is also clear that more space is accorded 'women' when these other agendas are dominated by a determination on the part of those in government to stay in power, and when women are courted to help achieve this end.

In Sweden political objectives, devised in the main by male politicians and male-dominated corporate actors, have never included sexual equality as a primary goal. Rather, it has been seen as a potential by-product of some other desired outcome, such as increased female work-force participation. Numbers of women have had a chance, and this is important, to capitalize on the improvements in social living standards which accompany the historical commitment to social equality. However, the politics of solidarity limits the kinds of recognition afforded 'women'.

Notes

1 It is fairly common to refer to Sweden's non-socialist parties as 'the bourgeois parties'. Historically, these include the Centre, the Liberal and the Moderate Parties. In the 1991 election, two new right-wing parties – the Christian Democrats and New Democracy – made their first appearance.

2 Current discussions are considering lowering the rate from 90 per cent of income to 80 per cent (Eveline, 1994c: 322, fn. 25).

3 In 1986, men took only 6 per cent of the days registered as paid by parental payment. The percentage of men taking parental payment was 23 per cent indicating that more men take out very few days. During the 1980s the proportion of men who took advantage of the benefit dropped by 3 per cent (Widerberg, 1991: 29; Statistics Sweden, 1990).

4 Joan Eveline (1994c: 303–4) teases out some of the ambiguities in the campaign. As she describes, the campaign used images of men, often bare-chested and hard-muscled, holding newborn infants. In her view, these images confirmed a stereotype of machismo. The campaign therefore activated a politics of persuasion, depicting 'fatherhood-as-rewarding' as compatible 'with the logic, the promise and the advantage of masculinity.'

5 Sweden has the highest sex segregation among OECD countries, with women congregating in low paid, low status (measured by current standards) jobs (Erneling, 1988: 17; Whitehouse, 1990: 359).

6 This was replaced in 1991 by the Equality in Working Life Act. In anticipation of Sweden joining the European Community, the Act was broadened to include indirect discrimination and work evaluations, bringing it into line with EC standards (Nielsen and Halvorsen, 1992: 9).

7 The term 'social partners' is commonly used to refer to the parties to a collective agreement, the unions and employers.

8 It is important to note that this quotation comes from a paper delivered to the University of Cape Town in 1975. In a more recent introduction (1984) Mitchell explained that 'In speaking of women in seventeenth-century England, I hoped to say something – very obvious – about how contemporary racist South Africa appears to liberals outside'. Her endorsement of liberal ideology was clearly strategic. The point here is that feminists, as much as social democrats and bourgeois politicians, use ideological categories for political purposes.

9 Dorothy Smith, in a 1987 unpublished piece entitled 'Feminist Reflections on Political Economy', used the phrase the 'main business' to explain why it had been so difficult to talk about women within the theoretical discourse of political economy. Quoted in Acker, 1989: 236, fn. 8.

10 The Equal Opportunities Commission, on motion of the Equality Ombudsman, can order defaulting employers, not subject to collective agreements, to take certain measures. The comprehensiveness of the collective agreement structure is probably at least partly responsible for the fact that in a 10-year period, not one decision was passed in a single case (Ministry of Public Administration, 1990: 14). Ingmarie Froman (1994: 2) reports that in 1992 'a law was passed obliging employers with more than ten employees to introduce an equal-opportunities plan.' The plan, however, does not have to be lodged anywhere; it has only to be kept on hand in case it is asked for. Since Sweden joined the European Community in 1995, collective agreements are subject to scrutiny by the Equality Ombudsman.

11 Under Section 4 of the Equality Act, employers are barred from offering 'inferior employment conditions' to 'either sex', a clause designed to cover equal pay guarantees. As with positive action, so with equal pay, however, conditions are to be judged 'equal' according to a collective agreement, or 'as of equal value according to an agreed work evaluation.' There are no requirements to the evaluation except 'that the bargaining parties agree' (Nielsen and Halvorsen, 1992: 15).

12 In 1989 women held 38 per cent of seats in the Swedish Parliament (Selbyg, 1989). In 1993 this had dropped to 33.5 per cent, which still compared favourably with 35.8 per cent in Norway, 29.3 per cent in the Netherlands, 13.2 per cent in Canada, 10.8 per cent in the United States, and 8.2 per cent in Australia (only Lower Chamber figures are offered here) (Department of the Parliamentary Library, Canberra, 1995).

13 Gerd Engman produced the study *Varannan Damernas* (*Ladies' Choice*; or *Every other Seat a Woman*, 1987) which proposed that efforts be made to increase women's representation on government committees and that success be monitored. There were veiled threats of legislation if the proportion of women had not reached 30 per cent by 1992. This target was reached on schedule (Froman, 1994: 4).

14 A Women's Party has in fact existed since 1985 to apply 'a women's perspective to society at large'. However, with only 140 members, it has not been large enough to be registered as a party, and hence has attracted little publicity (Eduards, 1992: 89).

7

The Politics of Transformation

This book describes the processes involved in the undermining and delegitimizing of affirmative action generally and affirmative action for 'women' in particular. It focuses upon the ways in which deployments of conceptual and identity categories have produced these results. Earlier chapters examined the effects produced by positioning the reform within notions of 'equal opportunity' and, most recently, in the last chapter, 'sexual equality'. This chapter, set in the Netherlands, illustrates that 'positive action' itself can be used to delimit reforms targeting 'women', supporting the contention that all concepts are susceptible to political manipulation.

The history of affirmative action in the Netherlands is a story of conceptual revision, a story captured in the chapter title, 'The Politics of Transformation'. Strong affirmative action for 'women', including targeted hiring and quotas, appeared on the political agenda in the 1970s. In fact, at that time, these reforms were considered almost non-controversial. Later this changed. In the end, except in isolated instances, they have disappeared, to be replaced by amorphous commitments to 'positive action'. Further, 'positive action' has come to replace a broader reform agenda so that it now represents the 'cutting edge' of the government's equality programme (Outshoorn, 1991). Examining how this has happened opens a window into the play of category politics.

Feminism in the Netherlands

The ways in which feminist discourses are shaped in part by dominant representations of conceptual and identity categories is a major theme in this book. In particular, I have stressed how being positioned outside spheres of political influence has impelled feminists to adopt justificatory stances which have unintended and problematic consequences – often limiting reform agendas and producing theoretical 'dilemmas'.

This positioning outside political influence has thrown up a range of possible ways of representing relations between 'women' and 'men'. Hege Skjeie (1991: 237) identifies two of these – a complementary 'difference' discourse and a conflictual 'difference' discourse. In the first, it is argued that 'women's' experiences differ from 'men's', producing 'different' values and perspectives which *complement* 'men's' values and perspectives and which ought therefore to be reflected in the political agenda. In the second, there is an emphasis on conflict and struggle, suggesting that 'women' are contending with 'men' for a share of influence and/or resources. In Sweden, we examined another kind of complementary discourse, where 'women' and 'men' are seen as working together towards a common goal of 'human' liberation (see Chapter 6). The approach adopted will depend upon country-specific and history-specific factors. The relative 'success' of the approach adopted will also be context dependent. Context here includes place and time.

The feminist movement in the Netherlands, as elsewhere, went through stages. The first stirrings in the 1960s echoed the American Betty Friedan (1965) with the emphasis on the discontent of the isolated housewife. The first feminist theoretician, Joke Smit, borrowed her ideas from the American sociologist, Helen Hacker, who described 'women' as a minority group (Outshoorn, 1987; see Chapter 2). 'Women' were seen as lagging behind 'men', as needing increased opportunities to join the economic and political mainstream. 'Women' could and would *persuade* 'men' of the need for change.

By the early 1970s, 'women' came to be thought of as oppressed *as a sex*, with analogies to the class analysis offered by Marxism. This was due to a growing belief in 'men's' vested interest in the sexual status quo and of their resistance to change. Power as domination entered the analysis. There were variations on this theme, emphasizing power either as structurally determined through capitalism or patriarchy, or as something individual men exercised over individual women. By the later 1970s, the emphasis had shifted from 'power over' to 'power to', and the idea of 'women's resistance' was added. For some this meant a recognition that 'women' could indeed pursue power – through entering politics, for example, or modelling themselves on the assertive male (Outshoorn, 1987: 27).

Despite these shifts it is possible to characterize the Dutch women's movement as predominantly socialist feminist with a strong radical feminist component.[1] Joyce Outshoorn (interview, 28 May, 1992) describes Dutch feminism as a distinct form of socialist feminism because of the easier link with radical feminism. She sets it off from British Marxist/socialist feminism which, probably due to the entrenched nature of the Marxist tradition, faced bitter conflicts with radical feminism. In the Netherlands, with a more recent and less doctrinaire socialist tradition, alliance was easier. In the analysis of the reasons for 'women's inequality', this alliance produced a consensus that it was crucial to consider the differential power between 'men' and 'women'. For feminists in the Netherlands, the most important factor in a power analysis is the recognition that the relationship between 'men' and 'women' is not just asymmetrical, but hierarchical (Outshoorn, 1987: 30). 'Women' constitutes a category in *opposition* to 'men', providing a direct contrast to the dominant representation of gender relations in Sweden, just examined in Chapter 6.

Dutch feminists have also been reluctant to take up the so-called 'special values' brand of feminism. According to Saskia Grotenhuis (1989: 535), '[F]rom the beginning, almost everybody in women's studies criticized all claims for the existence of an authentic femininity, for a feminine rationality, or feminine reasoning in feminist research. The influence here of Marxist feminism is obvious.'

In the 1970s the women's movement had a broad agenda for change. There were two main organizations: the more traditional Man–Woman–Society (*MVM*) and the more radical *Dolle Mina*. As in early feminism elsewhere, there was a strong emphasis on the need to challenge traditional sex roles and sex role stereotypes. This led to an interest in consciousness-raising. Other reforms common to early feminist campaigning in the Netherlands and elsewhere included a demand for child care and abortion reform. The influence of Marxism showed in the strong interest in the importance of paid work for women's liberation. Marxism, mainly through the writing of Engels, stressed that 'women' would never be free until they had attained economic independence from 'men'. This became a dominant demand of Dutch feminism and to an extent, as we shall see, allowed feminist demands to be represented as contained within the goverment's commitment to economic independence for all 'citizens'.

The American example also exerted an influence on the reform agenda. *MVM* took the idea of affirmative action from the United States and pressed for targeted hiring and quotas. In 1975 the Women's Section of the Labour Party demanded 'preferential' hiring. The same year the party agreed to a rule that 25 per cent of electoral candidates and party officials should be women.

Outshoorn (1991: 108-9) describes how socialist feminists managed to infiltrate the early committees set up to coordinate efforts to redress 'women's' inequality. Both *MVM* and *Dolle Mina* had many socialist feminist members. When the Socialist–Christian Democrat coalition decided to set up a Committee on the Status of Women in 1975, in response to pressure from the *MVM* and on the occasion of the United Nations Women's Year, many members were recruited from *MVM* and from the Labour Party. They took a power analysis and the idea of 'positive discrimination' with them.[2] The first document prepared by this Emancipation Committee listed 'temporary preferential hiring' as a policy instrument. The demand was legitimized by pointing to similar practices in the United States. The first government paper on 'women's' policy, in 1977, similarly incorporated 'positive discrimination' as a necessary reform.

Discursive openings

At first sight the Netherlands is an unlikely setting for the successful introduction of such a controversial reform as strong affirmative action.

By most indicators the Netherlands is quite a traditional society. The model of the male breadwinner and female homemaker was particularly well entrenched in the 1960s and 1970s, and is still endorsed by a sizable portion of the population (Holtmaat, 1991; Sainsbury, 1994; Knijn, 1994). This is due partly to strong religious currents, both Calvinist and Catholic, and partly to the fact that, until recently, it has been an affluent society where comparatively fewer women have felt compelled or enticed to engage in paid labour.

In 1991 women's labour force participation rate was 38.8 per cent, compared to 59.7 per cent in Australia, 66.9 per cent in Canada, 63.7 per cent in the United Kingdom, and 80.3 per cent in Sweden.[3] In addition, compared to surrounding countries in Europe, there are more women in part-time work than in any other country. Over half of the women working in paid jobs work part-time (Verleggen, 1991).

It is possible that it was precisely this backwardness in terms of women's labour force participation which convinced the government that dramatic measures were needed. Early government documents high-lighted the problems caused by too few women in the labour force. As one example, in the description of the brief of the Women's Emancipation Council, set up in 1981 to advise the government on emancipation policy, it was noted that the 'increasing "de-greening" [fewer children] and simultaneous "graying" of society' made solving the distribution of labour and income 'more and more urgent' (Women's Emancipation Council, 1985: 3). Here the concern was with having an adequate labour force to fund the extensive welfare provisions that had been established. Of course, any decision to integrate 'women' into the labour force would always be tinged with ambivalence, given the strength of the Christian Democratic Party and its commitment to traditional sex roles (Middendorp, 1991: 105).

The ambivalence underlying the government's attitude to the family is indicated in the two-tier social welfare system (Holtmaat, 1992). The first tier, social security, is tied to labour force participation, and hence only women in paid labour can make claims upon it. The second tier, social assistance, offers basic maintenance, and is predicated on the under-standing that this is a safety-net which comes into action only when the family fails to support its members. Ruth Lister (1990) notes the way in which insurance-based unemployment schemes on this model constitute 'women' as second-class citizens.[4]

Other welfare policies send mixed messages to women. Compared to the United States, maternity leave benefits are generous. Paid maternity leave is available for 16 weeks, and parents may work a shortened week for a period of six months during the first four years of their child's life.[5] And yet child care facilities are sadly inadequate. The best estimate, according to Rosi Braidotti (1991: 16), is that there is provision for only 1.5 per cent of children under three years old, and a further 10 per cent attend playgroups for a few hours a day.[6] Despite these contradictions, the expressed concern about the need for more 'women' in the labour force allowed feminists to put a case for strong measures to make this happen.

The character of Dutch politics created other discursive openings. The Dutch political system is best known for the phenomenon of 'pillarization' – the division of the national income among separate and often conflicting groups. The tradition owes its origins to early competition among diverse religious groupings. While recent studies suggest its influence may have been exaggerated, there seems to be wide acceptance that the Dutch 'deal with their differences by sharing, that is, distributing wisely the available capital – be it material or symbolic' (Braidotti, 1991: 4; see Middendorp, 1991). The accompanying commitment to freedom of expression and openness to dissent have led Gisela Kaplan (1992: Chapter 5) to characterize the Dutch political system as 'creative traditionalism'.

Joyce Outshoorn (interview, 28 May, 1992) feels that women activists were able to capitalize on this tradition. She explained that they made a claim to categorical standing for 'women' on these grounds and won a hearing. There are similarities here to the appeals by Norwegian women to the tradition of social representation for geographical areas, as we shall see in Chapter 8, and to the way in which Canadian women were able to point to the acceptance of Francophones as a distinctive collectivity requiring targeted reforms.[7]

As noted previously, the fact that women activists have felt constrained to find an analogy of some sort, analogies which are always inexact, upon which to base their claims to categorical recognition for 'women', creates practical and theoretical dilemmas. In the Netherlands, a claim for 'women' with analogies to religious groupings creates some of the same dilemmas faced by Canadian women. 'Women' is neither *like* a French-Canadian 'nation' nor *like* a Dutch church; women are members of both these entities which complicates any comparisons (see Chapter 4 for more detail). Still, there were discursive openings here that women activists could and did exploit.

It was also important that in 1974, for the first time, the Christian Democrats were in coalition with the Labour Party rather than with the Liberals. The slogan of the Cabinet, 'redistribution of knowledge, power and income', made it easier to demand a 'share' for 'women' through affirmative action (Outshoorn, 1991: 110).

Reshaping the reform agenda

Positive action reforms in the 1970s targeted the national civil service (Outshoorn, 1991: 112). The decision to concentrate reform efforts at this level had two causes. First, it fitted in nicely with the idea that government and bureaucracy ought to reflect the varied interests of the population (see discussion in Chapter 2; see also Burton, 1991: 39–45).

Hence, it could build upon the notion of 'pillarization'. Second, it left undisturbed the more controversial arena of private enterprise. Here, as we shall see, the government has never moved beyond voluntarism. It would be a mistake, therefore, to overstate the government's commitment to 'positive discrimination'. From the outset, the reform was tinged with reservations. These became explicit after the Liberals and Christian Democrats came to power in 1977. In 1980 the Ministry of Cultural Affairs, Recreation and Social Welfare stipulated in their policy statement, *Emancipation in the Netherlands* (1980: 12), that, as far as 'preferential treatment' or 'positive discrimination' is concerned, the government 'favours a very reserved policy': 'In the government's opinion, such measures should be subject to severe conditions.'

In this same period, an attempt was made to draft an all-inclusive antidiscrimination bill,[8] along the lines of legislation being introduced in many countries at that time. Following on this model, the 1981 proposal dropped the focus on 'women' and their lack of power, and introduced gender-neutral language. Even the reference to the possibility of 'positive discrimination' became gender neutral. Influential feminist civil servants, recruited from *MVM*, managed to put a stop to this development. The 1983 positive action plan for the civil service returned the emphasis to the need to 'prefer' 'women'. Significantly, however, 'preferential hiring' and quotas had been replaced by the mild injunction that 'women' should be invited to apply in job advertisements (Outshoorn, 1991: 114).

During this period the language of 'positive discrimination' became the language of 'positive action', and the notion of targeted hiring was watered down. There were several influences in this direction.

By the early 1980s the topic of quotas had attracted a great deal of debate in the United States. The popular press, academic literature and the government administration, now headed by Reagan, made it clear that the reform was becoming politically unpopular. Since the United States had been an influence in the original appeals to use quotas, it was to be anticipated that these currents would cause waves in the Netherlands. American multinationals, meanwhile, brought the notion of affirmative action with them, but now it meant something different. The idea of using targeted hiring and/or quotas to redress inequality had been replaced by proposals which, it was argued, followed good managerialist principles. It was now described as to a company's benefit to tap the nation's resources and provide 'opportunities' for 'women' to 'get ahead'. Hence, 'women' should be 'recruited' and 'offered' training programmes. Reforms like child care and maternity leave might also then make 'good business sense'. Quotas became a measure of 'last resort', though references to 'targets' were permitted (Outshoorn, 1991: 115).

The representation of women as an 'untapped resource', a discourse which, as we have seen, proved popular in Australia (Chapter 5), fitted nicely the Dutch government's desire to increase women's labour force participation. A 1981–1982 interim Socialist/Christian Democratic cabinet moved 'women's policy' to the Department of Social Affairs and Employment, indicating a view of the issue as predominantly to do with 'women's' employment prospects and their need to enter the labour market. This theme carried over to the first 1982 Lubbers administration, a coalition between Liberals and Christian Democrats, which retained power until 1989.

This regime was characterized by a general swing to the right, paralleling developments both in the United States and in the European Community. Privatization, deregulation, decentralization became the catchwords in government documents. A move away from the Dutch commitment to comprehensive social protection became apparent in cutbacks in government spending and reduced welfare provisions. Economic recession became the explanation for these changes. According to Casper Wiebrens (1988: 132), 'Traditionally one of the more generous welfare states, the country has recently begun to modify its social security system to meet some of the burdens of generous and indexed benefit systems, high unemployment and disability costs, and high inflation.'

There continued to be a battle or at least a debate about the meaning of these changes for 'women's' equality measures, however, reflecting the lingering influence of old-time feminist civil servants. Annelien Kappeyne van de Coppello, the State Secretary for Social Affairs between 1982 and 1986, prepared the 1985 Equal Rights Policy Plan. She paid particular attention to the potentially negative effects, first, of privatization, given the lack of government control over equal rights in private enterprise; second, of deregulation, arguing that 'the government must keep sight of the fact that ensuring equal rights for men and women is an essential and indispensable part of its equal rights policy'; and, third, of decentralization, noting a conflict 'if impulses from central government have to guarantee that the lower-tier authorities pay heed to equal rights in their policy' (Ministry of Social Affairs and Employment, 1985: 18–19).

Still a dominant theme in this and subsequent equality documents is the emphasis on integration of 'women' into the labour market and, more generally, on 'women's' economic independence. Now this had long been and remains a demand of the women's movement, in the Netherlands and elsewhere. Socialist feminists in particular, who as already mentioned dominated the Dutch women's movement, had long pursued this reform. In fact, there is a debate currently in the Netherlands about whether the women's movement ought to take responsibility for the reduction of the reform agenda to this single demand. Outshoorn (1991: 111) refers to her disagreement with B.P. Sloot who holds the women's movement responsible for the 'issue modification' which took place.

The matter is clearly more complicated than this. As mentioned in the previous chapter, feminists manoeuvre within and against dominant discourses simultaneously. Here is one instance where there was a congruence in the simple demand for economic independence. However, the women's movement had always had a much broader agenda, including a challenge to sex roles, attempts to get men to participate in domestic labour and demands for social supports, such as child care, for family responsibilities. Few then would have accepted the particular interpretation of 'economic independence' which now appeared in policy documents, an interpretation emphasizing the need for 'citizens' to support themselves and not to rely on government supports. Still, the way in which a Marxist-informed feminist analysis could be repositioned as aligned with a neoliberal economic analysis exemplifies the theoretical hazards involved in pursuing 'anomalous analogies', in this case talking about 'women' as a class (see Chapter 2).

The government's concerns are obvious. The slogan which has come to dominate the 1980s and beyond is 'economic independence for the 1990 generation'; the reason, as stipulated in the 1985 Equal Rights Plan – 'the unacceptably high social costs in the form of a greater claim on social security benefits' (Ministry of Social Affairs and Employment, 1985: 20).

Changes in family formation practices are part of the explanation for the government's determination to make 'women' self-supporting. As noted above, there were early concerns about the 'de-greening' of the population because of the declining birth rate, and the accompanying greying of the population, with the consequent growth in demands on the social security system. As elsewhere, a working population is needed to fund these benefits, and 'women' are seen to provide a readily available labour pool. In addition, following the liberalization of divorce laws in 1971, the number of divorces has jumped markedly, and many divorced wives have fallen back on public assistance. Wiebrens (1988: 133) records a rise from 46.3 divorces per 10 000 married males in 1971 to 83 per 10 000 in 1981. As in many other countries, women form the majority of those dependent on social benefits. In 1990, one out of every ten women, between the ages of 28 and 44, depended on minimum social benefits in the Netherlands.

The 1985 Equal Rights Policy Plan proposed revisions to social security provisions such that 'the new generation entering the labour market, both men and women, would be first of all obliged to acquire an adequate income from work instead of claiming a family supplement from their partner.' There was also mention of the government's plan to 'restrict the right to alimony or maintenance upon divorce' (Ministry of Social Affairs and Employment, 1985: 38). Now, it seems, the government has decided to force ex-husbands or ex-wives to pay for the social allowance accorded the dependent spouse. It has recently been proposed that even women with children under 12 ought to be required to pursue a job if they are to be entitled to government support.[9]

The Equal Rights Plan then was 'determined by the efforts to reduce the burden of social security charges and to conduct a socio-economic policy designed to bring about structural recovery in the Dutch economy.' The message addressed to 'women' was that in the future, 'adults will usually be expected to maintain themselves by working' (Ministry of Social Affairs and Employment, 1985: 6–7).

By the next policy statement on 'women's' inequality, in 1989, the reservations regarding privatization, deregulation and decentralization had disappeared. The document jacket declared that the government's overall goal '[is] to create the opportunity for everyone in the Netherlands to live an independent life.' There was also a restatement of the commitment to 'economic independence for the 1990 generation', offered as an explanation of the government's attention to 'girls" education and the desire to encourage 'women' into 'men's' jobs and into entrepreneurial activities (Ministry of Social Affairs and Employment, 1989: 9).

Parts of the women's movement are very concerned about some of these developments. The van de Coppello document (Ministry of Social Affairs and Employment, 1985: 11) made it clear that, in the drive to economic independence, provision had to be made for the 'older generation' of married women who 'based their plans for life on certain expectations'. Some recent analyses also express reservations about the move towards 'individualization' of social security benefits. Riki Holtmaat (1992) is concerned that transferring the characteristics of a right to social insurance, based on dominant notions about independence and autonomous citizenship, to social assistance would mean that the dependence that is central in many women's lives would be disregarded: 'This would lead to a formal equality that does not do justice to the circumstances of women's lives today' (see also Meehan, 1992: 59). Speaking for the Emancipation Council, Frank Boddendijk (1992: 80) wishes to see the drive towards 'women's' financial independence accompanied by a shortening of the daily/weekly (paid) working hours to allow 'men' to share domestic labour. These voices are unlikely to be heard in the current economic and political climate.

It is interesting to note that the power analysis which entered Dutch equality policy in the early days is still retained in current government documents. In fact, *Women and the State*, a pamphlet produced by the Ministry of Social Affairs and Employment (1989), clearly reflects that conflictual approach between 'men' and 'women' in the series of cartoons used to illustrate it. In these cartoons, a woman with a broom in hand is seen slowly whittling away at a stone pedestal, atop of which is perched a man. The pedestal is engraved with the logo 'MAN'. In the last cartoon, the pedestal topples and the man falls.

However, there is a new emphasis on the deep structural nature of the power imbalance between 'men' and 'women' and an accompanying suggestion that change will 'take time'. Here is another instance of the way in which the notion of structural discrimination can be appropriated by those opposed to change (see Chapter 2). And, not surprisingly, 'women's' economic independence is held up as the key to the problem (Ministry of Social Affairs and Employment, 1985 and 1989).

'Positive action' is retained in these documents as a desirable policy, but it too has been redefined. It is now officially described as 'a coherent arrangement of measures aimed at removing the inferior position of a group of people in an organisation.' Applied to 'women', it means 'encouraging and helping women to take up jobs, and to keep moving upward in the organisation and to continue working.' Targets have replaced quotas (Ministry of Social Affairs and Employment, 1989: 16). The reform has been simultaneously broadened and narrowed. It has been broadened in the sense that it is now seen as the fundamental approach to change. It has been narrowed in the way in which other items have been removed from the agenda and in the shift from hiring and/or promotion quotas to pledges of encouragement. As Joyce Outshoorn (1991: 117) says, positive action now sits comfortably within the current political discourse of less state intervention.

The reference to positive action as a reform for 'a group of people' in an inferior position in an organization is also significant. While, in contrast to the United States, positive action was first introduced in the Netherlands as a reform for 'women' and not for some other identity category, this has changed. The influx of migrant workers has led to a concern regarding their underrepresentation in better status and better paid jobs. Hence, most positive action programmes now include 'ethnic minorities' as a target group. While this is doubtless a worthwhile gesture, 'women' as a separate category has been displaced in the reform agenda, paralleling developments in Canada (see Chapter 4). Els Oosterman of the FNV (Confederation of Trade Unions) explained that 'ethnic minorities' have become the priority (interview, 29 May, 1992). In this case, she maintained, it is easier for good Calvinists to salve their consciences since ethnic minorities are few in number and have poor qualifications. Unlike 'women' then, they present little threat.

The impact of the identification of target categories other than and in addition to 'women' is a continuing theme in this study. I have noted several times that the way in which policy creates categories of 'women' or 'Blacks' and here 'ethnic minorities' prevents us from recognizing and dealing with the complex problems of people who refuse to fit neatly into these categories. Policy, it seems, is highly insensitive to the postmodern insight into our 'multiple subjectivities', highlighting the dangers in ignoring the interaction between political processes and identity formation.

Of most interest here is that this lack of sensitivity has particular effects for some women. In the Netherlands, no differentiation is made between ethnic minority women or ethnic minority men, despite the fact that statistics indicate that minority women are clearly worse off when it comes to job prospects. The existence of a positive action programme targeting 'women' means that other targeted groups are considered to be constituted solely by 'men'. As Oosterman says, 'ethnic minorities' are defined as 'men'. We have already seen how in the United States and in Canada (Chapters 3 and 4) the separate targeting of 'women' alongside other identity categories makes some women, those who experience multiple oppression, disappear. Counter-intuitively, a policy which appears to be addressed to a wider range of inequalities removes some women from consideration.

Positive inaction

Positive action remains today on the policy agenda in the Netherlands. In fact, the phrase is ubiquitous in policy documents, and union and university publications. A peripheral glance at this literature leaves the impression that there is a genuine commitment to redress 'women's' inequality. Experience suggests otherwise. Almost invariably, the reforms are mild, weakly applied or avoided altogether.

The Ministry of Home Affairs has a Positive Action Bureau, concerned with increasing the numbers of 'women' and 'ethnic minorities' in the public service. It recently produced a handbook stating as its objective 'to arrive at a proportional distribution of women in all functions and at all levels of the administration' (Ministry of Home Affairs, 1989). Joke Verplanke of the Positive Action Bureau (interviewed 26 May, 1992) described the model employed in the public service as containing 'not very hard targets' and no sanctions. Departments are asked to make a plan of action, with a growth objective of one half of one per cent of women per year (this was increased to one per cent in 1993). As an additional goal, there should be an increase of one and one half per cent of women in certain salary ranges. However, departments are autonomous, Verplanke explained, in line with recent moves towards decentralization, and her office can only offer advice. Ministries have to report to her and she, in turn, reports to Parliament.

As far as procedures are concerned, Departments are permitted to hire a woman over an equally qualified man, but there are no instructions to this effect. The document outlining how to set target figures for 'women, handicapped, and ethnic minorities in public administrations' accepts at the outset that 'the supply of skilled women's labour is inadequate'. Hence, departments are expected only to set targets in line with their calculations of the available pool of female talent. They are advised to do this by determining the average age at which a certain cohort would have finished their studies and adding to this an expected number of years of experience (Ministry of Home Affairs, 1989). It is difficult to see how such calculations can do anything other than capture the current inequities facing women. The limitations of setting targets to match 'availability' is apparent also in Canada (see Chapter 4).

'Positive action' has also been broadened in certain ways. Child care and parental leave, for example, are counted as policy instruments. While these reforms are doubtless needed, the implications of bracketing them with 'positive action' should be considered. They become in this interpretation add-ons for 'women', rather than essential social security policies.[10] In this way the reforms reinforce the conventional division of domestic labour.

Figures which claim to illustrate the success of the programme show differences by Ministry.[11] In Home Affairs itself there was a jump in the proportion of women employed from 34 per cent in 1989 to 40 per cent in 1990. Another success story is the Ministry of Cultural Affairs, Health and Welfare which rose from 37.7 per cent to 39.1 per cent. These are ministries where women have always congregated. Changes in the Military and Justice (Police) Ministries are, by contrast, negligible. According to Verplanke (interviewed 26 May, 1992), the key to success is the presence in positions of authority of strong women pressing for change. She also emphasized that the current political climate in the Netherlands was not conducive to further reform at this time. It is, she explained, a 'more conservative part of the cycle', a 'no nonsense period'. The shortage of resources has also meant tensions between her area and those of her colleagues working for positive action for ethnic minorities. She concluded that, as far as 'women' are concerned, 'our measures right now are kind of sweet!' (implying that they are inoffensive).

As with government departments, Dutch universities are permitted to implement an 'everything else being equal' rule to redress 'women's' underrepresentation. This means that, if a male and female candidate are judged to have equal qualifications, the woman can be hired as part of a positive action programme. The problem is that 'qualifications' are seldom judged to be exactly equal – and there are no sanctions. The ways in which qualifications are measured are also contentious.[12] One study at the University of Leiden concluded that departments were either ignorant of the rule or ignored it. As a result, between 1970 and 1988, one woman was appointed for every six men. A disappointed observer concluded: 'At this point, we must conclude that you can put anything on paper; paper will not blush' (Grotenhuis, 1989: 531).

The University of Amsterdam has gone beyond the 'equal qualifications' rule. There, the pool of qualified applicants for each discipline is calculated and, if a faculty falls short of its 'quota', it can be instructed to include a clause in the advertisement that, in the first round, only women's applications will be considered. The faculty could also choose to advertise for a woman, but this is seldom done. Representatives of the Positive Action Bureau (interviewed 21 May, 1992) at the University feel some progress has been made, but they doubt that the reform is achieving its purpose. They noted that often the first round, the one where women applicants are assessed, produces no likely candidates and the selection committee then proceeds to examine the men's applications. In fact, it seems that often the standards are falsely high at the outset and, once women applicants have been dismissed, the standards are lowered to fill the position. The Bureau wants to make it compulsory for women applicants to remain in contention until the standard of the applicant has been decided.

The 'first round' reform was extremely controversial when it was first proposed, and a good deal of opposition remains. In 1989 the Arts Faculty challenged the provision as contravening the European Community's Equal Treatment Directive. The Faculty lost when the court decided that the measure was permitted within the exemption which allows positive action to increase equal opportunity. The Positive Action Bureau remains reluctant, nonetheless, to impose the provision because they feel that nothing will be accomplished without goodwill. The more recent decision by the European Court of Justice which declared targeted hiring 'sex discrimination' (see Chapter 2) probably means that the University of Amsterdam policy would not withstand another challenge.

For private enterprise and lower levels of government, the Ministry of Social Affairs and Employment has introduced a grants scheme for those who wish to pursue positive action. As this measure indicates, the approach to private enterprise is voluntaristic. There is not even a compulsory reporting system such as exists for many companies in Canada, the United States and Australia. Janny Dierx (interviewed 25 May, 1992), working in the Department for the Coordination of Emancipation Policy, Ministry of Social Affairs and Employment, explained that the government does not interfere with the collective agreements negotiated between employers and unions; these are left to the 'social partners'. In the competition for grants, employers tend to count everything they have done for 'women', such as child care, as points for positive action. Contract compliance, which has existed for some companies in the United States from the 1960s and in Canada from 1986, and which has recently been introduced by the Australian government, was being considered for 'ethnic minorities', but not for 'women'. There was an agreement between unions, the government, and employers to reserve 60 000 jobs for 'ethnic minorities' in 1993–1994.

It is heartening to see that the current Emancipation Council endorses a form of contract compliance to get political parties and schools to guarantee a number of positions for women. Frank Boddendijk (1992: 81) of the Council for Emancipation suggested that some government grants be tied to certain prerequisites which enable women to retain or to obtain access to important posts. It is interesting that Boddendijk feels that the theory regarding women's inequality has progressed from a model of assimilation in the 1970s to one which currently demands 'societal transformations'. However, he makes no mention of the early endorsement of quotas.

Some enterprises have taken the initiative and formulated their own rules for the promotion of 'equal opportunities' or 'positive action', terms which have come to mean much the same thing. Albertine Veldman (1991: 72) notes that, to an extent, the discussion surrounding such reforms suggests that 'the social-economic interests of organisations seem to coincide with government (legislation) policy'. The reasoning goes that stereotypes and prejudices based on sex-differences 'directly contradict efficient human resources management that requires maximilisation (*sic*) of all potential human capital.' The dominant discourse here, as in the United States, Canada and Australia, is a managerialist one which emphasizes the need for 'women' as an economic resource. Despite the apparent coincidence of goals between employers and government, Veldman's study of one Dutch multinational with an excellent reputation in the field of 'emancipation-management' showed disappointing results. The company had had a positive action plan for 'women' for some time. A key part of this plan was the so-called 'ladies' programme' which stressed career development. Despite these 'efforts', the percentage of women managers, around 4 or 5 per cent, changed little over the period and remains below the Dutch average of 8 per cent.

Veldman set out to explain this 'failure'. She emphasized several factors. Despite the stated commitment to equal opportunity, she found that among managerial personnel there remained entrenched attitudes about the desirable division of labour and sex stereotypes. Neither men nor women, for example, questioned the responsibility of 'women' for house and children. Hence, 'women' are allowed to 'aspire to a career' but this is presented as a 'choice' and it is left up to them to resolve the problems of combining paid work and family responsibilities. The inadequate child care facilities, commented on earlier, make this difficult. Organizational values and structures also serve to maintain the sexual status quo. For example, it is 'freely admitted that part-timers are not appointed to managerial positions'. The assumption is that to 'get ahead' the employee must be completely available to the company. Ninety per cent of part-timers in the company are women (Veldman, 1991: 73). Finally, the company's reputation for 'being good' on 'equal opportunities' means that most employees feel that any problems have been solved. Some men and women even express the view that 'women' now have enormous advantages due to company policy. We have seen several times how an 'equal opportunity' discourse scripts the 'beneficiaries' of the policy as in some way 'advantaged'.

Further study revealed that there was great ignorance at every level about the positive action plan. According to Veldman (1991: 76), this is not surprising since the plan is exceedingly vague: '[I]t formulates goals, but not measures calculated to achieve such goals'. Nor is the programme mentioned in personnel guidelines. No one seemed willing to take responsibility for the implementation of any rules relating to the programme. Veldman concludes that, although 'equal opportunity' has been formalized, there is no real support in the organizational culture.

Feminists in Dutch trade unions started talking about positive action in earnest around 1985.[13] At that time, they had to counter 'positive discrimination' charges, and did so by explaining that 'women' had some catching up to do. They pointed out that equal treatment of unequals would only perpetuate inequality. They emphasized that it was inappropriate to portray 'women's' inequality as somehow their own fault due to their lack of initiative, that the problems went deeper and were indeed structural. They won this argument through their statistical demonstration of the sex segregation of the labour force. Hence, a first strategy became integrating 'women' into 'men's' jobs.

Els Oosterman of the FNV points out that unions which accepted this agenda had their own motivation for pursuing reform: it provided an opportunity to intervene in personnel policy, something they had previously been stopped from doing. This of course also explained why many employers were so opposed.

The FNV conducted a pilot project on affirmative action to see just how implementation could be assured. The experience revealed that any such attempt required a large investment of time, and that union representatives had to be on the scene, keeping employees informed. Given the current style of centralized organization, designed to facilitate negotiation for collective agreements at a national level, this kind of close supervision was not feasible.

The ways in which positive action came to be understood also created problems for supporters. The idea that it meant simply getting 'women' into 'men's' jobs attracted limited enthusiasm since many women did not find these jobs, or the general workplace culture which surrounded them, appealing. Male unionists also emphasized that the primary goal was to move 'women' into higher status jobs, pointing out that this simply catered for white-collar women, not 'workers'. For some, then, the reform became tinged with elitism, an image that has proved difficult to shake off. This interpretation also tended to set 'career women' against 'other women', undermining solidarity.

Attempts to introduce quotas were defeated. 'Targets' meant that never enough women entered an enterprise to make a real difference to the workplace culture. Moreover, even within the unions, where one might have expected greater efforts, little change has occurred. Men continue to dominate the top positions. Union women have become disheartened and have begun to seek alternative reform strategies. Oosterman explained that a new and larger 'umbrella' is required. She and her women union colleagues have decided to focus on 'broad organizational change', taking as a guide a recent (1991) publication produced by the Organization for Economic Co-operation and Development (OECD), entitled *Shaping Structural Change: The Role of Women*. This, a report produced by a high-level group of experts for the Secretary-General of the OECD, focuses on labour conditions and the labour process, and stresses the need to facilitate a combination of family responsibilities with paid labour. The FNV is paying particular attention to sexual harassment and the need to revalue 'women's' jobs.

The problem has become, says Oosterman, to locate affirmative action in this larger agenda. If we call all these reforms 'kinds' of affirmative action, they will face the stigmatization which has become associated with this programme. At the same time, if affirmative action is replaced by 'broad organizational change', some of the political discussion which she believes is necessary, in particular that 'men' continue to resist 'women's' entry in many domains and profit from their exclusion, becomes neutralized. At least, she says, when the phrase 'positive discrimination' was used, you could talk about overt discrimination. Now, everything has become 'structural' and diffuse.

The meanings of 'positive action'

The union experience illustrates the way in which 'positive action' has 'been given' a meaning that limits its impact. A dominant neoliberal discourse proved useful in portraying targeted hiring and quotas as unfair manipulation of already fair processes. This view found a ready home in the managerialist approach to the reform. The focus shifted to measures such as training programmes which would 'help' 'women' to become competitive. In this understanding 'women' become the problem and integration into existing structures the goal.

Because targeted hiring and quotas were defeated, the potential flow-on effects in workplace culture that might have followed from a large increase of female personnel never occurred. Without these changes, it became easier to label the reform inadequate and elitist. Moreover, once positive action was endorsed officially, it was assumed that all that needed to be done had been done. The kinds of problems of implementation which this chapter illustrates were not identified. Hence, women who 'failed' were seen as responsible for that 'failure', for making 'choices' which did not work to their advantage.

For all these reasons, some women became reluctant to associate themselves with the reform. They feared the label 'token', or the assumption that they had been appointed 'only' because they were women. I have noted several times the way in which dominant understandings of affirmative action contribute 'to a low sense of self-worth in victims of discrimination and to the public impression of them as inferior' (Edelman, 1988: 26).

Since the meanings attached to positive action effectively determine its impact, it is crucial to uncover how these meanings are produced. Veldman (1991: 78) emphasizes the power of those in charge in the organization to 'discursively constitute the problem and its solution'. Hence, she concludes that the law is defeated by the very power relations it aimed to undermine.

It is also clear that the media has played an active role in shaping the discourses around positive action. A great deal of attention has been directed to a few cases in the Netherlands. These include the episode referred to above where the Arts Faculty at the University of Amsterdam challenged the quota rule. The most notorious case, however, and the one which comes to everyone's lips in the Netherlands when the subject is raised is the 'Barlios affair'. This concerned the appointment of a woman under a positive action programme to a director's position in an elite public secondary school. The case was twice brought before the Equal Opportunity Commission by men who felt aggrieved, and twice their complaints were dismissed. Half a year later the woman left, driven out by the negative publicity.

Odille Verhaar has studied the ways in which the media debate was mobilized and the kinds of arguments raised. She emphasizes that the terms were predefined and closed to challenge. In particular, there were appeals to an empirical concept of 'equality'. The notion that 'merit' was a 'real' and measurable thing went unchallenged. Not surprisingly, some women on the staff were quoted as saying that they wished to be appointed only if they were deemed to be capable by these standards, standards which remained ill-defined.[14]

Conclusion

The Netherlands case illustrates how defenders of positive action for 'women' have been impelled to present the reform within established conceptual categories instead of showing the ways in which these terms are used by social actors to defend a particular way of viewing the world. A first step in reopening the debate involves stepping outside of the discourses which have claimed the spotlight to date, including 'managerialism', 'equal opportunities', 'careerism' and 'elitism'. By stepping outside of discourses, I mean that women activists have to cease setting their *own* arguments in the *terms* of those discourses.

The original commitment to targeted hiring was lost because it was described as incompatible with a fundamental notion of 'equal opportunity'. Instead of contesting this notion, it was accepted that such a fundamental precept as 'equal opportunity' could not be challenged. In the process 'positive action' was tamed. Much the same thing happened in the United States. To re-situate affirmative action it is necessary to demonstrate the unfairness that hides behind commitments to 'equal opportunity'. We need to unpack such theoretical concepts to reveal the investments lurking behind their invocation.

The Netherlands case illustrates that problems of implementation are tied to modes of representation, and confirms the highly political character of conceptual categories. Hence, it highlights the need to be placed where these modes of representation are determined. This includes at the very least political parties, the bureaucracy, universities, unions, large corporations and the media. An awareness of the workings of category politics produces good reasons to support strong affirmative action for 'women' to guarantee representation in these arenas.

Notes

This chapter reproduces in part material from an article entitled 'Positive Action in the Netherlands' which appeared in *Nemesis: Netherlands Feminist Law Journal*, January/February, 1994.

1 Here socialist feminism identifies a strand of feminism which sees economics as the chief cause of women's subordination, while radical feminism views women's oppression as the root of all systems of oppression (Tuttle, 1987: 267). The particular way in which these notions blend in the Netherlands highlights the dangers of insisting on sharp divisions among feminisms, particularly out of context.

2 This phrase, 'positive discrimination', is widely used in the Netherlands to describe positive action. While I argue in Chapter 2 that this use is unwise, later in this chapter a feminist trade unionist offers another perspective.

3 For Australia, Canada, the United Kingdom and Sweden the percentages are for 1988 (Whitehouse, 1990).

4 Such schemes operate in the United States, Canada, Sweden and Norway. Australia, by contrast (Shaver, 1993), has a single assistance-based scheme.

5 In personal correspondence (2 January, 1993) Els Oosterman explains that parents who wish to work a shortened week must work a minimum of 20 hours and any leave is unpaid. Hence, only relatively well-off women can benefit from this rule.

6 Els Oosterman feels that Braidotti is slightly too negative with her child care figures, though the situation is dismal. According to Oosterman, child care centres have places for only 5 per cent of children under four years of age (personal correspondence, 2 January, 1993).

7 By targeted reforms here I mean language bills, such as Bill 101, which protect French-speaking language rights and which have on occasion been referred to as Canada's first affirmative action programmes. It should be noted, however, that Francophones have been unsuccessful in bids to become a targeted employment equity category. See Chapter 4.

8 The proposal for a general antidiscrimination law ran into difficulties due to an attempt to include sexual preference among the provisions. The Christian Democrats, responding to their large Church lobby, rejected the idea. The problem was that both the Catholic and Protestant Churches felt that this could lead to interference with their control over their schools, a right protected by the Constitution. In this instance, pillarization worked against change.

9 According to Els Oosterman (personal correspondence, 2 January, 1993), it is as yet unclear whether this proposal will be accepted. There continues to be some ambivalence about the determination to get women into the labour market. It should not be forgotten that many Christian Democrats continue to believe in the model of the nuclear family with a male breadwinner and a female homemaker.

10 Riki Holtmaat made this point in interview, 28 May, 1992.

11 I say 'claim' here because, as I argue elsewhere, saying that an increase in the proportion of women hired or promoted proves the success of a positive action programme means that other factors explaining this increase, say for example the superior qualifications of some women applicants, disappear from the record.

12 For a discussion of the gendered character of university appointment procedures, see Bacchi, 1993.

13 The following account draws heavily on an interview (29 May, 1992) with Els Oosterman of the Women's Secretariat, FNV, the largest trade union confederation in the Netherlands.

14 Verhaar feels that we ought not to underplay the significance of the fact that the school concerned was an elite school. This, she argues, facilitated the appeal to a merit discourse. Interview with Odille Verhaar, 27 May, 1992.

8

The Politics of Difference

A central argument in this book is that being aware of the play of category politics assists feminists in developing strategies for change. At the very least, an increased sensitivity to the ways in which categories are deployed for political purposes provides a caution against believing that winning recognition of 'women', for example through affirmative action, will necessarily produce desired results. There remains a need to assess continually the meanings attached to terms like 'affirmative action' and 'women', and to examine how rhetorical commitments to 'women' take effect.

It is also important to recognize that feminists, like any social group, are positioned within specific historical and political circumstances. These will affect the strategies they adopt. The hope in this study is that a close examination of some of these strategies will help feminists elsewhere to reflect upon the reasons they pursue particular political options, and the possible dangers in some of those choices.

In the current debate about feminism's relationship to the category 'woman'/'women', some have argued that women activists have little choice but to invoke some notion of 'women'. Naomi Schor, you may recall (see Chapter 1), puts the question thus: 'can there be a feminist politics that dispenses with the notion of Woman?' (Schor, 1994: xiii). Biddy Martin answers this question in the negative: '[W]e cannot afford to refuse to take a political stance "which pins us to our sex" for the sake of an abstract theoretical construct' (in Doane and Hodges, 1987: 12–13). Teresa de Lauretis (1989: 31) has suggested that feminists need to 'take the risk of "essentialism"'. She describes a case-study not unlike the one offered in this chapter, in which Italian feminists appeal to a notion of a female social subject modelled on the archetype of 'woman' as 'a consciously political formulation of the specific difference of women in a particular historical location.'

Laying claim to 'women' can, of course, mean many things. It can mean drawing upon an archetype of 'woman', described in Chapter 1, and claiming that indeed 'women' possess special nurturing characteristics which the world sorely needs. This can then become the basis for demands for increased representation in political parties and elsewhere. Or, laying claim to 'women' can mean suggesting that despite 'differences' among women, they have enough in common to join together to make political claims.

The message in this volume is that feminists need to reconsider the amount of time and energy invested in debating meanings of 'woman'/ 'women' and pay more heed to the ways in which 'women' is taken up and used in political debate. The lesson is that particular meanings will have certain uses at certain times and in specific places, but that shifting political winds may necessitate a willingness to rethink those meanings. Appeals to an archetype, where they appear to be useful, are indeed practical and strategic, but they are not essentialist. The reasoning behind this claim was laid out in Chapter 1.

Norway and the discussions there around positive action have been selected to test the usefulness of an appeal to 'women's' ontological 'difference' from 'men'. In the main Norwegian feminists have emphasized 'women's' particular experiences, values and 'knowledges' in making political claims. The feminist scholar, Beatrice Halsaa (1991a: 45), makes this clear. In Norway, she explains, 'Women's demands have to a large extent been legitimized by reference to the female culture and to care as a specific woman-quality.'

These characteristics are seen to be due to an unexplored combination of biological and environmental influences. A recent quote from Prime Minister, Gro Harlem Brundtland (1991: 74), illustrates this form of argument:

> I believe that all women, regardless of origin or background, feel that there are some matters in which we take a greater interest than men. This is related to our role as women and mothers and our closeness to new life and future generations. It is also related to the fact that in virtually every part of the world, the day-to-day activities of the family are mainly the responsibility of women.

In contrast to the conflictual model in the Netherlands (Chapter 7), which positions 'women' and 'men' in competition for power, the suggestion in Norway is that 'women's' 'difference' *complements* 'men's' values and perspectives. This complementary model is different again from the one offered in Sweden, where the emphasis is on 'women's' and 'men's' shared humanity and not on the 'differences' between them. The demand in Norway is for increased recognition of 'women's' important 'difference'. This is clearly an appeal to the archetypical 'woman' mentioned above. It is an attempt to use a traditional representation of 'women' to win improved status, representation and living conditions for designated members of that category.

The assertion that 'women' have particular values and perspectives because they are mothers and carers has proved useful in several ways. It has served as an important rallying cry to mobilize numbers of women. It has also allowed women activists to tap into a tradition of social or descriptive representation in Norway to claim positive action in political representation, government-funded research targeting 'women', university courses for 'women' – even a 'Women's' University.

However, claims in other areas, specifically for positive action in private enterprise, have faced constraints similar to those we have found operating elsewhere, and for similar reasons – the priority assigned to labour market politics. It is also clear that some of the changes in government organization accompanying the swing to the right are making it difficult to maintain a commitment to 'women'. We shall also see that the emphasis on 'women' as carers and nurturers is being transformed into an emphasis on 'children', 'family' and 'fathers', with some worrying effects.

Mobilizing 'difference'

To a certain extent the successful mobilizing of women's groups across Norway owes a great deal to one woman, former politician and academic, Berit Ås. Of course, the kind of organization politics available to Ås could hardly be replicated in larger countries, or populations with dramatically diverse ethnic backgrounds. Norway's population is commonly described as 'small and homogeneous'. There are approximately four million people (Kissman, 1991: 193).

In 1978–1979 Ås developed a nine-point strategy for action for women. She chose as a starting place: 'Find out how women in the district or country have been mobilized before. Find an historical case which they know and build on earlier accepted preconditions' (1981, 1986). A decade earlier Ås (interviewed 15 June, 1992) had employed this very strategy secretly to organize a number of linked women's groups which brought together women from different ideological persuasions and across party lines. She asked them to find only three things upon which they could agree. These – a demand for better education, personal independence, and higher representation of women everywhere – became the basis for action. A programme which could unite conservative women and socialists like Ås herself had to be minimalist. There were conflicting points of view on a range of issues, including abortion (Stromberg, 1980: 44). 'Women' are not a homogeneous grouping but, as Ås proved, numbers of women could be united around particular claims.

The key point of agreement was that the women consulted wished to increase the representation of women in positions of power, particularly in politics. They united behind this demand because they recognized the need to make women players in category politics, though they would not have used those words. It was felt that invoking a traditional image of 'women' as society's carers provided the best chance of justifying recognition of 'women' as a group. Much of the basis for this conviction lay with Berit Ås's notion of a 'female culture'. Ås wrote a key article in 1975 arguing that 'women' had distinctive, positive characteristics. In particular, care was held to be a special womanly quality, for a mixture of biological and sociological reasons. This notion attracted supporters among women who continued to emphasize the importance of 'woman's' mothering role, and among those who believed that 'women' represented more positive life-creating virtues than did 'men'.

According to Beatrice Halsaa (1991b), the idea of a 'female culture' had particular appeal for many Norwegian women, because of the material and economic conditions of their lives. That is, Norway lagged behind the other Scandinavian countries in women's labour force participation.[1] Comparatively, then, it was a more traditional society. More women continued to be full-time housewives; many worked part-time. In 1991 48 per cent of all employed women worked part-time, compared to 8 per cent of men (Ministry of Children and Family Affairs, 1991: 21). Child care provisions were sadly inadequate.[2] Hence, the question of who was to do the caring in society and the need to give that role value became extremely pertinent. Kissman (1991: 194) describes Norwegian women activists as rallying around 'organization of life' issues.

Ås's (1986: 181) motives in invoking a 'female culture' were, as ever, strategic. She felt that women needed to see themselves as powerful and creative. They needed an image which moved beyond the patriarchal ones available, 'women' as subordinate or 'women' as oppressed. She felt that the traditional characterization of 'women' as nurturant could provide the basis for a dynamic political movement. Her tactics proved to be very successful. Using the notion of 'women's' distinctive experiences and values, she mobilized a campaign to increase women's representation in local government. This was achieved through a careful application of Norway's distinctive electoral rules.

Norway, like the other Scandinavian countries, employs a system of proportional representation which, it has been suggested, works to increase women's representation. The argument is, and the figures bear it out, that parties presenting lists to electors find it easier and politically wiser to include women than in first-past-the-post systems (Lakeman, 1982: Chapter 8). Parties indicate their preferences through the ranking of candidates. In Norway, additional preference is indicated through cumulating names, listing the names more than once on the ballot, usually consecutively. Another distinctive Norwegian feature is that voters can actively construct ballots to their personal preference, transferring names from other party ballots onto the ballot they have chosen, crossing out names and cumulating names themselves (Ås, 1991).

In the lead-up to the 1971 local elections, Ås and her co-organizers instructed women voters on how to construct party ballots which would lead to women being elected. This resulted in a number of so-called 'women's coups'. In 1971 women won the majority in three important councils, the City Councils of Oslo, Trondheim and Asker. The electoral laws have since been modified to limit the extent to which voters can influence outcomes.

Ås was also instrumental in the introduction of positive action for 'women' within Norway's political parties. By her own account (interview, 15 June, 1992), the move started when she was asked to chair a new party, the Democratic Socialists, after she had been ejected from the Labour Party for her opposition to Norway's membership in the Common Market. She agreed to do so with one precondition, that the new party's by-laws include the rule that women be represented by no less than 40 per cent on all party levels.

Other parties became concerned that they might lose many women's votes if they did not follow suit, and so adopted a 40/60 per cent rule for gender representation. These included the Liberals, the Socialist Left, Labour and the Marxist Leninists. The Christian People's Party now employs the principle, though it does not appear in the by-laws. The Centre Party, formerly the Farmers' Party, has formally adopted the 40/60 rule, and the Conservatives apply it in a *de facto* manner, though there is still opposition to the principle of 'quotas'. According to Hege Skjeie, 'the sequential adoption by different Norwegian parties of formal regulations which specify 40/60 percent gender quotas for party elective positions can be interpreted as a sign of competition working in women's favor' (1991: 237).

The winning of positive action for 'women' in the political parties was due to more than pragmatism, however. The idea that society 'divided' into competing social categories was well accepted. As Gro Brundtland (1991: 72) explains, quotas had long been used in Norway 'to ensure that sparsely populated districts and various geographical interests are heard'. Moreover, there is a wide community acceptance that 'women' represent 'different' 'interests'. According to recent research, around two-thirds of Norwegian Parliamentarians accept the existence of gender-structured interests, though 'there was a comparatively large group who could not specify their content' (Skjeie, 1991: 238).

In addition, as Berit Ås (1991: 30) points out, social democracy did not exert the ideological hegemony in Norway which it did in Sweden. Class divisions, it seems, while important, are not as significant in Norwegian politics. Hence, there has been more space to put the case for the political significance of gender.[3] The strong Nordic commitment to equality meanwhile provided a useful opening (Halsaa, 1991b: 26).

The result is that Norway leads the world in female representation in parliament and in community councils. Between 1989 and 1992, women held 36 per cent of the seats in parliament, 39 per cent of the seats in county councils, and 28 per cent of those in municipal councils. In 1987 the famous Brundtland 'women's' cabinet had 44.4 per cent women. The next non-socialist coalition cabinet maintained the tradition with 42.1 per cent women and, when Gro Brundtland returned to power in 1991, 47.4 per cent of the cabinet were women.[4]

The acceptance of 'women' as a separate political category also led to the introduction of a Royal Resolution in 1973, imposed by the Labour

Party, calling for all nominating agencies to put forward both women and men when invited to send a representative to central-government committees and boards. The goal was to guarantee that both sexes were represented (Halsaa, 1991b: 25–6, 35). In 1981 a provision was added to the Equal Status Act that both sexes, as far as possible, should be equally represented. This was strengthened in 1988 with wording in the Equal Status Act which requires a minimum of 40 per cent representation of each sex on every committee (Ministry of Children and Family Affairs, 1991: 7).

Another area where the difference/complementarity argument has proved effective is in gaining resources and recognition in Norway's important research institutions. 'Women's' particular experiences, it is maintained, need to have research focused upon them; otherwise a vital component of the social mix is excluded. Some also suggest that 'women's' experiences produce distinctive approaches to knowledge and distinctive knowledges. Norway has a large publicly-funded research sector and an equally significant privately-funded 'institute sector'. 'Women's' research is well represented in both areas. The Norwegian Research Council for Science and the Humanities (NAVF) has enouraged 'women's' research through its scholarship programme and through the establishment of the Secretariat for Women and Research in 1977. The Secretariat has become an important lobbying agency, and now issues its own journal, *Nytt om kvinneforskning* (*News on Feminist Research*).[5]

Norway also led the world in introducing in 1975 a special course in 'women's law' in the University of Oslo Law School. This became a special section for 'women's law' in 1978. The scholar, Tove Stang Dahl, who was the instigating force behind these moves, wrote a book in 1987 explaining what was meant by 'women's law'. Here she emphasized that traditional ways of organizing law had little to do with 'women's' lives and that there was a need to offer alternative organizing categories to those commonly used in law schools. She argued that, since 'women' experience unjust distribution of resources in money, time and work, categories such as 'housewives' law', and 'paid work law' are more appropriate than 'tax law' or 'contract law'. The starting point, according to Stang Dahl (1987), should be the 'needs and wants of women in general'. A new publication, called *Birth Law* (Hellum, 1992), takes as its empirical starting point the female body, another idea which comes originally from Stang Dahl (Christensen et al., 1988: 11). Norway also established a 'Women's University' in 1983 which has since received separate funding from the government.

All of these initiatives can be seen as outcomes of the particular recognition of 'women' as a category with special experiences, knowledges and values. Difference/complementarity has indeed provided a useful claim in some areas. However, the usefulness of this kind of argument is currently being disputed. According to Hege Skjeie (1991), there is great ambiguity about just what it means to assert that 'women' have particular values and perspectives, and the political consequences of invoking such an argument are uncertain.

'Women' and 'equal status'

As in Sweden, in the 1960s and early 1970s, as a result of a period of boom, accentuated in Norway by the discovery of off-shore oil, those in government and a number of business leaders agreed that there was a need to encourage 'women' to join the labour force. As mentioned previously, Norway lagged behind the other Scandinavian countries in recruiting women to paid labour. Hence, there was some agreement that a concerted effort would be required. This decision coincided with the first stirrings of the revived women's movement and created some common ground. This in part explains the amount of research on 'women's' work commissioned by public authorities. Here a coincidence of goals led to public funding of 'women's' research (Leira, 1986: 5).

There was also some agreement that a key necessity was to encourage 'women' into nontraditional jobs (Norwegian Research Council for Applied Social Science, 1985). This emphasis is reflected in the development of 'equal status' legislation in the later 1970s. The view at the time was that inappropriate gender stereotypes were precluding 'women' from taking up certain occupations, and discouraging 'men' from entering occupations traditionally designated 'female'. Hence, the solution to recruiting 'women' and to ending the sex segregation of the labour market was to challenge sex roles.

These were, of course, familiar arguments. A sex roles approach to gender equality had, as we have seen, become popular in nearby Sweden and overseas. The argument also had appeal because it seemed to suggest that both 'men' and 'women' were disadvantaged in certain ways by current societal expectations, and both 'men' and 'women' would benefit from proposed changes. In the process, the focus on 'women' and their needs became diffused in gender-neutral language. The women's movement was wary about this shift and battled to retain an awareness that indeed 'women' were the ones suffering discrimination and oppression. This battle surfaced, as it had in Sweden, over the framing of Norway's first equality legislation, the Equal Status Act of 1978.

The origins of this legislation can be traced to the Norwegian Labour Party's election programme in 1973, where the voters were promised a 'statutory prohibition of discrimination against *women* in all sectors of society, and in particular in the labour market' [my italics] (Nielsen and Halvorsen, 1992: 10; Halvorsen, 1989: 20). A committee from several ministries produced a draft report in 1974 which outlawed 'sex discrimination' and called for 'equal treatment of men and women' in employment and education. The major trade union organization, the LO (Confederation of Trade Unions), was also involved in producing the draft.

The feminist community was dissatisfied with the draft proposal. Four feminist lawyers, including Tove Stang Dahl, produced a pamphlet highlighting the limitations of 'equal treatment' as a principle. They pointed out that treating unequals equally simply perpetuated inequality, and demanded that the legislation leave adequate room for positive measures, that is positive action, to address 'women's' inequality. They also wished the legislation to return to the original determination to outlaw discrimination against *'women'*. The bill did not pass but was sent back to the committee where a revised draft was produced. The main provisions and trends, however, remained the same. At this point representatives from the Labour Party and the Conservative Party compromised and the bill was accepted.

In accordance with the decision to integrate 'women' into the labour market, the principal aim of the Equal Status Act was 'to grant women equal access to education and employment through legal rules establishing the principle of equal formal treatment' (Skjeie, 1992: 161). This followed the European pattern where an Equal Treatment Directive had been introduced in 1976 (see Chapter 2). The Act applies to 'working life', education and 'organizations', but is not to be applied 'in respect of family life and purely personal relationships' (Ministry of Consumer Affairs, 1985: 4–5).

The concerns of the women's movement were captured and contained within two clauses. The objective of the Act, as stated in Article 1, combined gender neutrality with a specific commitment to address *'women's'* inequality. Article 1 reads: 'This Act shall promote equal status between the sexes and aims particularly at improving the position of women' (Halsaa, 1991b: 18). The general clause, Article 3, prohibiting discrimination, was written in gender-neutral language, but left an opening for 'different treatment' which 'promotes equal status between the sexes'. The gender-specific phrasing in Article 1 was indeed a victory, one that has only recently been accomplished in Sweden (see Chapter 6), and one which is replicated in no other Western democracy. According to the Equal Status Ombud,[6] Ingse Stabel (1991: 131), it 'provides the framework for introducing positive action in favour of women', and allows her to dismiss complaints by men that such measures discriminate against them. Still, as we shall see, the provision remains susceptible to political machinations.

The unions were prepared to give ground on the opening article *in exchange* for increased influence over the equal pay provision. Hege Skjeie has found that this, Article 5, was drafted by a smaller group than the rest of the bill, and that LO was heavily represented in this group (in Halvorsen, 1989: 22). In the first instance the LO wished only to have an 'equal pay for equal work' provision, but was more or less compelled to follow the ILO directive which called for 'equal pay for work of equal value'. However, as Skjeie (1992: 164) says, 'no further concessions were granted'.

Article 5 contains the ambiguous wording that 'Women and men employed *by the same employer* shall have equal pay for work of equal value', narrowing considerably the possibility of broad work evaluations (Ministry of Children and Family Affairs, 1991: 8; my italics). More significantly, the LO succeeded in inserting a clause which removed the Equal Status Board's right to intervene in collective agreements, paralleling the situation in Sweden.[7] Ombud, Ingse Stabel (1991: 132–4), has pointed out the severe restrictions these arrangements imposed on her ability to enforce the Equal Status Act. She explained that employers continue to insist that they are observing the Act if they pay men and women, who are doing the *same* work, equally. And, so long as wage negotiations are supervised by the Labour Disputes Court rather than the Equal Status Board, any attempt on her part to apply a broader interpretation of 'equal pay for work for equal value' is doomed to fail.[8] Specifically, she has drawn attention to her inability to affect collective wage agreements, and has suggested a more activist, interventionist role for the Ombud.

This, however, seems unlikely to come to pass. In the words of one researcher into the subject,

> not even as good a cause as justice for women workers could bring the social democrats to breach (sic) with the tradition of the past 60–70 years with foundations in theories about social classes, but lacking in recognition of gender as an important entity. (Halvorsen, 1989: 22)

While a class discourse may not be as dominant in Norway as in Sweden, leaving a space to claim legitimacy for 'women' as a political category, this space has always been narrow.

Plans of positive inaction

In 1977 the Ministry of Consumer Affairs and Government Administration set up a separate Department for Family and Equality Issues to initiate 'sex equality' measures. These took the form of a 'Plan of Action', introduced by the Labour government in 1981. It suggested the use of 'quotas' in admission to certain educational courses where women were seriously underrepresented, and in the hiring of some public servants. In Norway the term 'quota' is used to refer to hiring procedures in which it becomes permissible to hire a 'person of the opposite sex' when that group is underrepresented and when they have either *adequate* or *equal* qualifications for the position being filled. The hiring of someone with *sufficient* qualifications is called a 'radical quota', and someone with *equal* qualifications a 'moderate quota'. It is important to remember that the term 'quota' is often used loosely.

The Labour Government tried to introduce a 'radical quota' in the recruitment to offices in the public service at the lowest levels, and a 'moderate quota' for the top level positions. The public service union baulked at the idea of a radical quota and delayed until the non-socialist Government came to power in 1985. The revised provision that 'Preferential treatment shall be used for "the underrepresented sex" in cases of *equal* qualifications, for offices at all levels' proved more acceptable (Halsaa, 1991b: 36–7). After some debate, local organizations were permitted to use a 'radical quota' for lower level positions, but most decided wisely that this might in fact have deleterious effects since, as a gender-neutral provision, it made it possible for men to infiltrate some women-dominated areas.

As the wording, 'underrepresented sex', indicates, the second Action Plan, prepared by the non-socialist Government, adopted gender-neutral language, even when referring to 'preferential treatment'. In addition, more responsibility was devolved to the various ministries to implement their own positive action measures. While the list of proposals may seem impressive, the results have proved disappointing. Hege Skjeie concluded that the guidelines were of little use:

> It is, unfortunately, difficult to conclude that the quota system has been an effective means for promoting equal status. Instead, this process illustrates how a quota decision is no guarantee for the use of the quota. In the best case, the quota directive in the agreement implies that individual preferential treatment may be used as an argument to hire a female applicant *who hardly can be ranged behind a male applicant*. . . . The 'quota'-label is itself misleading; it gives the impression of a far more active policy to recruit women. (In Halsaa, 1991b: 37; my italics)

In the university sector, where employment guidelines specify the use of a 'moderate quota', the rule is seldom applied, and has attracted much controversy in the few cases where it has been used. At the University of Oslo, the provision has been invoked only once. It then proved so controversial that the male candidate who had been bypassed was offered another post.[9] As a result, the figures for women in senior university posts are not much different from those elsewhere. As of 1987, women constituted 4.6 per cent of the professoriate. This figure rose to 8 per cent as a result of the government's decision, prompted by cross-party support among women politicians, to use a special fund to promote appropriately qualified women associate professors to the level of professor. Since that single action, monies for this purpose are now equally available to 'women' and 'men'.

Given the lack of control over collective agreements, there has been little attempt to use positive action in private enterprise. As a result it is not surprising that 1987 figures register that women occupy only 3 per cent of leading positions in this domain (Ministry of Children and Family Affairs, 1991: 6). Prime Minister Brundtland (1991: 72) has explained, 'There are clear differences between the proportion of women in political and public life, where quotas have been applied, and in the private sector, which is not regulated this way.'

From 'equal status' to 'family affairs'

With the onset of the recession in the later 1970s, the impetus to increase 'women's' labour force participation abated somewhat. In fact, women were among the first laid off (Aga, 1986: 88). Still, it would have been difficult to remove the commitment to 'women's' labour force participation at this stage. More and more women were entering paid labour for a variety of reasons, and the trend was well established in other industrialized countries. Nonetheless, there are some changes in the language surrounding 'women's' position in society which hint at subtle shifts in policy direction.

Introducing the second Action Plan in 1985, the then Ministry of Consumer Affairs and Government Administration explained: 'Women's contribution to the economy is now of such importance that an active equal status policy is absolutely vital for continued growth and development.' There was a suggestion, however, that a new focus was required:

> To date, the policy on equal status has focused on the situation of women, mainly in relation to education and employment. Great importance is attached to motivating women to choose untraditional forms of education and occupation . . .
> The future policy on equal status requires research so as to achieve a broader political area of impact and a wider range of objectives and instruments adjusted to new challenges. The society is not organized to meet the increased challenges created by equal status between the sexes. For example, who will carry out the caring work? (Norwegian Research Council for Applied Social Science, 1985: 5–6)

There is much in this statement to recommend it. In fact, it captures the principal complaint of many Norwegian feminists and feminists elsewhere that, unless some changes are made to the ways in which paid work and domestic responsibilities are distributed, attempts to integrate 'women' into existing work structures will create more problems for many women than they solve. The Ministry even noted that it was now crucial 'to draw attention to the importance of women's traditional duties and the resources which men represent as carers.'

However, the document also hints at the discursive shift underway in Norway replacing 'women' with 'children's rights', 'fathers' rights' and the 'family'. This is indicated in some significant and ominous name changes in Norway's 'Public Gender Equality Machinery'. In 1991 the Department of Family and *Gender Equality* became the Department of *Family Affairs and Child Care*. It resides within the Ministry of *Children and Family Affairs* (Equal Status Council, 1991: 120; my italics). Some recent public statements indicate that these changes represent an attempt to reinforce traditional sex roles while causing some attrition to the status attached to the category 'mother'. For example, some of the positions defended by the Commissioner for Children,[10] Trond-Viggo Torgersen (1991: 80–2), sound vaguely familiar and a little disturbing. He takes as his starting point 'the modern dilemma that arises when childrens' (*sic*) needs conflict with their parents' time and work'. He is concerned that due to technological inventions and a declining birth rate 'many women have thus lost a natural career choice, housewife'.

Among the reforms Torgersen considers 'politically discussable' to realign family and paid work responsibilities are: 'Transferring resources from the older established to the young establishing themselves in the form of favourable state establishment-loans, larger tax deductions for parents of small children, higher child support benefits, a salary for *those women who prefer to stay home* and care for their children' (my italics). This clear endorsement of traditional sex roles by someone with such high standing suggests that future prospects for Norwegian women are as yet undecided. Other parts of Torgersen's statement sound more forward-looking. He admits that, until 'women' have higher wages, 'One cannot simply afford choosing father as the one to stay at home'. But again the language here is disconcerting. He refers, for example, to the need to help 'men' 'to *capture* the arena of children' (my italics).

In Norway and elsewhere women activists are increasingly concerned about the recent trend among some men to demand their 'rights' to have access to their children. In fact in 1989 women MPs crossed party lines to protest against a ministerial proposal to grant visiting rights to fathers who had not lived with their child after its birth. The initiative for the proposal came from the state agency of the children's ombud on the grounds that this would be in the best interests of the children concerned (Skjeie, 1991: 248). Women MPs protested that the suggested change reflected not the child's interest but the father's. Some of the concerns were that the provision could apply in rape cases and in other cases where the mother had good grounds for denying the father access (Ministry of Children and Family Affairs, 1991: 35).

A recent suggestion that fathers be offered four weeks' paid parental leave which will be lost to the mother if it is not taken up has received mixed reactions among feminists for related reasons (Stoltenberg, 1991: 128).[11] While a large number feel it may be the only way to provide fathers with the necessary incentive to assume a share of childrearing responsibility, some see no reason why mothers should lose the benefit.[12] Others are concerned that forcing fathers to stay with their children is dangerous given the recent evidence of child sexual abuse.

This same subject of fathers' access to children caused tensions among those on the Men's Role Committee. This was a government initiative which followed the Swedish lead in focusing on the need to change 'men's' behaviour in order to alter sex roles and sex-role expectations (Halsaa, 1991b: 23).

The shift from 'women' as a category to 'family' and to 'men' has been accompanied by a new emphasis on 'conflicting interests' between groups of women. For example, the 1991 Report from the Ministry of Children and Family Affairs (Part 1, Introduction) to the United Nations highlighted 'a complex and problematic field of conflicts of interest between groups of women, in particular in relation to the enhancement of economic rights for women who perform care-related work in the home.' We have seen elsewhere how 'exceptional women' are often set against 'traditional women' discursively, and how affirmative action for 'women' as a reform is undermined in this representation (see Chapter 3).

The minority Labour Government handed down a Green Paper in 1992 which illustrates the swing away from a focus on 'women's' concerns. This paper had been long awaited and was expected to indicate what would follow the second Action Plan which expired in 1990. In an interview with Gerd Vollset (18 June, 1992) – Assistant Director General, Department of Family Affairs and Kindergarten, Ministry of Children and Family Affairs – the person behind the Green Paper, the new trend became apparent. Vollset informed me that there were no plans for a third Action Plan. In fact, there was some talk about disbanding the Equal Status Council. And, as far as 'positive action' was concerned, although Article 1 specifying the focus on *'women's'* inequality would be retained, it would be made clear that 'positive action' could be applied to 'men' as well as to 'women'. Quotas could then be used for 'men' in certain areas of education, and in hiring for public care work. The women's movement is currently mobilizing to challenge these changes.

Several factors help explain the swing away from the categorical recognition of 'women'. Vollset noted that the trend established in the second Action Plan towards decentralization of responsibility for equality issues would be continued. This can be seen as in part due to the current rise of neoliberal thinking. Beatrice Halsaa (1991b: 2) notes that in Norway, as elsewhere, 'The right-wing critique of the expansion of the public sector, and of the underestimation of individual responsibility, is gaining weight'. Equality issues may be suffering from the fallout accompanying this change.

It is also important to note that those now appointed to handle 'sex equality', even when they are women, are less likely to have a personal commitment to the issue. Halsaa is concerned that civil servants who take up this responsibility have no training for the task. And, in contrast to the late 1970s, many now have no personal ties to the women's movement. Without this background, they are less likely to see 'women' as a legitimate political category and more likely to be influenced in their decision making by their investments in other identity categories.

Finally, it is possible to suggest that the decision of the women's movement to emphasize 'women's' difference/complementarity created an opening for the shift to 'family affairs' which is now displacing the focus on 'women' as a category. We have seen why, strategically, this particular representation of 'women' was made. It certainly made sense given the historical and material conditions in Norway. It also aroused less antagonism than a conflictual representation and even won some men supporters. But when women's groups, as is happening increasingly in Norway and Sweden, wish to demand categorical recogniton for 'women' – not 'carers', not 'mothers' – they meet greater resistance. The Norwegian feminist scholar, Hanne Haavind (interviewed 11 June, 1992), perceptively notes that there is an odd 'discrepancy between the legitimization of a discourse which says we need a woman here (because she is a woman), and disconfirmation of the same argument when she says something about the *claims* of women.' This 'odd discrepancy' takes us to the heart of category politics. When women claim a category status which challenges *'men's'* status and/or the status of those groups men deem to be socially relevant, be these classes or unions or employers, that claim is delegitimized or displaced.

I am not suggesting that Norwegian feminists are paying the price for 'taking the risk of "essentialism"'. Rather it is important to draw attention to the reasons they felt compelled to characterize 'women' *in any particular manner*. This, as I have argued, is because they were located outside political processes and hence became appellants. Those who sit in judgement – who are mostly men – are assumed to represent 'general interests', to stand above 'personal commitments'. Hence, they are not asked to justify their overrepresentation.

One strategy in this situation, which has been recommended throughout, is making 'men' visible as a category and calling them to task for their domination of positions of power, wealth and influence. While this rhetorical reversal in no way guarantees that invocation of the category 'men' will have progressive effects, it serves a useful purpose. Making 'men' visible allows feminists to see that their disputes about the ontological status of 'woman'/'women' are a direct effect of *feeling compelled* to justify their claim to categorical recognition. While at one level it is necessary to engage in category politics, at another level much more is gained from exposing the effects of its practices.

It is significant that it is a Labour Government, *albeit* a minority government, and one headed by a woman, which is initiating the move away from 'women' to gender-neutral positive action. While historically Labour has often taken the lead in introducing 'sex equality' issues and while there appears to be an ideological residue in the dispute over publicly-funded versus at-home care (discussion to follow), more marked is the increasing convergence between the major parties on approaches to take to 'women's' inequality and the question of priority (Skjeie, 1991). Regardless of party 'ideology',[13] there is more concern with economic issues.

Have women mattered?

There is increasing disquiet among some sections of the Norwegian women's movement that talk about 'women's' difference/complementarity is both ambiguous and politically dangerous. The chief concern is that the description contains insufficient content to judge political programmes. It is becoming increasingly clear that women elected to public office do not necessarily agree on political issues of key importance to many women, and that some do not see themselves as representing 'women' at all. Because Norway has led the world in the numbers of women elected to parliament, it provides an interesting test-case for women elsewhere who feel that all that is needed in their own countries to redress 'women's' inequality is a similar increase in women's representation.

Hege Skjeie (1991) has conducted the most comprehensive study of the behaviours of Norwegian women politicians. She has found there is no guarantee that they put 'women' ahead of party loyalty. Rather it depends upon the case in hand. That is, there is agreement on some issues, but 'ideology' continues to cause dispute on others.

In the 1980s women MPs crossed party lines three times. The first of these was to change procedures for calculating pension benefits to include periods of unpaid care work for children. Another was to win government funding to have a certain percentage of qualified women academics promoted to the rank of professor, to remedy their serious underrepresentation. A third, which proved unsuccessful, was to protest the piece of legislation which guaranteed the biological father access to 'his' child/children even if he had had no role in their upbringing (Skjeie, 1991: 247–9).

Increased representation of women within parties has also had some effect on party platforms. Skjeie (1992: 177) points out that those parties with the longest tradition of 'integration politics', referring to the integration of women into party ranks and offices, have the longest tradition of supporting policies, specifically child care and parental leave, to promote 'women's' labour market participation. Meanwhile, the one Norwegian party that has remained male-dominated, the right-wing Progress Party, continues to express the view that programmes to increase 'women's' economic independence do not belong to the field of party politics.

The fact that both Labour and non-socialist governments now include demands for child care and parental leave indicates a degree of convergence in accepting that many women will now engage in paid labour. But this does not necessarily mean agreement about the form that labour will take. Child care can be seen, for example, as a means of facilitating the sharing of paid labour *between* spouses, with the woman working part-time, not necessarily increasing *'women's'* full-time labour force participation. So too parental leave can be seen as a form of funding for maternal care, since parents are, in effect, paid to stay home and mothers are most likely to use the benefit. This means that even those who wish to maintain traditional sex roles can accommodate reforms which are most often associated with more progressive political visions. I have drawn attention to this point at several places in the text (see Chapters 3 and 5).

According to Skjeie (1991: 243), the fact that 'ideology' continues to exert some influence on this issue shows up, however, when parties are forced into an either/or choice. For example, there is consensus that care work needs to be done, and that public funding is essential. But currently there is a dispute over the form this funding should take. As in Sweden, socialists tend to support a substantial increase of state subsidies to child care centres, while non-socialists favour a substantial cash transfer to families with preschool children, which the parents may decide how to use. The fear of socialists and of many feminists, discussed earlier, is that a lump-sum payment may be used in ways which reinforce 'women's' domestic role. This division reflects a modified version of the old ideological tension between socialists, who wished to encourage 'women's' labour force participation, and non-socialists, who continued to support a traditional nuclear family with the man the breadwinner and the wife at home.

The important point here is that *women* in political parties are dividing along traditional party lines on the issue. So, while women politicians may agree about the need for a focus on 'care' and 'care work', the content of these categories remains abstract. When they are given content, a division arises between those who stress the reconciliation of care and career, and those who stress care within the family.

Do women then make a 'difference'? It seems that they have been influential in raising the profile of 'women' as a political category and in drawing attention to the importance of 'caring work', though there is little agreement about how this is to be best performed. In the current debate over whether it is ever appropriate to talk about a notion of 'women's interests', the Norwegian example seems to confirm Anna Jónasdóttir's (1991: 156 ff.) view that women can be mobilized behind a belief that it is vital to increase their representation, even if they do not agree on a whole range of other issues. However, the basis of that mobilization will reflect particular historical and cultural conditions.

In Norway, where many women continue to lead lives dominated by domestic responsibilities, they have rallied beneath a banner which places value on those responsibilities. They join together on issues which concern the arrangements around childbirth and child care. They have campaigned for equal pay and have expressed a keen desire for some form of economic independence, while *at the same time* 'sticking to the needs of caring' (Halsaa, 1991b: 41). Some Norwegian feminists, however, are dissatisfied with the performance of their women politicians, and are reframing their rhetoric accordingly. But the shift is neither total nor unambiguous. For many, there lingers an attachment to the notion of 'women's' distinctive caring virtues. This could be because they recognize that their claim to political legitimacy depends upon community attitudes which position 'women' as 'different'. It is interesting in this context to note that for some years Norwegian feminists have adopted the practice of retaining the word 'women's' for national publications and for the 'Women's' University, while using the term 'feminist' for overseas consumption (see note 5, this chapter).

Berit Ås (1988: 30) is now talking about the need to replace the concept of 'female culture' with the idea of a 'feminist culture'. She wants a broader and more political agenda, but the traits she highlights, including a commitment to 'peace with the earth', and basic human characteristics like 'solidarity, beauty, and creativity', are often associated with traditional notions of 'womanly' virtue.

Another leading feminist scholar, Beatrice Halsaa (1988), has written an article describing a 'Feminist Utopia'. Here she distinguishes between feminism and what she calls 'womanism' which accepts that there are two distinctive kinds of individuals, male and female. Feminism, as distinct from womanism, argues that society is 'not only based on the power of men over women (patriarchy); but human relationships are in general characterized by subordination, competition and violence.' Interestingly, however, Halsaa founds her feminist utopia on a 'female standard' based upon 'the rearing and caring of children, about preparing for birth and death, about structuring society around concrete life processes.' Her vision then continues to capture parts of the Norwegian difference/complementarity agenda. In one place she states explicitly, a feminist utopia 'is based on the *value of differences* between men and women.'

And Tove Stang Dahl (1989: 12) now refers to a 'women's – or feminist – perspective', implying that these are one and the same thing. But Stang Dahl calls for a re-evaluation of domestic labour rather than integrating 'women' into the labour force, because 'this [meaning the re-evaluation of domestic labour] is what the women want.' She also asserts that 'women will never participate "on a par with men" in waged labour and public affairs since we necessarily must – and gladly – give much of our energy to the work of birth.' She feels that this analysis best reflects the interests of Norwegian women.

The interesting point here is that a prominent figure like Stang Dahl can endorse the alternative of recognizing domestic labour *over* integrating 'women' into the labour force. This is an alternative feminists in most industrialized countries shy away from, due to the fear that it would entrench traditional sex roles. The specific historical and material conditions in Norway, including the lag in industrialization, the lower proportion of women in paid labour, and the continuing obligation for most women to combine paid and unpaid labour, are responsible for Stang Dahl's willingness to pursue this alternative.

In personal correspondence (30 October, 1992) Hege Skjeie makes the important point that this question – 'how to organize/finance the public concern for women's care work/tasks' – is indeed the hard question when we discuss 'women's interests'. Feminists in every country face the dilemma of attempting either to make social institutions more responsive to people's need and desire to spend more time with family or loved ones, or pursuing some form of recognition for those who undertake this responsibility, who are in the vast majority women. Some in Norway have chosen the second option, capitalizing on the association between 'women' and caring work – 'women's' 'difference'.

The dispute over whether women activists ought or ought not to use a rhetoric of difference/complementarity reflects the irreconcilable conflicts in most women's lives given current paid work and family care arrangements. The rhetoric can in some circumstances draw attention to those conflicts; it is less clear if it can be useful in resolving them. As Trudie Knijn (1994: 204, 192) says, the problem is that women are 'supposed to resolve the contradiction between care and autonomy themselves, which is an insurmountable task.' Moreover, the dilemma is represented as one of individual choice between motherhood and career, or some combination of both, without any acknowledgement of the social conditions that limit choice (see Bacchi, 1990).

Conclusion

The case of Norway may provide a lesson here. Basing political claims on representations of the archetypical 'woman' has brought some political victories. However, it has also provided an opening for the creation of a refashioned political category, 'family'. This in turn has made it possible to argue that 'men' have 'rights' to the 'families' to which they claim they have been denied access. Not only is the focus on 'women' lost, but 'men' are situated as the ones 'disadvantaged' by 'women's' claims. We have seen this pattern emerging in each of the countries studied. Norway provides only the clearest example of how this can happen.

To intervene in these discourses, an analysis such as this suggests that feminists keep an eye on the particular ways in which category politics is played out in different locales. We need to be able to see the shifts in positionings which take place in particular settings, and how these are achieved. And, we need to retain flexibility to redefine the interests at stake, and to reposition 'men' and 'women' accordingly.

Notes

1 In 1960 Sweden and Finland had an overall labour force participation rate for married women of 23.3 per cent and 25.9 per cent respectively, compared to 9.5 per cent in

Norway. By 1970, including all married women who worked at least 1000 hours per year, the employment rate in Norway was 22 per cent, compared to 38 per cent in Sweden and 53 per cent in Finland. By 1978 the overall participation rates of women aged 15 to 74 were 53.2 per cent in Finland, 60.7 per cent in Sweden, and 51.9 per cent in Norway (Bjoru and Skrede, 1980).

2 As of 1989, of all children under 7 years of age, only 34 per cent were in child care centres. Only 6 per cent of the children under 2 years were in such institutions. A government report in that year concluded that a major barrier to women entering paid labour 'is the lack of kindergartens and other child-care assistance' (Equal Status Council, 1990: 11).

3 It should be noted that this does not mean that 'class' arguments will not be marshalled against 'women' in some strategic contests. As Elizabeth Fürst explained, in her current campaign to point out the gender bias in academic appointments, one critic emphasized the need to increase the representation of 'working-class men', not 'bourgeois women'. Seminar at the Women's Centre for Research, University of Oslo, 22 June, 1992.

4 All the Scandinavian countries have high female representation in parliament compared to most other Western countries. In Norway, Sweden and Finland, the proportion of women is between 35 and 40 per cent (Brundtland, 1991: 73). For figures on the Netherlands, Canada, Australia and the United States, see Chapter 6, note 12.

5 The journal title should translate as 'News on *Women's* Research', but 'News on *Feminist* Research' is the translation offered by the authors of the pamphlet from which this information is taken. The political reasons for this will be discussed below (Eeg-Henriksen and Schiotz, 1991).

6 There was a conscious decision to create the term 'Ombud' to avoid the clearly gendered 'Ombudsman', again indicating a greater willingness to take on openly the kinds of gender issues the women's movement was raising (Ministry of Consumer Affairs, 1985: 8–9).

7 Article 14 stipulates that 'questions that involve the validity, interpretation or continued existence of a collective wage agreement, shall be brought before the Labour Disputes Court. This court is considered to have exclusive competence with regard to such agreements' (Halvorsen, 1989: 10).

8 Statistics show that women in the same trade or industry, and on the same level of work, still earn an average of 15 per cent less than their male colleagues (Ministry of Children and Family Affairs, 1991: 9).

9 Interview in Oslo with Live Hov, Equal Status Representative, University of Oslo, 9 June, 1992.

10 Norway appointed the first Commissioner for Children in 1981.

11 In Sweden, as noted in Chapter 6, one month of parental leave is now set aside for fathers.

12 Interview in Oslo with Sigrun Hoel, staff member of the Equal Status Ombud's Office, 4 June, 1992.

13 Quotation marks are used here to indicate the way in which this study problematizes 'ideology' by highlighting that ideological claims often serve as rhetorical devices in political contests.

Conclusion: No Final Curtain

Two concerns are central to this book: first, the importance of recognizing the political uses of categories; second, the impact of these usages on feminist debates. I have concentrated on exposing the effects of conceptual categories, such as 'equal opportunity', 'sexual equality', 'positive discrimination' and 'positive action' in the disputes around affirmative action, and the roles of identity categories, in particular 'women', in these and surrounding discourses. I have highlighted how these have been invoked in a variety of settings to undermine challenges to existing relations of domination.

Context is crucial to these stories. Though there are important similarities in the narratives, it would have been impossible to predict in advance the exact shifts and subtle nuances in the deployments of categories which we have observed. History and historical contingency, due to things like the impact of separatist stirrings in Canada, the history of slavery in the United States, and 'pillarization' in the Netherlands, produce a rich complexity in the configuration of category politics.

Within this complexity I have uncovered patterns, and there are doubtless others which have gone unremarked. These patterns, while not unsurprising, were certainly not expected. My excursions to countries like Sweden and Norway were planned in the fond hope that somewhere I would discover a place where women mattered. I found places, like Australia and Norway, which *said* that 'women' mattered. In Australia federal affirmative action legislation targets 'women', but this legislation provides the rationale for doing little about women in other contexts. In Norway quotas have increased the representation of women in parliament and political parties, but positive action will soon be extended to 'men'.

I found other places, like Sweden, where 'mothers' mattered to an extent. Because of the desire to increase women's workforce participation while maintaining a growing population, generous parental leave provisions are in place and public child care is well funded. However, women still perform the bulk of domestic labour, the workforce is highly sex segregated, and certain issues, such as sexual harassment and domestic violence, have had difficulty finding their way onto the political agenda.

I found no place which gave due weight to the kinds of concerns the women's movement has been raising for decades – the need to address the domestic division of labour, the need to look to the differences among women, the need to recognize the combination of factors which lock women into positions of subordination. I discovered instead a tokenism and manipulation of issue representation which was disconcerting.

Similarly, with affirmative action, I went looking for exemplars. I deliberately sought out countries with worldwide reputations as leaders in the design and implementation of affirmative action programmes. I discovered instead a disturbing commonality in themes – a general acceptance that only 'soft' affirmative action was permissible; that if 'strong' affirmative action was agreed upon, it had to be gender neutral; a positioning of affirmative action recipients as 'needy' and receiving beneficence; a transmutation of affirmative action into human resource management; and a growing emphasis on ingroups, especially on 'white men', as 'disadvantaged' by affirmative action policies.

The message I kept hearing was depressingly repetitive. 'Women' did not matter. Political agendas were determined for other purposes. These were predominantly economic in nature. No simple capitalist conspiracy here though. An economic agenda could mean, as in Sweden, an attempted *modus vivendi* between employers and unions. An economic agenda could mean, as in the Netherlands, ensuring sufficient resources to fund welfare measures.

In these economic agendas, a single figure loomed large – the self-sufficient individual. The ubiquity of the model of the self-sufficient individual lies behind the common characterization of affirmative action as 'beneficence' to the 'needy'. In this model equal opportunity works; all comers have a 'fair go' on a 'level playing field'. Those who fail to 'measure up' may receive a species of charity but stronger 'intervention' is condemned as unfair since it disrupts unduly the rules of the game. This self-sufficient individual lives 'his' life at home uninterrupted, and in the workforce unimpeded. Val Plumwood (1995: 107) identifies this unifying subject as the 'Man of Property' whose perspective connects these areas – the so-called 'private' economy and the private household or domestic sphere – in terms of his interest in protecting them both from democratizing political arrangements.

The dilemmas facing women who aspire to become like this self-sufficient individual confirm his gender as male. The most significant discursive transformation I discovered over the past 20 years (longer in Sweden) in all the countries examined was the 'creation' of 'women' as 'equally' self-sufficient. Of course, due to a range of indicators – wages, positioning in the labour market, sex segregation of the labour force – this transformation is often described as 'incomplete'. Other indicators, however, especially the rigidity of the sexual divison of domestic labour, suggest that this transformation will remain incomplete and discursive.

Examining the construction and deployment of categories in affirmative action debates exposes some of the discursive shifts which have led to the dominance of current understandings. It allows us to see how terms are devised and meanings imputed to produce certain political effects. The implications of this insight are manifold. Here I reflect upon three of these: the need to expose the political uses of constructed conceptual and identity categories, to be wary of the defensive posture, and to intervene in category politics with an eye to strategy.

Feminists and other social theorists have an important role to play in exposing the political uses of constructed conceptual and identity categories. We need close studies of these practices in order to identify more clearly the issues at stake and to free us from some of our pre-suppositions about categories. Revealing the ways in which conceptual and identity categories serve as tokens in political contests allows us to see that categories are not real – they serve functions. This realization highlights the role of categorizers.

It is indeed the case that identity involves differentiation, just as categorizing necessarily involves inclusion and exclusion, but not all of us are placed equally in these processes. Categorizing is the preserve of those who dominate our academies, legislatures, media, unions and boardrooms, and these are predominantly white middle-class males.

I have placed particular emphasis upon the importance of the categories created in social and political theory, identifying theorists as political actors. Returning to a point made in Chapter 1, thinking about theory as a verb (see McClure, 1992) usefully shifts the emphasis from a reified product to the producers of theory and raises questions about their motivations in theorizing. It also raises question about the usefulness of the theory produced.

Feminists have displayed increasing scepticism of the terms of analysis employed in much malestream theory. They have pointed in particular to the inappropriateness of dichotomous thinking (see Clough, 1994: 144 and *passim*). The analysis of conceptual categories in this book is lodged within this tradition. It highlights the political uses of dichotomies such as 'equal opportunity'/'equal results', 'public'/'private', 'individualism'/'collectivism'. It also asks what we do when we discover a lack of fit between women's lives and analyses which assume such binaries. One reaction is to see what it is about women which stops them from fitting these categories. Another, and the one I would recommend pursuing, is suggesting that the categories are themselves inadequate. This leads to questions about their origins, the ways they are deployed in political debate, and the political purposes they serve.

I go further to suggest that the scepticism feminists have brought to dichotomies be broadened to include all concepts/categories, including some old standbys such as 'ideology'. I ask that we step back from assumptions about the ways in which ideas work to examine how conceptual categories such as 'social democracy' or 'equal opportunity' are deployed in political discourse and with what effects. Theories and ideologies, I argue, can be invoked instrumentally to achieve particular aims.

A sharpened awareness of the political uses of categories ought to produce reflection upon how one positions one's arguments in relation to the conceptual terrain. I stress in particular the dangers inherent in a defensive posture. This refers to the tendency to modify one's arguments in order to exploit what appear to be discursive openings. We have seen both proponents of affirmative action and advocates for 'women' engaging in this process. To rehearse Connolly (1993: 1), '[For] to adopt without revision the concepts prevailing in a polity is to accept terms of discourse loaded in favor of established practices.' This is so in part because of the subtle ways arguments shift in the process of adaptation. Constituting affirmative action 'beneficence' in order to make it congruent with 'equal opportunity' is an obvious example. Calling 'women' a 'class', a 'minority', or 'nurturers' also opens the door to unintended and adverse positionings while closing the door on particular kinds of claims. As a 'class', economic location is privileged; as a 'minority', 'culture' assumes a hegemonic role; as 'nurturers', appeals to 'family' are facilitated.

Some feminists criticize affirmative action for being assimilationist (see Chapter 2). Dominant understandings of the reform as these appear in this volume clearly strengthen this case. However, the analysis I offer reveals how affirmative action has come to mean simply entrance to existing institutions. I have shown how many reformers sought to give affirmative action legitimacy by fitting it to equal opportunity, a presumed given, and that this had the effect of reshaping the reform agenda – from targeted hiring/promotion to targeted recruiting and training.

Of course, some might argue that targeted hiring/promotion is *more* assimilationist than 'softer' reforms since this is less likely to change the fundamentals of institutional practice. Kathleen Jones (1993) argues convincingly that getting women into authority can never be simply an additive move, however, since what they represent challenges the traditional foundations of authority. Jones, K. (1993: 170) examines the symbolic 'feminine' for new models of decision making, exploring the ways in which what has been characterized as a 'female' emphasis on relationships over rules or abstract rights modifies how authority is constituted.

I would also suggest that opening up for discussion the meaning of merit creates the possibility of challenging assumptions about what makes a person valuable as an employee. As we saw in Chapter 2, some feminists accept that affirmative action candidates must be meritorious by current standards; but others have insisted that we rethink the grounds on which we assign rank and reward. These questions, to quote Clare Burton again, relate to 'the exercise of power at the work place, how jobs are organised and practised, and the fundamental preconditions for the development of alternative arrangements' (1987: 432).

So affirmative action as a reform is itself up for grabs. It can be interpreted in ways which push beyond assimilation. The point is to observe how the marshalling of conceptual categories serves to define a project in a particular way and to challenge them when they work against progressive goals. For the category 'women' I make the point that we can neither eliminate nor ignore it. But instead of agonizing over its abstract content, I think more effort ought to be expended on studying how it is used and challenging uses which undermine feminist objectives.

As an example from the book, feminists ought to challenge the ways in which the separate listing of target groups in antidiscrimination and affirmative action legislation allows multiply-oppressed women to fall through the cracks. This is a practical as well as a theoretical issue, demonstrated by the attempt of the Australian Law Reform Commission (1994: 65–8) to come to terms with exactly this situation. It was suggested that, since there were separate legislative instruments for sex and race discrimination in Australia, provision be made for complaints by one person 'under each head' to be heard together (see also Chapter 3, note 8).

A sensitivity to category politics should reduce anxieties about the content of categories. I began this book discussing the tension I had discovered between some feminist theory and practice around affirmative action, and by implication other policies targeting 'women'. The tension revealed itself as the endorsement by many feminists of affirmative action for 'women', a term which had become suspect in much feminist theory. I would argue that looking at the ways in which 'women' operates in political discourse bypasses this tension. We have no option but to contest uses of a category when it is invoked in ways that undermine feminist goals.

I also suggest that more attention be paid to the consequences of being categorized. A number of authors, and they have been duly acknowledged in the text, have emphasized the importance of drawing attention to those who refuse identification, those who operate behind a mask of anonymity while setting society's rules. Most usefully, Martha Minow (1990) has insisted that we recognize that those of us constituted 'different' are so only to those who have had the power to so constitute us.

Feminists have been more sensitive than most to the repercussions of being 'outside-named'.[1] In fact, it is just this realization which has produced the feminist conundrum referred to at several places in this text – how to work with and through the designation 'woman' or 'women', given its historical associations.

My argument is that we need to focus more attention on the practices which have produced this 'dilemma' and that this exercise is liberating. Once we realize, not that we have little choice but to invoke existing categories, but that all categories – old and new – are up for grabs and that any can be used for or against us, a certain freeing sensation is produced and some agonizing hopefully reduced. Our dilemmas are practical, not ontological. Hence, it is important to remain flexible, to be willing to shift explanation and change definitions when circumstances are propitious.

The reference here to 'our' dilemmas is meant to capture a wide range of activists working for progressive change. As I am aware of the way in which constructed boundaries between groups prevent progressive alliances, I insist that, when 'women' is used with these effects, for example to divert attention from the particular situation of multiply-oppressed women, we need to challenge its usage. My position is not that feminists need simply to campaign for 'women' but that women need *to engage in the politics surrounding uses of the category 'women'*.

I am also sensitive to Toni Williams's (1990) claim that women activists are compelled to shape their arguments in particular ways to conform to legal categories. But I do not agree that this forces us into essentialist claims. Recognizing and asserting the reasons for adopting particular stances means emphasizing the *political* content of the categories we use. This includes 'women'. This kind of argument is, to repeat, not a version of what has been called 'strategic essentialism', which seems to suggest that essences exist. Being aware of category politics produces strategy without essences. An essence by any other name is someone else's category.

Where does this argument lead? What space is left to reclaim and rework 'women' (or 'Blacks', or 'Aborigines', or 'the disabled' for that matter), and 'affirmative action'? A study which emphasizes discourse and representation to my mind must recognize that, in an age of transnational corporations and mass media communication, certain members of our society have more power to disseminate messages than other members, and these messages, as I have discussed them, are narrow and selective. Without doubt the degree to which these representations dominate current understandings is disheartening to those pursuing change.

My hope is that drawing attention to the ways in which this occurs strengthens the case for demanding access to those places where discursive construction and dissemination take place. There are 'understandings' here which need to be contested and they can only be contested from within – universities, parliaments, board rooms, work councils. This, I contend, is the case for affirmative action and the case for 'women'.

Note

1   Jenson and Mahon (1993: 78) discuss the process and effects of 'outside-naming'. The process involves the labelling of 'relatively powerless collectivities' by 'external forces'. Resistance, these authors say, generally takes on a 'wider significance – and empower[s]

the actors involved – only when such resistance includes a claim to a preferred name.' They offer as an example that to become autonomous actors women have had to displace 'other identities, such as wives, mothers, or guardians of the "private" world of hearth and home.' I suggest that recognizing the effects of the politics of 'other-naming' is more important than the assigned names, and that appeals to 'assigned names' can at times be useful.

Bibliography

Abele, Francis (1991) 'The Politics of Fragmentation', in F. Abele (ed.) *How Ottawa Spends: The Politics of Fragmentation 1991–1992*. Ottawa: Carleton University Press.

Abella, Rosalie S. (1984) *Report of the Commission on Equality in Employment*. Ottawa: Supply and Services Canada.

Abella, Rosalie S. (1987) 'Employment Equity – Implications for Industrial Relations', Industrial Relations Centre Reprint Series No. 73, Kingston: Queen's University.

Abella, Rosalie S. (1991) 'Equality and Human Rights in Canada: Coping with the New Isms', *University Affairs*, 22: 21–5.

Acker, Joan (1987) 'Hierarchies, Jobs and Bodies: An Outline for a Theory of Gendered Organizations'. Paper to the American Sociological Association Annual General Meeting, Chicago.

Acker, Joan (1989) *Doing Comparable Worth: Gender, Class and Pay Equity*. Philadelphia: Temple University Press.

Affirmative Action Agency (1992a) *Affirmative Action into the 90s: Discussion Paper*. Canberra: Australian Government Publishing Service.

Affirmative Action Agency (1992b) *Quality and Commitment: The Next Steps. The Final Report of the Effectiveness Review of the Affirmative Action (Equal Employment Opportunity for Women) Act 1986*. Canberra: Australian Government Publishing Service.

Affirmative Action Agency (1994) *Annual Report, 1993–94*. Sydney: Affirmative Action Agency.

Aga, Synnova (1986) 'Women's Attempts to Break Down Sex Barriers in the Labour Market', in Arnlaug Leira (ed.) *Work and Womanhood: Norwegian Studies* (2nd edn). Oslo: Institute for Social Research, Report 8/83.

Agocs, Carol (1986) 'Affirmative Action, Canadian Style: A Reconnaissance', *Canadian Public Policy*, 12(1): 148–62.

Agocs, Carol, Burr, Catherine and Somerset, Felicity (1992) *Employment Equity: Cooperative Strategies for Organizational Change*. Ontario: Prentice-Hall.

Almbladh, Ingrid (1983) *New Proposed Amendments to Sweden's Penal Code Regulations on Sexual Misconduct*. Stockholm: The Swedish Institute.

Altmann, Carol (1995) 'Labor's Policy of Negative Action', *The Advertiser*, 2 September.

Andersen, Bent Rold (1986), 'Rationality and Irrationality of the Nordic Welfare State', in Stephen Graubard (ed.) *Norden: The Passion for Equality*. Oslo: Norwegian University Press. pp. 112–42.

Anderson, Benedict (1983) *Imagined Communities*. London: Verso.

Ås, Berit (1975) 'On Female Culture: an attempt to formulate a theory of women's solidarity and action', *Acta Sociologica*, special issue on Women's Studies, 18(2&3): 142–61.

Ås, Berit (1981) 'A Five-Dimensional Model for Change: Contradictions and Feminist Consciousness', *Women's Studies International Quarterly*, 4(1): 101–14.

Ås, Berit (1986) 'Mobilizing Women for Action', in Aisla Thomson (ed.) *The Decade for Women*. Toronto: Canadian Congress for Learning Opportunities for Women. pp. 177–87.

Ås, Berit (1988) 'Managing visions from invisibility to visibility. Women's impact on the nineties', speech given in the New Church in Amsterdam, Bernardijn ten Zeldam stichting.

Ås, Berit (1991) 'Preference Voting Rules in Norway', unpublished typescript.

Atcheson, M. Elizabeth, Eberts, Mary and Symes, Beth (1983) *Women and Legal Action: Precedents, Resources and Strategies for the Future*. Ottawa: Canadian Advisory Council on the Status of Women.

Bacchi, Carol (1986) 'The Woman Question in South Australia', in Eric Richards (ed.) *The Flinders History of South Australia*. Sydney: Oxford University Press.

Bacchi, Carol (1990) *Same Difference: Feminism and Sexual Difference*. Sydney: Allen & Unwin.

Bacchi, Carol (1991a) 'Survey Examines Staff and Student Attitudes to Affirmative Action', *Lumen: The University of Adelaide Magazine*, 20(2): 8–11.

Bacchi, Carol (1991b) 'Every Man for Himself', *Lumen*, 20(5): 3–7.

Bacchi, Carol (1991c) 'Discrimination and Justice', *Lumen*, 20(6): 3–6.

Bacchi, Carol (1992a) 'Affirmative Action – Is It Really Un-American?', *International Journal of Moral and Social Studies*, 7(1): 19–31.

Bacchi, Carol (1992b) 'Do Women Need Equal Treatment or Different Treatment?', *Australian Journal of Law and Society*, 8: 80–94.

Bacchi, Carol (1993) 'The Brick Wall: Why So Few Women Become Senior Academics', *The Australian Universities' Review*, 36(1): 36–41.

Bacchi, Carol and Marquis, Vicky (1994) 'Women and the Republic: "Rights" and Wrongs', *The Australian Feminist Review*, 19: 93–114.

Backhouse, Constance (1989) 'Roberts *v.* Ontario (Ministry of Health)', *Canadian Human Rights Reporter*. 10: D/6353-D/6375.

Bagguley, Paul, Mark-Lawson, Jane, Shapiro, Dan, Urry, John, Walby, Sylvia and Warde, Alan (1990) *Restructuring: Place, Class and Gender*. London: Sage.

Baines, Beverley (1987) 'Gender and the Meech Lake Committee', *Queen's Quarterly*, 94(4): 807–16.

Baker, Judith (ed.) (1994) *Group Rights*. Toronto: University of Toronto Press.

Bannerji, Himani (ed.) (1993) *Returning the Gaze: Essays on Racism, Feminism and Politics*. Toronto: Sister Vision Press.

Becker, Lawrence (1993) 'Affirmative Action and Faculty Appointments', in Steven M. Cahn (ed.) *Affirmative Action and the University: A Philosophical Inquiry*. Philadelphia: Temple University Press. pp. 93–110.

Begin, Monique (1992) 'The Royal Commission on the Status of Women in Canada: Twenty Years Later', in C. Backhouse and D.H. Flaherty (eds) *Challenging Times: The Women's Movement in Canada and the United States*. Montreal: McGill and Queen's University Press. pp. 21–38.

Benhabib, Seyla (1989) 'Liberal Dialogue Versus a Critical Theory of Discursive Legitimation', in N. Rosenblum (ed.) *Liberalism and the Moral Life*. Cambridge, MA: Harvard University Press. pp. 143–56.

Billig, Michael, Condon, Susan, Edwards, Derek, Gane, Mike, Middleton, David and Radley, Alan (1988) *Ideological Dilemmas: A Social Psychology of Everyday Thinking*. London: Sage.

Bjoru, Kirsten and Skrede, Kari (1980) *A Decade of Transition: Changes in the Labour Force Participation and Family Adjustment of Norwegian Women in the Seventies*. Oslo: Institutt for anvendt sosialvitenskapelig forskning.

Black, Donald (1989) *Sociological Justice*. New York: Oxford University Press.

Black, M. and Coward, R. (1981) 'Linguistics, Social and Sexual Relations: a Review of Dale Spender's Man-Made Language', *Screen Education*, 39: 69–85.

Blackman, Danny (1984) 'Women and the Accord', *Australian Left Review*, 89: 17–23.

Blackmore, Jill and Kenway, Jane (1988) 'Rationalisation, Instrumentalism and Corporate Managerialism: the Implications for Women of the Green Paper in Higher Education', *The Australian Universities' Review*, 31(1): 42–9.

Blishen, Bernard (1986) 'Continuity and Change in Canadian Values', in Alan Cairns and Cynthia Williams (eds) *The Politics of Gender, Ethnicity and Language in Canada*. Toronto: University of Toronto Press. pp. 8–23.

Bloom, Alan (1987) *The Closing of the American Mind*. New York: Simon and Schuster.

Boddendijk, Frank (1992) 'The Netherlands: From Theory to Practice', *Women of Europe*, 70: 77–82.

Bottomley, Gill (1994) 'Living Across Difference: Connecting Gender, Ethnicity, Class and Ageing in Australia', in Norma Grieve and Ailsa Burns (eds) *Australian Women: Contemporary Feminist Thought*. Melbourne: Oxford University Press. pp. 59–69.

Brah, Avtar (1992) 'Difference, Diversity and Differentiation', in James Donald and Ali Rattansi (eds) *'Race', Culture and Difference*. London: Sage. pp. 126–45.

Braidotti, Rosi (1991) 'Introduction: Dutch Treats and Other Strangers', in Joke J. Hermsen and Alkeline Van Lenning (eds) *Sharing the Difference: Feminist Debates in Holland*. London: Routledge. pp. 1–18.

Braithwaite, Valerie (1992) *First Steps: Business Reactions to Implementing the Affirmative Action Act*. A Report to the Affirmative Action Agency. Canberra: Research School of Social Sciences, Australian National University.

Breton, Raymond (1986) 'Multiculturalism and Canadian Nation-Building', in Alan Cairns and Cynthia Williams (eds) *The Politics of Gender, Ethnicity and Language in Canada*. Toronto: University of Toronto Press. pp. 25–56.

Brodsky, Gwen and Day, Shelagh (1989) *Canadian Charter Equality Rights for Women: One Step Forward or Two Steps Back?* Ottawa: Canadian Advisory Council on the Status of Women.

Broom, Dorothy (1992) 'The Body in Question', *Australian Left Review*, April, pp. 10–11.

Brundtland, Gro Harlem (1991) 'Women in Politics – Participation, Power and Results', in Equal Status Council, *Women and Democracy: Participation and Welfare*. Conference in Oslo, November. pp. 70–7.

Bryson, Valerie (1992) *Feminist Political Theory: An Introduction*. London: Macmillan.

Bumiller, Kristin (1988) *The Civil Rights Society: The Social Construction of Victims*. Baltimore, MD: Johns Hopkins University Press.

Burgmann, Meredith (1984) 'Black Sisterhood: Urban Aboriginal Women and Their Relationship to the White Women's Movement', in M. Simms (ed.) *Australian Women and the Political System*. Melbourne: Longman Cheshire. pp. 20–47.

Burstein, Paul (1985) *Discrimination, Jobs, and Politics: The Stuggle for Equal Employment Opportunity in the United States since the New Deal*. Chicago, IL: University of Chicago Press.

Burt, Sandra (1986) 'Women's Issues and the Women's Movement in Canada since 1970' in Alan Cairns and Cynthia Williams (eds) *Constitutionalism, Citizenship and Society in Canada*. Toronto: University of Toronto Press. pp. 115–65.

Burton, Clare (1987) 'Merit and Gender: Organisations and the Mobilisation of Masculine Bias', *Australian Journal of Social Issues*, 22(2): 424–35.

Burton, Clare (1988) *Redefining Merit*, Monograph No. 2, Affirmative Action Agency. Canberra: Australian Government Publishing Service.

Burton, Clare (1991) *The Promise and the Price: The Struggle for Equal Opportunity in Women's Employment*. Sydney: Allen & Unwin.

Burton, Clare (1992) 'Comments on "Managing Diversity"'. Paper presented at National EEO Directions Conference, Perth. Unpublished Paper.

Burton, Clare (1995) *An Equity Review at the University of South Australia*. June. Adelaide: University of South Australia.

Butler, Judith (1990) *Gender Trouble: Feminism and the Subversion of Identity*. New York: Routledge.

Butler, Judith (1992a) 'Contingent Foundations: Feminism and the Question of "Postmodernism"', in Judith Butler and Joan W. Scott (eds) *Feminists Theorize the Political*. New York: Routledge. pp. 3–21.

Butler, Judith (1992b) 'The Body You Want: Liz Kotz Interviews Judith Butler', *Artforum* 31(3): 82–9.

Cahn, Steven M. (ed.) (1993) *Affirmative Action and the University: A Philosophical Inquiry*. Philadelphia, PA: Temple University Press.

Calasanti, Toni and Bailey, Carol (1991) 'Gender Inequality and the Division of Household Labor in the United States and Sweden: A Socialist-Feminist Approach', *Social Problems*, 38(1): 34–53.

Canada (1990) *Beneath the Veneer: Report of the Task Force on Barriers to Women in the Public Service*. Ottawa: Canadian Government Publishing Service.

Canada (1991) *Employment Equity: A Guide for Employers*. Ottawa: Supply and Services Canada.

Canada (1992) *A Matter of Fairness: Report of the Special Committee on the Review of the Employment Equity Act*. Hon. Alan Redway, Chairman. Ottawa: Queen's Printer.

Canada (1993) *Employment Equity: The Federal Contractors Program: 1986–1991*. Ottawa: Minister of Supply and Service.

Canadian Advisory Council on the Status of Women (CAC) (1992) *Re-evaluating Employment Equity*. A Brief to the Special House of Commons Committee on the Review of the Employment Equity Act. Ottawa: CACSW.

Canadian Advisory Council on the Status of Women (CAC) (1993) *Expanding our Horizons: The Work of the Canadian Advisory Council on the Status of Women and its Context*. Ottawa: CACSW.

Canadian Alliance for Visible Minorities (1992) *Revised Brief on Employment Equity Legislation of Ontario*. Ottawa: Canadian Alliance for Visible Minorities.

Canadian Congress for Learning Opportunities for Women (1992) *More than Numbers: A Review of the Employment Equity Act*. Brief No. 92.1 to the Special Committee on the Review of the Employment Equity Act. Toronto: CCLOW.

Canadian Labour Congress (CLC) (1985) *Submission to the Legislative Committee on Bill C-62* (An Act Respecting Employment Equity). Ottawa: CLC.

Canadian Labour Congress (CLC) (1992) *Submission to the Special Committee on the Review of the Employment Equity Act*. Ottawa: CLC.

Carty, Linda (ed.) (1993) *And Still We Rise: Feminist Political Mobilizing in Contemporary Canada*. Toronto: Women's Press.

Carty, Linda and Brand, Dionne (1993) 'Visible Minority Women: A Creation of the Canadian State', in Himani Bannerji (ed.) *Returning the Gaze: Essays on Racism, Feminism and Politics*. Toronto: Sister Vision. pp. 169–81.

Castelli, J. (1990) 'Education Forms Common Bond', *HRMagazine*, June: pp. 46–9.

Caudron, S. (1993) 'Training Can Damage Diversity Efforts', *Personnel Journal*, 72(4): 51–62.

Chandran, E. (1990) *Reservations of O. B. Cs (Mandal Commission Report)*. New Delhi: Cosmos.

Chertos, Cynthia H. (1983) 'Hard Truths for Strategic Change: Dilemmas of Implementing Affirmative Action', *Women's Studies International Forum*, 6(2): 231–41.

Christensen, Anna, Stang Dahl, Tove, Eckhoff, Torstein and Eriksson, Lars D. (1988) 'Methodology of Women's Law', *Working Papers in Women's Law*, No. 27. Oslo: Institute of Women's Law, University of Oslo.

Christofides, L.N. and Swidinsky, R. (1994) 'Wage Determination by Gender and Visible Minority Status: Evidence from the 1989 LMAS', *Canadian Public Policy*, 20(1): 34–51.

Clough, Patricia Ticineto (1994) *Feminist Thought: Desire, Power, and Academic Discourse*. Oxford: Blackwell.

Cockburn, Cynthia (1991) *In the Way of Women: Men's Resistance to Sex Equality in Organizations*. London: Macmillan.

Connolly, William (1993) *The Terms of Political Discourse* (3rd edn). Oxford: Blackwell. (1st edn, 1974.)

Conway, Jill Kerr (December 1993/January 1994) 'Blinky Bill and the Forgotten Females', *The Independent Monthly*, pp. 79–82.

Crenshaw, Kimberle (1988) 'Race, Reform, and Retrenchment: Transformation and Legitimation in Antidiscrimination Law'. *Harvard Law Review*, 101(7): 1331–87.

Crenshaw, Kimberle (1989), 'Demarginalizing the Intersection of Race and Sex: A Black Feminist Critique of Antidiscrimination Doctrine, Feminist Theory and Antiracist Politics', *University of Chicago Legal Forum*, 139–67.

Cuneo, Carl (1990) *Pay Equity: The Labour-Feminist Challenge*. Toronto: Oxford University Press.

Dahl, Hans Fredrik (1986), 'Those Equal Folk', in Stephen Graubard (ed.) *Norden: The Passion for Equality*. Oslo: Norwegian University Press. pp. 97–111.

Dahlberg, Anita (1982) 'The Equality Act', Offprint from Ruth Nielsen (ed.) *Women's Law in Scandinavia*, Copenhagen. Stockholm: Swedish Centre for Working Life.

Dahlberg, Anita (1984) *Summary of the Research Report on the Equality Ombudsman*. Stockholm: Swedish Centre for Working Life.

Davis, Fania E. (1993) *Affirmative Action in the United States and its Application to Women in Employment*. Equality for Women in Employment: An interdepartmental project. Geneva: International Labour Office, Working Paper.

Dawkins, John S. (1987) *Higher Education: a Policy Discussion Paper*. Canberra: Australian Government Publishing Service.

Dawkins, John S. (1988) *Higher Education: a Policy Statement*. Canberra: Australian Government Publishing Service.

de Beauvoir, Simone (1952) *The Second Sex*. New York: Vintage Books.

de Lauretis, Teresa (1989) 'The Essence of the Triangle or, Taking the Risk of Essentialism Seriously: Feminist Theory in Italy, the United States, and Britain', *Differences*, 1(2): 3–37.

de Tocqueville, Alexis (1946) *Democracy in America*. London: Oxford University Press.

Delgado, Richard (1984) 'The Imperial Scholar', *University of Pennsylvania Law Review*, 132(3): 561–78.

Department of Employment, Education and Training (1988) *Australian Women's Employment Strategy*. Canberra: AGPS.

Department of the Parliamentary Library (1995) *Research Note: Women in the Parliaments of the World*, No. 13, Canberra.

Doane, J. and Hodges, D. (1987) *Nostalgia and Sexual Difference*. New York: Methuen.

Docksey, Christopher (1987) 'The European Community and the Promotion of Equality', in Christopher McCrudden (ed.) *Women, Employment and European Equality Law*. London: Eclipse Publications.

Donald, James and Rattansi, Ali (eds) (1992) *'Race', Culture and Difference*. London: Sage.

Dovidio, J., Mann, J. and Gaertner, S. (1989) 'Resistance to Affirmative Action: The Implications of Aversive Racism', in F.A. Blanchard and F.J. Crosby (eds) *Affirmative Action in Perspective*. New York: Springer-Verlag. pp. 83–102.

Duclos, Nitya (1993) 'Disappearing Women: Racial Minority Women in Human Rights Cases', *Canadian Journal of Women and the Law*, 6(1): 25–51.

Dumont, Louis (1972) *Homo Hierarchicus: the Caste System and its Implications*. Trans. Mark Sainsbury. Chicago, IL: University of Chicago Press. First published 1966.

Edelman, Murray (1988) *Constructing the Political Spectacle*. Chicago, IL: University of Chicago Press.

Editorial (1995) *The European Journal of Women's Studies*, 2(4): 419–21.

Eduards, Maud (1989) *Women's Participation and Equal Opportunities Policies*. Stockholm: The Swedish Institute.

Eduards, Maud (1991) 'The Swedish Gender Model: Productivity, Pragmatism, and Paternalism', *West European Politics*, 14(3): 166–81.

Eduards, Maud (1992) 'Against the Rules of the Game: On the Importance of Women's Collective Actions', in Maud Eduards, Inga Elgqvist-Saltzman, Eva Lundgren, Christina Sjoblad, Elisabeth Sundin and Ulla Wikander (eds) *Rethinking Change: Current Feminist Research*. Uppsala: HSFR. 83–104.

Eduards, Maud and Elman, Amy (1994) 'Unprotected by the Swedish Welfare State: A Survey of Battered Women and the Assistance They Received', in Marianne Githens, Pippa Norris and Joni Lovenduski (eds), *Different Roles, Different Voices: Women and Politics in the United States and Europe*. New York: HarperCollins College Publishers. pp. 161–70.

Eduards, Maud, Halsaa, Beatrice and Skjeie, Hege (1985) 'Equality: How equal?', in Elina Haavio-Mannila, Drude Dahlerup, Maud Eduards, Esther Gudmundsdottir, Beatrice

Halsaa, Helga Maria Hernes, Eva Hanninen-Salmelin, Gergthora Sigmundsdottir, Sirkka Sinkknoen and Torild Skard (eds) *Unfinished Democracy: Women in Nordic Politics*. Oxford: Pergamon Press. pp. 134–59.

Edwards, John (1987) *Positive Discrimination, Social Justice and Social Policy: Moral Scrutiny of a Policy Practice*. London: Tavistock.

Eeg-Henriksen, Fride and Schiotz, Aina (1991) 'Women's Studies in Norway: Content and Development during the Last Fifteen Years', in Solveig Bergman (ed.) *Women's Studies and Research in the Nordic Countries*. Uppsala, Sweden: Center for Women Scholars and Research on Women. pp. 35–45.

Ehrenreich, Barbara (1989) *Fear of Falling: The Inner Life of the Middle Class*. New York: Pantheon Books.

Eisenberg, Avigail (1994) 'The Politics of Individual and Group Difference in Canadian Jurisprudence', *Canadian Journal of Political Science*, 27(1): 3–21.

Eisenstein, Hester (1986) 'Feminist Judo: Throwing with the Weight of the State', *Australian Left Review*: 20–2.

Eisenstein, Zillah R. (1988) *The Female Body and the Law*. Berkeley, CA: University of California Press.

Employment and Immigration Canada (1991a) *Consultations in Preparation for the Review of the Employment Equity Act*. Ottawa: Minister of Supply and Services.

Employment and Immigration Canada (1991b) *Employment Equity: A Guide for Employers*. Ottawa: Supply and Services Canada.

Employment and Immigration Canada (1991c) *Employment Equity: Federal Contractors Program: Questions and Answers*. Ottawa: Supply and Services Canada.

Employment and Immigration Canada (1992a) *Annual Report: Employment Equity Act*. Ottawa: Minister of Supply and Services.

Employment and Immigration Canada (1992b) *Employment Equity: The Federal Contractors Program: 1986–1991*. Ottawa: Supply and Services Canada.

Engman, Gerd (1987) *Varannan Damernas (Every Other Seat a Woman)*. Stockholm: SOU.

Engstrom, Lars-Goran (1976) *New Penal Provisions on Sexual Offenses Proposed in Sweden*. Stockholm: The Swedish Institute.

Equal Opportunities Ombudsman (1980) *The Act Concerning Equality Between Women and Men at Work*. Stockholm, Sweden: JänO, The Equal Opportunities Ombudsman.

Equal Status Council (1990) *Women's Status in Norway*. Oslo: Equal Status Council.

Equal Status Council (1991) *Women and Democracy: Participation and Welfare*. Conference in Oslo, November. Oslo: Equal Status Council.

Equal Status Ombud (1989) *The Norwegian Equal Status Act: With Comments*. Revised Edition, Oslo: Equal Status Ombud.

Erneling, Christina (1988) 'Equality Between Women and Men in Sweden – Myth or Reality?' *Canadian Woman Studies*, 9(2): 16–18.

Esping-Andersen, Gøsta (1990) *The Three Worlds of Capitalism*. Cambridge: Polity Press.

European Parliament (1993) Report of the Committee on Women's Rights on the assessment of women's unwaged work. Opinion of the Committee on Social Affairs, Employment and the Working Environment for the Committee on Women's Rights. Conclusions adopted 23 September 1992. Brussels: European Parliament.

Evans, Gareth (1974) 'Benign Discrimination and the Right to Equality', *Federal Law Review*, 6: 26–83.

Eveline, Joan (1993) 'The Politics of Advantage', *Political Theory Newsletter*, 5 (1): 53–67.

Eveline, Joan (1994a) 'The Politics of Advantage', *Australian Feminist Studies*, special issue: *Women and Citizenship*, 19 (Autumn): 129–54.

Eveline, Joan (1994b) 'Normalization, Leading Ladies and Free Men: Affirmative Actions in Sweden and Australia', *Women's Studies International Forum*, special issue: *Women in a Changing Europe*, 17(6): 157–68.

Eveline, Joan (1994c) 'The Politics of Advantage: Managing "Work" and "Care" in Australia and Sweden'. PhD dissertation, Murdoch University, Perth, Western Australia.

Eveline, Joan (1995a) 'Surviving the Belt Shop Blues: Women Miners and Critical Acts', *Australian Journal of Political Science*, 30(1): 91–107.

Eveline, Joan (1995b) 'Care with Compliance: Changing the Worlds of Men'. Administration and Compliance Series, Working Paper No. 25, Research School of Social Sciences, Australian National University.

Eveline, Joan, Booth, Michael and Chadwick, Rona (1989) *A Tiger By the Tail: Report to the Workers on their Interviews on Women in the Workforce at ADM Expressed during 1988 to Joan Eveline and Michael Booth*. Perth, Western Australia: Murdoch University.

Ezorsky, Gertrude (1992) *Racism and Justice: The Case for Affirmative Action*. Cambridge, MA: Harvard University Press.

Fabian, Johannes (1983) *Time and the Other: How Anthropology Makes its Object*. New York: Columbia University Press.

Falk, Jill (1988) 'Women in Swedish Universities – A Major "Minority" of Growing Importance', *Canadian Woman Studies*, 9(2): 19–22.

Findlay, Sue (1988) 'Facing the State: The Politics of the Women's Movement Reconsidered', in Heather J. Maroney and Meg Luxton (eds) *Feminism and Political Economy: Women's Work, Women's Stuggles*. Toronto: Methuen. pp. 31–47.

Findlay, Sue (1990) 'Employment Equity and the Ontario College of Art', *FUSE*, Summer: pp. 25–37.

Findlay, Sue (1993a) 'Democratizing the Local State: Issues for Feminist Practice and the Representation of Women', in Gregory Albo, David Langille and Leo Panitch (eds) *A Different Kind of State? Popular Power and Democratic Administration*. Toronto: Oxford University Press. pp. 155–64.

Findlay, Sue (1993b) 'Problematizing Privilege: Another Look at Representation', in Linda Carty (ed.) *And Still We Rise: Feminist Political Mobilizing in Contemporary Canada*. Toronto: Women's Press. pp. 207–24.

Fish, Stanley (1989) *Doing What Comes Naturally: Change, Rhetoric, and the Practice of Theory in Literary and Legal Studies*. Durham: Duke University Press.

Forbes, Ian (1989) 'Unequal Partners: The Implementation of Equal Opportunities Policies in Western Europe', *Public Administration*, 67: 19–38.

Foster, Victoria (1992) 'Different but Equal?: Dilemmas in the Reform of Girls' Education', *Australian Journal of Education*, 36(1): 53–67.

Fox-Genovese, Elizabeth (1986), 'Women's Rights, Affirmative Action, and the Myth of Individualism', *The George Washington Law Review*, 54(2&3): 338–74.

Francis, L.P. (1993) 'In Defense of Affirmative Action', in S.M. Cahn (ed.) *Affirmative Action and the University: A Philosophical Inquiry*. Philadelphia, PA: Temple University Press.

Friedan, Betty (1965) *The Feminine Mystique*. Harmondsworth: Penguin. First published 1963.

Froman, Ingmarie (1994) 'Sweden for Women', *Current Affairs*, No. 407. Stockholm: Swedish Institute.

Frye, Marilyn (1992) 'Getting it Right', *Signs*, 17(4): 781–93.

Fullinwider, Robert K. (1980) *The Reverse Discrimination Controversy: A Moral and Legal Analysis*. New Jersey: Rowman and Littlefield.

Fürst, E. (1985) *Retratten Från Mansjobben*. Göteborg: Sociologiska Institutionen, Göteborgs Universitet.

Fürst, E. (1988) *I Reserv Och Reservat*. Göteborg: Sociologiska Institutionen. Göteborgs Universitet.

Fuss, Diana (1989) *Essentially Speaking: Feminism, Nature and Difference*. New York: Routledge.

Gallie, W. B. (1955–56) 'Essentially Contested Concepts', *Proceedings of the Aristotelian Society*, 56: 167–98.

Game, Ann (1984) 'Affirmative action: Liberal rationality or challenge to patriarchy?' *Legal Service Bulletin* (Australia), 9(6): 253–7.

Garber, Marjorie (1992) *Vested Interests: Cross Dressing and Cultural Anxiety*. New York: Routledge.

Gatens, Moira (1991) *Feminism and Philosophy: Perspectives on Difference and Equality*. Cambridge: Polity Press.

Gelb, Joyce (1990) *Feminism and Politics: A Comparative Perspective*. Berkeley, CA: University of California Press.

Goetz, Anne Marie (1988) 'Feminism and the Limits of the Claim to Know: Contradictions in the Feminist Approach to Women in Development', *Millennium: Journal of International Studies*, 17(3): 477–96.

Goldman, Alan H. (1976) 'Affirmative Action', *Philosophy and Public Affairs*, 5: 178–95.

Gradin, Anita (1985) *Side by Side: A Report on Equality between Women and Men in Sweden*. Stockholm, Sweden: Gotab.

Graham, Dee L.R., Rawlings, Edna and Rimini, Nelly (1988) 'Survivors of Terror: Battered Women, Hostages, and the Stockholm Syndrome', in Kersti Yllo and Michele Bogard (eds) *Feminist Perspectives on Wife* Abuse. Newbury Park, CA: Sage. pp. 217–33.

Graubard, Stephen (ed.) (1986) *Norden: The Passion for Equality*. Oslo: Norwegian University Press.

Groll, Lennart (1980) *Freedom and Self-discipline of the Swedish Press*. Stockholm: The Swedish Institute.

Grotenhuis, Saskia (1989) 'Women's Studies in the Netherlands: A Successful Institutionalization?' *Feminist Studies*, 15(3): 530–42.

Gunew, Sneja and Yeatman, Anna (1993) *Feminism and the Politics of Difference*. Sydney: Allen & Unwin.

Gustafsson, B. and Uusitalo, H. (1988) 'The Welfare State and Poverty in Finland and Sweden from the Mid-1960s to the Mid-1980s', *Review of Income and Wealth*, 36(3): 249–66.

Gustafsson, Siv (1983) 'Equal Opportunity Policies in Sweden', in M. Schmid (ed.) *Discrimination and Equalization in Selected Countries*. Berlin: Wissenschaftszentrum.

Hacker, Andrew (1992) 'The New Civil War', *New York Review of Books*, 23 April: 30–3.

Hacker, Helen (1951) 'Women as a Minority Group', *Social Forces*, 30: 60–9.

Hagman, Ninni (1990) 'If Half of Them Were Women'. Paper presented to a Conference on Equal Advances in Education Management, Vienna. Unpublished paper.

Halsaa, Beatrice (1988) 'A Feminist Utopia', *Scandinavian Political Studies*, 11(4): 323–36.

Halsaa, Beatrice (1991a) 'The Women's Movement in Norway', in Equal Status Council, *Women and Democracy: Participation and Welfare*. Conference in Oslo, November. pp. 39–47. Oslo: Equal Status Council.

Halsaa, Beatrice (1991b) 'Policies and Strategies on Women in Norway: the Role of Women's Organizations, Political Parties, The Government'. Revised version of paper presented at the Workshop on 'Policies and Strategies related to Women's Issues', Lima, Peru 23–28 Sept. 1989. Lillehammer: Oppland College.

Halvorsen, Marit (1989) *Sex and Salary: A Study of the Equal Pay Provision of the Norwegian Equal Rights Act*. Copenhagen: Centre for Samfundsvidenskabelig.

Harding, Sandra (1986) *The Science Question in Feminism*. Ithaca, NY and London: Cornell University Press.

Harris, Catherine Rossi (1994) 'Achieving High Quality Affirmative Action Programmes'. Paper delivered at the 'Women in the Workplace: the Economic Imperative Conference', 17 October. Sydney. Unpublished paper.

Harvard Law Review (1989) 'ReThinking Weber: The Business Response to Affirmative Action', 102(3): 658–71.

Harvey, Edward B. and Blakely, John H. (1993), 'Employment Equity Goal Setting and External Availability Data', *Social Indicators Research*, 28: 245–66.

Heins, Marjorie (1987) *Cutting the Mustard: Affirmative Action and the Nature of Excellence*. Boston, MA and London: Faber and Faber.

Held, David (1991) *Political Theory Today*. Cambridge: Polity Press.

Hellum, Anne (ed.) (1992) *Birth Law*. Oslo: Norwegian University Press.

Henriques, J., Hollway, W., Unwin, C., Venn, C. and Walkerdine, V. (eds) (1984) *Changing the Subject: Psychology, Social Regulation and Subjectivity*. London: Methuen.

Herman, Didi (1994) *Rights of Passage: Struggles for Lesbian and Gay Legal Equality*. Toronto: University of Toronto Press.

Hindess, Barry (1990) 'Political Equality and Social Policy', *Thesis Eleven*, 25: 114–21.

Hirdman, Yvonne (1987) *The Swedish State and the Gender System: A Theoretical and Empirical Sketch*. The Study of Power and Democracy in Sweden, Report No. 9. Uppsala, Sweden.

Hirdman, Yvonne (1990) *The Gender System: Theoretical Reflections on the Social Subordination of Women*. The Study of Power and Democracy in Sweden, Report No. 40. Uppsala, Sweden.

Hirst, Paul (1990) *Representative Democracy and its Limits*. Cambridge: Polity Press.

Hoagland, Sarah L. (1988) *Lesbian Ethics: Toward New Value*. Palo Alto, CA: Institute of Lesbian Studies.

Holgate, Alina and Karen Milgrom (1985) *She Works Hard for the Money . . . Equal Pay for Women*. Melbourne: Women's Legal Resources Group.

Holtmaat, Riki (1991) 'Flexible Labour and Economic Independence of Women', unpublished paper. Faculty of Law, University of Leiden, The Netherlands.

Holtmaat, Riki (1992) 'To Care for a Right: the analysis of the political-legal discourse on social assistance'. English summary of PhD dissertation, University of Leiden.

Howe, R. Brian (1991) 'The Evolution of Human Rights Policy in Ontario', *Canadian Journal of Political Science/Revue Canadienne de Science Politique*, 24(4): 783–802.

Huggins, Jackie (1994) 'A Contemporary View of Aboriginal Women's Relationship to the White Women's Movement', in N. Grieve and A. Burns (eds) *Australian Women: Contemporary Feminist Thought*. Melbourne: Oxford University Press.

Irigaray, Luce (1985) *The Sex Which Is Not One*. New York: Cornell University Press.

Iyer, Nitya (1993) 'Categorical Denials: Equality Rights and the Shaping of Social Identity', *Queen's Law Journal*, 19: 179–207.

Jackson, Bailey W., LaFasto, Frank, Schultz, Henry G. and Kelly, Don (1992) 'Introduction: Diversity, an Old Issue with a New Face', *Human Resource Management*, 31(1&2): 21–34.

Jackson, Peter and Penrose, Jan (eds) (1993) *Constructions of Race, Place and Nation*. London: UCL Press.

Jay, Nancy (1981) 'Gender and Dichotomy', *Feminist Studies*, 7(1): 38–56.

Jenson, Jane (1991), 'Citizenship and Equity: Variations across Time and in Space', in Janet Hiebert (ed.) *Political Ethics: A Canadian Perspective*, Vol. 12. Toronto: Dundurn Press. pp. 195–228.

Jenson, Jane and Rianne Mahon (1993) 'Representing Solidarity: Class, Gender and the Crisis in Social-Democratic Sweden', *New Left Review*, 201: 76–100.

Johnson, Carol (1990) 'Whose Consensus? Women and the ALP', *Arena*, 93: 85–104.

Johnson, Carol (1992) 'Other Times: Thatcher, Hawke, Keating and the Politics of Identity', Annual Conference of the Australasian Political Studies Association, Australian National University, October; forthcoming in Geoff Stokes (ed.) *The Politics of Identity in Australia*. NSW: University of NSW.

Johnson, Carol (1993a) 'Fightback and Masculine Identity: A Postscript on the 1993 Election', *Australian Feminist Studies*, 17: 81–92.

Johnson, Carol (1993b) 'Shaping the Future: Women and Australian Political Discourse'. Paper presented to the Annual Conference of the Australasian Political Studies Association, Monash, 29 September–1 October. Forthcoming (1996) in Barbara Sullivan and Gillian Whitehouse (eds) *Governing Gender: Sex, Politics and Citizenship in the 1990s*. Randwick: University of New South Wales Press.

Johnson, Carol (1994) 'Women and Economic Citizenship'. Paper presented to the Women, Power and Politics Conference, Adelaide, 8–11 October, 1994. Published (1995) with some modifications in *Just Policy*, 2: 11–16.

Johnson, Roberta Ann (1990) 'Affirmative Action Policy in the United States: its impact on women', *Policy and Politics*, 18(2): 77–90.

Jónasdóttir, Anna (1991) *Love, Power, and Political Interests*. Sweden: Örebro Studies, No. 7. Örebro, Sweden: University of Örebro.

Jones, Alison (1993) 'Girls' School Achievement', Keynote address to Education Review

Office National Conference, Auckland, 14 December. Unpublished paper. Education Faculty, University of Auckland.

Jones, Kathleen (1990) 'Citizenship in a Woman-Friendly Polity', *Signs*, 15: 781–812.

Jones, Kathleen (1993) *Compassionate Authority: Democracy and the Representation of Women*. New York: Routledge.

Junor, A., Barlow, K. and Patterson, M. (1993) *Service Productivity: Part-time Women Workers and the Finance Sector Workplace*. Canberra: Equal Pay Unit, Commonwealth Department of Industrial Relations, Equal Pay Research Series, No. 5.

Kagod, S.K. (1991) *A Workshop for Managing Diversity in the Workplace*. San Diego, CA: Pfeiffer.

Kaplan, Gisela (1992) *Contemporary Western European Feminism*. London: Allen & Unwin. pp. 149–78.

Kenway, Jane (1989) 'Yes Minister – But . . .! Women, Research and Higher Education – Before and After Dawkins', in A. Junor and J. O'Brien (eds) *The Reshaping of Australian Higher Education, 1988–1989*. Sydney: Sydney College of Advanced Education. pp. 123–35.

Kenway, Jane and Blackmore, Jill (1988) 'Gender and the Green Paper: Privatisation and Equity', *The Australian Universities' Review*, 31(1): 49–56.

King, Deborah K. (1989) 'Multiple Jeopardy, Multiple Consciousness: The Context of a Black Feminist Ideology', in Micheline R. Malson, Jean F. O'Barr, Sarah Westphal-Wihl and Mary Wyer (eds) *Feminist Theory in Practice and Process*. Chicago, IL: University of Chicago Press. pp. 76–105.

Kingdom, Elizabeth (1991) *What's Wrong with Rights? Problems for Feminist Politics of Law*. Edinburgh: Edinburgh University Press.

Kissman, Kris (1991) 'Women Caregivers, Women Wage Earners: Social Policy Perspectives in Norway', *Women's Studies International Forum*, 14(3): 193–9.

Kluegel, J. (1985) 'If There Isn't a Problem, You Don't Need a Solution', *American Behavioral Scientist*, 28(6): 761–84.

Kluegel, J. and Smith, E. (1983) 'Affirmative Action Attitudes: Effects of Self-Interest, Racial Effect, and Stratification Beliefs on Whites' Views', *Social Forces*, 61(3): 797–823.

Knijn, Trudie (1994) 'Social Dilemmas in Images of Motherhood in the Netherlands', *The European Journal of Women's Studies*, 1(2): 183–206.

Knopff, Rainer (1989) *Human Rights and Social Technology: The New War on Discrimination*. Ottawa: Carleton University Press.

Kome, Penney (1983) *The Taking of Twenty-Eight: Women Challenge the Constitution*. Toronto: The Women's Press.

Kramar, R. (1987) 'Affirmative Action: A Challenge to Australian Employers and Trade Unions', *The Journal of Industrial Relations*, 169–89.

Kukathas, Chandran (1992) 'Are There Any Cultural Rights?' *Political Theory*, 20(1): 105–39.

Kymlicka, Will (1989) *Liberalism, Community, and Culture*. Oxford: Clarendon Press.

Kymlicka, Will (1992) 'The Rights of Minority Cultures', *Political Theory*, 20(1): 140–6.

Lacey, Nicola (1987) 'Legislation against Sex Discrimination: Questions from a Feminist Perspective', *Journal of Law and Society*, 14(4): 411–21.

LaChapelle, Caroline (1982) 'Beyond Barriers: Native Women and the Women's Movement', in M. Fitzgerald, C. Guberman and M. Wolfe (eds) *Still Ain't Satisfied*. Toronto: The Women's Press. pp. 257–64.

Lake, Marilyn (1986) 'The Politics of Respectability: Identifying the Masculinist Context', *Historical Studies*, 22: 116–31.

Lakeman, Enid (1982) *Power to Elect: The Case for Proportional Representation*. London: Heinemann.

Lakoff, George (1987) *Women, Fire, and Dangerous Things: What Categories Reveal About the Mind*. Chicago, IL and London: University of Chicago Press.

LaRue, Linda (1976) 'The Black Movement and Women's Liberation', in Sue Cox (ed.) *Female Psychology: The Emerging Self*. Chicago, IL: Science Research Association. pp. 216–25.

Law Reform Commission (1994) *Equality Before the Law: Justice for Women*. Report No. 69, Part I. Sydney: Commonwealth of Australia.

Leck, Joanne and Saunders, David (1992) 'Hiring Women: The Effects of Canada's Employment Equity Act', *Canadian Public Policy*, 18(2): 203–20.

Legge, K. (1995) 'Boys will be boys', *The Weekend Australian Magazine*, 11–12 March: 19–21.

Leira, Arnlaug (ed.) (1986) *Work and Womanhood: Norwegian Studies* (2nd edn). Oslo: Institute for Social Research, Report 8/83.

Leira, Arnlaug (1989) *Models of Motherhood: Welfare State Policies and Everyday Practices: The Scandinavian Experience*. Oslo: Institute for Social Research.

Leon, Renee (1993). 'W(h)ither Special Measures? How Affirmative Action for Women Can Survive Sex Discrimination Legislation', *The Australian Feminist Law Journal*, 1: 89–114.

Lerner, Melvin (1980) *The Belief in a Just World: A Fundamental Delusion*. New York: Plenum Press.

Lester, Richard A. (1974) *Antibias Regulation of Universities: Faculty Problems and Their Solutions*. A Report Prepared for The Carnegie Commission on Higher Education. New York: McGraw-Hill.

Liberal/National (1994) *The Things That Matter: Encouraging, Supporting and Protecting the Things that Matter to the Australian People*. Canberra: Liberal/National.

Lie, Suzanne Stiver and O'Leary, Virginia (eds) (1990) *Storming the Tower: Women in the Academic World*. London: Kogan Page.

Linner, Birgitta (1967) *Sex and Society in Sweden*. New York: Pantheon.

Lister, Ruth (1990) 'Women, Economic Dependency and Citizenship', *Journal of Social Policy*, 19(4): 445–67.

Livingston, John (1979) *Fair Game: Inequality and Affirmative Action*. San Francisco, CA: W.H. Freeman.

Lloyd, Genevieve (1984) *The Man of Reason*. London: Methuen.

Lukes, Steven (1991) 'Equality and Liberty – Must they Conflict?', in David Held (ed.) *Political Theory Today*. Cambridge: Polity Press.

Lynch, Frederick (1989) *Invisible Victims: White Males and the Crisis of Affirmative Action*. New York: Greenwood Press.

Mahoney, Kathleen (1993) 'International Strategies to Implement Equality Rights for Women: Overcoming Gender Bias in the Courts', *The Australian Feminist Law Journal*, 1: 115–38.

Malveaux, Julianne (1991) 'Why Are the Black Conservatives All Men?' *Ms. Magazine*, March/April, pp. 60–61.

Marshall, T.H. (1950) *Citizenship and Social Class and Other Essays*. Cambridge: Cambridge University Press.

Maslen, Geoff (1995) 'Gender roles swapped', *Campus Review*, 5(2): 1–2.

McClure, Kristie (1992) 'The Issue of Foundations: Scientized Politics, Politicized Science, and Feminist Critical Practice', in Judith Butler and Joan Scott (eds) *Feminists Theorize the Political*. New York: Routledge. pp. 341–68.

McCrudden, C., Smith, D.J. and Brown, C. (1991) 'Groups versus Individuals: the Ambiguity behind the Race Relations Act', *Policy Studies*, 12(2): 26–35.

McDermott, Patricia (1992) 'Employment Equity and Pay Equity: And Never the Twain Shall Meet?', *Canadian Woman Studies/Les Cahiers de la Femme*, 12: 24–7.

Meehan, Elizabeth (1992) 'European Community Policies on Sex Equality: A Bibliographic Essay', *Women's Studies International Forum*, 15(1): 57–64.

Meekosha, Helen and Pettman, Jan (1991) 'Beyond Category Politics', *Hecate*, 17(2): 75–92.

Middendorp, C. P. (1991) *Ideology in Dutch Politics: The Democratic System Reconsidered 1970–1985*. Assen/Maastricht: Van Gorcum.

Mill, John Stuart (1983) *The Subjection of Women*. London: Virago.

Ministry of Children and Family Affairs (1991) *The UN Convention on the Elimination of All Forms of Discrimination Against Women, Norway, Third Report (1987–1990)*. Oslo: Ministry of Children and Family Affairs.

Ministry of Consumer Affairs (1985) *The Norwegian Equal Status Act*. Oslo.

Ministry of Cultural Affairs, Recreation and Social Welfare (1980) *Emancipation in the Netherlands*. Prepared for World Conference of the United Nations Decade for Women, Copenhagen, Denmark, July. Rijswijk, The Netherlands: Ministry of Cultural Affairs, Recreation and Social Welfare.

Ministry of Education (1984) *A Way to Equality – Affirmative Action*. Stockholm, Sweden: Ministry of Education.

Ministry of Home Affairs (1989) *Basic Overview of Target Figures*. June. The Hague, The Netherlands: Produced by the Information Centre, Ministry of Home Affairs.

Ministry of Labour (1986) *The Changing Role of the Male*. Summary of a report by the Working Party for the Role of the Male. Stockholm: Ministry of Labour.

Ministry of Public Administration (1990) *Third Periodic Report on the Convention on the Elimination of All Forms of Discrimination Against Women*. Stockholm: Ministry of Public Administration.

Ministry of Social Affairs and Employment (1985) *Design of an Equal Rights Policy Plan*. The Hague, The Netherlands: Ministry of Social Affairs and Employment.

Ministry of Social Affairs and Employment (1989) *Women and the State: Dutch Government Policy for the Advancement of Women*. The Hague, The Netherlands: Ministry of Social Affairs and Employment.

Minow, Martha (1990) *Making All the Difference: Inclusion, Exclusion, and American Law*. Ithaca, NY: Cornell University Press.

Mitchell, Deborah (1991) *Income Transfers in Ten Welfare States. Studies in Cash and Care*. Aldershot: Avebury.

Mitchell, Juliet (1984) 'Women and Equality', in *Women: The Longest Revolution*. London: Virago. pp. 55–97.

Moens, Gabriel (1985) *Affirmative Action: The New Discrimination*. Sydney: CIS (Centre for Independent Studies).

Moens, Gabriel (1989) 'Affirmative Action: Success or Failure?', *Policy*, Autumn: 15–18.

Moore, Henrietta (1988) *Feminism and Anthropology*. Cambridge: Polity Press.

Moreton-Robinson, Aileen (1992) 'Masking Gender and Exalting Race: Indigenous Women and Commonwealth Employment Policies', *Australian Feminist Studies*, 15: 5–10.

Morgan, Nicole (1988) *The Equality Game: Women in the Federal Public Service (1908–1987)*. Ontario: Canadian Advisory Council on the Status of Women.

Morris, Cerise (1980) 'Determination and Thoroughness: The Movement for a Royal Commission on the Status of Women in Canada', *Atlantis*, 5(2): 1–21.

Mossman, Mary Jane (1989) 'Individualism and Community: Family as a Mediating Concept', in Allan C. Hutchinson and Leslie J.M. Green, *Law and the Community: The End of Individualism?* Toronto: Carswell. pp. 205–18.

Mulhall, Stephen (1987) 'The Theoretical Foundations of Liberalism', *European Journal of Sociology*, 28: 269–95.

Myrdal, Gunnar (1946) *An American Dilemma: The Negro Problem and Modern Democracy* (2nd edn). New York: Harper and Brothers. (1st edn, 1944.)

Naffine, Ngaire (1994) 'Possession: Erotic Love in the Law of Rape', *The Modern Law Review*, 57: 10–37.

Nagel, Thomas (1979) *Mortal Questions*. Cambridge: Cambridge University Press.

National Action Committee on the Status of Women (1992a) *Not Another Hundred Years*. NAC Brief to the Parliamentary Committee Reviewing the Employment Equity Act by Judy Rebick and Phebe Poole. Ottawa: NAC.

National Action Committee on the Status of Women (1992b) *Justice Works*. Reponse of the NAC to 'Working Towards Equality', Ontario's Discussion Paper on Employment Equity Legislation. Ottawa: NAC.

National Action Committee on the Status of Women (1992c) 'NAC says No – The Charlottetown Agreement Threatens Equality Rights'. Ottawa: NAC.

National Employment Equity Network (1990) *Results of National Meeting*. Ottawa: NEEN.

National Swedish Board of Education (1977) *Instruction Concerning Interpersonal Relations*. Stockholm: Libutbildningsforlaget.

Newman, Gun (Equal Opportunity Ombudsman) (1990) *Tio ar med Jämställdhetslagen*. Gothenburg, Sweden: Jäm O, The Equal Opportunities Ombudsman.

Ng, Roxana (1990) 'Immigrant Women: The Construction of a Labour Market Category', *Canadian Journal of Women and the Law*, 4(1): 96–112.

Ng, Roxana (1993) 'Sexism, Racism and Canadian Nationalism', in Sneja Gunew and Anna Yeatman (eds) *Feminism and the Politics of Difference*. Sydney: Allen & Unwin. pp. 197–211.

Nielsen, Ruth (1983) *Equality Legislation in a Comparative Perspective – Towards State Feminism?* Copenhagen: Women's Research Centre in Social Science.

Nielsen, Ruth and Halvorsen, Marit (1992) 'Sex Discrimination Between the Nordic Model and European Community Law', in Niklas Bruun (ed.) *The Nordic Labour Relations Model*. Aldershot, Hants.

Niland, C. and Champion, R. (1990) *Equal Employment Opportunity Programs for Immigrants: The Experience of Thirteen Organizations*. Commonwealth of Australia: Bureau of Immigration Research.

Norwegian Research Council for Applied Social Science (1985) *Research to Promote Equal Status and Gender Equality*. Program Memorandum, Oslo: NORAS.

Oakley, Ann (1994) *Scenes Originating in the Garden of Eden*. London: Flamingo.

O'Brien, Mary (1984) 'The Commatization of Women: Patriarchal Fetishism in the Sociology of Education', *Interchange*, 15(2): 43–60.

O'Shane, Pat (1976) 'Is There Any Relevance in the Women's Movement for Aboriginal Women?' *Refractory Girl*, 12: 31–5.

Office of the Status of Women (1988) *A Say, a Choice, a Fair Go: The Government's National Agenda for Women*. Canberra: AGPS.

Okin, Susan Moller (1979) *Women in Western Political Thought*. Princeton, NJ: Princeton University Press.

Okin, Susan Moller (1989) *Justice, Gender and the Family*. New York: Basic Books.

Okin, Susan Moller (1991) 'Gender, the Public and the Private', in David Held (ed.) *Political Theory Today*. Cambridge: Polity Press. pp. 67–90.

Olsen, Frances (1985) 'The Myth of State Intervention in the Family', *University of Michigan Journal of Law Reform*, 18(4): 835–64.

Orford, Anne (1994) 'Liberty, Equality, Pornography: The Bodies of Women and Human Rights Discourse', *The Australian Feminist Law Journal*, 3: 72–102.

Organization for Economic Co-operation and Development (1991) *Shaping Structural Change: The Role of Women*. Report by a high-level group of experts to the Secretary-General. Geneva: OECD.

Outshoorn, Joyce (1987) 'Power as a Political and Theoretical Concept in "Second-Wave" Feminism', in Monique Leyenaar, Kathy Davis, Claudine Helleman, Jantine Oldersma and Dini Vos (eds) *The Gender of Power: A Symposium*. Leiden: Vakgroep Vrouwenstudies FSW. pp. 25–33.

Outshoorn, Joyce (1991) 'Is This What We Wanted? Positive Action as Issue Perversion', in Elizabeth Meehan and Selma Sevenhuijsen (eds) *Equality, Politics, and Gender*. London, Sage. pp. 104–21.

Ozga, Jenny (1987) 'Studying Education Policy through the Lives of the Policy-makers: An attempt to Close the Macro–micro gap', in Stephen Walker and Len Barton (eds) *Changing Policies, Changing Teachers: New Directions of Schooling?* Milton Keyes: Open University Press. pp. 138–50.

Pal, Leslie A. (1993) *Interests of State: The Politics of Language, Multiculturalism, and Feminism in Canada*. Montreal: McGill-Queen's University Press.

Patai, Daphne (1983) 'Beyond Defensiveness: Feminist Research Strategies', *Women's Studies International Forum*, 6(2): 177–89.

Pateman, Carole (1981) 'The Concept of Equity' in P.N. Troy (ed.) *A Just Society? Essays on Equity in Australia*. Sydney: George Allen & Unwin.

Pateman, Carole (1983) 'Feminist Critiques of the Public/Private Distinction', in Stanley Benn and Gerald Gaus (eds) *Private and Public in Social Life*. London: Croom Helm.

Pateman, Carole (1988) *The Sexual Contract*. Cambridge: Polity Press.

Peattie, Lisa and Rein, Martin (1983) *Women's Claims: A Study in Political Economy*. Oxford: Oxford University Press.

Persson, Inga (1990) 'The Third Dimension – Equal Status between Women and Men', in Inga Persson (ed.) *Generating Equality in the Welfare State: The Swedish Experience*. Oslo: Norwegian University Press.

Persson-Tanimura, Inga (1988) *Economic Equality for Swedish Women – Current Situation and Trends*. The Study of Power and Democracy in Sweden, Report No. 27. Uppsala, Sweden.

Peterson, V. Spike (1992) 'Security and Sovereign States: What Is at Stake in Taking Feminism Seriously', in V. Spike Peterson (ed.) *Gendered States: Feminist (Re)Visions of International Relations Theory*. Boulder, CO and London: Lynne Rienner Publications.

Petersson, Olof (1991) *Makt: En Sammanfattning Av Maktutredningen*. Stockholm, Sweden: Allmannaforlaget.

Pettman, Jan (1992a) 'Gendered Knowledges: Aboriginal Women and the Politics of Feminism', in Bain Attwood and John Arnold (eds) *Power, Knowledge and Aborigines*. (A special edition of *Journal of Australian Studies*, 35: 120–31). La Trobe: La Trobe University Press.

Pettman, Jan (1992b) *Living in the Margins: Racism, Sexism and Feminism in Australia*. Sydney: Allen & Unwin.

Phillips, Rhys (1984) 'Equity in the Labour Market: The Potential of Affirmative Action', in Rosalie Abella, *Report of the Royal Commission on Equality in Employment*. Ottawa: Supply and Services Canada.

Phillips, Susan (1991) 'How Ottawa Blends: Shifting Government Relations With Interest Groups', in Francis Abele (ed.) *How Ottawa Spends: The Politics of Fragmentation 1991–1992*. Ottawa: Carleton University Press. pp. 183–227.

Plumwood, Val (1995) 'Feminism, Privacy and Radical Democracy', *Anarchist Studies*, 3: 97–120.

Premfors, R. (1981) 'National Policy Styles and Higher Education in France, Sweden and the UK', *European Journal of Higher Education*, 16(2): 143–262.

Prentice, Alison, Bourne, Paula, Brandt, Gail Cuthbert, Light, Beth, Mitchinson, Wendy and Black, Naomi (1988) *Canadian Women: A History*. Toronto: Harcourt Brace Jovanovich.

Pringle, Rosemary and Watson, Sophie (1992) '"Women's Interests" and the Post-Structuralist State', in Michèle Barrett and Anne Phillips (eds) *Destabilizing Theory: Contemporary Feminist Debates*. Cambridge: Polity Press. pp. 53–73.

Public Service Commission of Canada (1993) *Beyond Perceptions: Towards Managing Diversity*. Ottawa: Public Service Commission of Canada.

Radin, Margaret (1991) 'Affirmative Action Rhetoric', *Social Philosophy & Policy*, 8(2): 130–49.

Rae, Douglas, Yates, Douglas, Hochschild, Jennifer, Morone, Joseph and Fessler, Carol (1981) *Equalities*. Cambridge, MA: Harvard University Press.

Rawls, John (1971) *A Theory of Justice*. Cambridge, MA: Belknap Press of Harvard University Press.

Razack, Sherene (1991) *Canadian Feminism and the Law: The Women's Education and Action Fund and the Pursuit of Equality*. Toronto: Second Story Press.

Razack, Sherene (1994) 'Collective Rights and Women: "The Cold Game of Equality Staring"', in Judith Baker (ed.) *Group Rights*. Toronto: University of Toronto Press.

Rehn, Gosta and Viklund, Birger (1990) *Changes in the Swedish Model*. Stockholm: Arbetslivcentrum.

Riley, Denise (1987) 'Does a Sex Have a History? "Women" and Feminism', *New Formations*, 1: 35–45.

Riley, Denise (1988) *Am I that Name? Feminism and the Category of 'Women' in History*. Houndmills: Macmillan.

Roberts, Barbara (1989) *Smooth Sailing or Storm Warnings? Canadian and Quebec Women's*

Groups on the Meech Lake Accord. Ottawa: Canadian Research Institute for the Advancement of Women.

Ronalds, Chris (1987) *Affirmative Action and Sex Discrimination: A Handbook on Legal Rights for Women*. Sydney: Pluto Press.

Rosenfeld, M. (1991) *Affirmative Action and Justice: A Philosophical and Constitutional Inquiry*. New Haven, CT: Yale University Press.

Ross, Dorothy (1991) *The Origins of American Social Science*. Cambridge: Cambridge University Press.

Ruth, Arne (1986), 'The Second New Nation: The Mythology of Modern Sweden', in Stephen Graubard (ed.) *Norden: The Passion for Equality*. Oslo: Norwegian University Press. pp. 240–82.

Sainsbury, Diane (1988) 'The Scandinavian Model and Women's Interests: The Issues of Universalism and Corporatism', *Scandinavian Political Studies*, 11(4): 337–46.

Sainsbury, Diane (1994) 'Gender and Comparative Analysis: Welfare States, State Theories, and Social Policies', in M. Githens, P. Norris and J. Lovenduski (eds) *Different Roles, Different Voices: Women and Politics in the United States and Europe*. New York: HarperCollins College Publishers. pp. 126–35.

Sandel, Michael (1982) *Liberalism and the Limits of Justice*. Cambridge: Cambridge University Press.

Sanders, Douglas (1991) 'Collective Rights', *Human Rights Quarterly*, 13: 368–86.

Sawer, Marian (ed.) (1985) *Program for Change: Affirmative Action in Australia*. Sydney: Allen & Unwin.

Schor, Naomi (1994) 'Introduction', in Naomi Schor and Elizabeth Weed (eds) *The Essential Difference*. Bloomington, IN: Indiana University Press. pp. vii–xix.

Schultz, Vicki (1992) 'Women "Before" the Law: Judicial Stories about Women, Work, and Sex Segregation on the Job', in Judith Butler and Joan Scott (eds) *Feminists Theorize the Political*. New York: Routledge. pp. 297–338.

Scott, Joan (1992) '"Experience"', in Judith Butler and Joan Scott (eds) *Feminists Theorize the Political*. New York: Routledge. pp. 22–40.

Selbyg, Arne (1989) 'Why Are Women in Power in the Nordic Countries but not in the United States?', *Scandinavian Review*, 77(4): 20–7.

Serdjenian, Evelyne (1994) *Inventory of Positive Action in Europe*. Women of Europe supplements, No. 42. Brussels: European Commission.

Sex Discrimination Act (1984). Canberra: Commonwealth of Australia.

Shaver, Sheila (1993) *Women and the Australian Social Security System: From Difference to Equality*. Social Policy Research Centre Discussion Papers, No. 41. Sydney: University of New South Wales.

Sheehy, Elizabeth A. (1991) 'Feminist Argumentation Before the Supreme Court of Canada in *R. v. Seaboyer; R. v. Gayme*; The Sound of One Hand Clapping,' *Melbourne University Law Review*, 18: 450–68.

Sheppard, Colleen (1993) 'Litigating the Relationship between Equity and Equality'. Study Paper prepared for the Ontario Law Reform Commission.

Sher, George (1975) 'Justifying Reverse Discrimination in Employment', *Philosophy and Public Affairs*, 4(2): 159–70.

Silen, Birgitta (1988) 'Women and Power', *Scandinavian Review*, 76(1): 91–101.

Simms, Glenda (1992) 'Beyond the White Veil', in Constance Backhouse and David H. Flaherty (eds) *Challenging Times: The Women's Movement in Canada and the United States*. Montreal: McGill-Queen's University Press. pp. 180–9.

Simons, Margaret A. (1979) 'Racism and Feminism: A Schism in the Sisterhood', *Feminist Studies*, 5(2): 384–401.

Sinclair, Amanda (1994) *Trials at the Top: Chief Executives Talk About Men, Women and the Australian Executive Culture*. Melbourne: University of Melbourne, The Australian Centre.

Skard, Torild and Haavio-Mannila, Elina (1986) 'Equality Between the Sexes – Myth or

Reality in Norden?', in Stephen Graubard (ed.) *Norden: The Passion for Equality*. Oslo: Norwegian University Press. pp. 143–75.

Skjeie, Hege (1991) 'The Rhetoric of Difference: On Women's Inclusion into Political Elites', *Politics and Society*, 19(2): 233–63.

Skjeie, Hege (1992) 'Ending the Male Political Hegemony: Changes in Party Politics 1970–90', in K. Strom and L. Svaasand (eds) *Challenges to Political Parties*. pp. 144–82.

Slack, Alison T. (1988) 'Female Circumcision: A Critical Appraisal', *Human Rights Quarterly*, 10: 437–86.

Smith, Dorothy (1988) 'Femininity as Discourse', in Leslie G. Roman and Linda K. Christian-Smith (eds) *Becoming Feminine: The Politics of Popular Culture*. London: Falmer Press.

Solomon, C.M. (1991) 'Are White Males Being Left Out?' *Personnel Journal*, November: 88–92.

Soper, Kate (1990) *Troubled Pleasures*. London: Verso.

Sowell, Thomas (1984) *Civil Rights: Rhetoric or Reality?* New York: William Morrow.

Spelman, Elizabeth V. (1988) *Inessential Woman: Problems of Exclusion in Feminist Thought*. Boston, MA: Beacon Press.

Stabel, Ingse (1991) 'The Norwegian Equal Status Act', in Equal Status Council, *Women and Democracy: Participation and Welfare*. Conference in Oslo, November. Oslo: Equal Status Council. pp. 130–5.

Stang Dahl, Tove (1987) *Women's Law. An Introduction to Feminist Jurisprudence*. Oslo: Norwegian University Press.

Stang Dahl, Tove (1989) 'Taking Women as a Starting Point: Building Women's Law', *Working Papers in Women's Law, no. 4*. Oslo: Institute of Women's Law, University of Oslo.

Starr, Paul (1992) 'Civil Reconstruction: What to Do Without Affirmative Action', *The American Prospect*, 7–14.

Stasiulis, Daiva (1987) 'Rainbow Feminism: Perspectives on Minority Women in Canada', *Resources for Feminist Research*, 16(1): 5–9.

Stasiulis, Daiva (1991) 'Symbolic Representation and the Numbers Game: Tory Policies on "Race" and Visible Minorities', in F. Abele (ed.) *How Ottawa Spends: The Politics of Fragmentation*. Ottawa: Carleton University Press. pp. 229–67.

Statement of Government Policy presented by the Prime Minister to the Swedish Parliament, 4 October 1991. Stockholm. Unpublished translation.

Statistics Sweden (1990) *Women and Men in Sweden*. Stockholm, Sweden: Statistics Sweden.

Stimpson, Catharine (1993) 'Rethinking Affirmative Action', *Change: The Magazine of Higher Learning*, 25(2): 4–5.

Stoltenberg, Karin (1991) 'An Outline of the Ministry's Work on Gender Equality' in Equal Status Council, *Women and Democracy: Participation and Welfare*. Conference in Oslo, November. Oslo: Equal Status Council. pp. 127–30.

Stromberg, Erling (1980) *The Role of Women's Organizations in Norway*. Oslo: Equal Status Council.

Sullivan, L. (ed.) (1988) 'The Federal Contractors Program', *The Equal Times*, 1(2): 16–20.

Summers, Anne (1975) *Damned Whores and God's Police: The Colonization of Women in Australia*. Harmondsworth: Penguin. Reprinted 1976, 1995.

Sundin, Elisabeth (1992) 'Equality Through Regional Policy: Report from a Swedish Project', in Maud Eduards, Inga Elgqvist-Saltzman, Eva Lundgren, Christina Sjoblad, Elisabeth Sundin and Ulla Wikander (eds) *Rethinking Change: Current Feminist Research*. Uppsala: HSFR. pp. 105–30.

Sundstrom, M. (1991) 'Part-Time Work in Sweden: Trends and Equality Effects', *Journal of Economic Issues*, 25(1): 167–78.

Swedish Institute (1990) 'Mass Media in Sweden', *Fact Sheets on Sweden*. Stockholm: Sverigehuset.

Swanton, Christine (1985) 'On the "Essential Contestedness" of Political Concepts', *Ethics*, 95(4): 811–27.

Tajfel, H. (1970) 'Experiments in Intergroup Discrimination', *Scientific American*, 223(5): 96–103.

Tanesini, Alessandra (1994) 'Whose Language?', in Kathleen Lennon and Margaret Whitford (eds) *Knowing the Difference: Feminist Perspectives in Epistemology*. New York: Routledge. pp. 203–16.

Tapper, Marion (1986) 'Can a Feminist be a Liberal?' *Australasian Journal of Philosophy*, supplement to 64: 37–47.

Taylor, Bron R. (1991) *Affirmative Action at Work: Law, Politics, and Ethics*. Pittsburgh, PA: University of Pittsburgh Press.

Taylor, Charles and Gutmann, Amy (1992) *Multiculturalism and 'The Politics of Recognition'*. Princeton, NJ: Princeton University Press.

Taylor, Jayne (1992) 'Listening to Women: Report of Program Review – Equal Opportunity for Women'. Adelaide: Women's Advisory Unit, South Australian Government.

Taylor-Gooby, Peter (1994) 'Postmodernism and Social Policy: A Great Leap Backwards?', *Journal of Social Policy*, 23(3): 385–404.

Thalberg, Irving (1973) 'Reverse Discrimination and the Future', *The Philosophy Forum*, 5: 294–308.

Thalberg, Irving (1980) 'Themes in the Reverse-Discrimination Debate', *Ethics*, 91: 138–50.

Thomas, D.Q. and Beasley, M.E. (1993) 'Domestic Violence as a Human Rights Issue', *Human Rights Quarterly*, 5: 36–62.

Thomas, R. Roosevelt (1990) 'From Affirmative Action to Affirming Diversity', *Harvard Business Review*, 2: 107–17.

Thomas, R. Roosevelt (1991) *Beyond Race and Gender: Unleashing the Power of Your Total Workforce by Managing Diversity*. New York: American Management Association.

Thompson, Herb M. (1984) 'Class and Gender in the Pilbara', *Arena*, 68: 124–40.

Thompson, John B. (1987) 'Language and Ideology: a Framework for Analysis', *Sociological Review*, 35(3): 516–36.

Thompson, William (1983) *Appeal of One Half of the Human Race, Women, Against the Pretensions of the Other Half, Men, to Retain Them in Political, and thence in Civil and Domestic Slavery*. London: Virago.

Thornton, Margaret (1991) 'The Public/Private Dichotomy: Gendered and Discriminatory', *Journal of Law and Society*, 18(4): 448–63.

Thornton, Margaret (1994) 'The Seductive Allure of EEO', in Norma Grieve and Ailsa Burns (eds) *Australian Women: Contemporary Thought*. Melbourne: Oxford University Press.

Toobin, Jeffrey (1994) 'X-Rated', *The New Yorker*, 3 October: 70–8.

Torgersen, Trond-Viggo (1991) 'Children, Time, Work', in Equal Status Council, *Women and Democracy: Participation and Welfare*. Conference in Oslo, November. Oslo: Equal Status Council. pp. 78–88.

Turpel, M.E. (1993) 'Patriarchy and Paternalism: The Legacy of the Canadian State for First Nations Women', *Canadian Journal of Women and the Law*, 6: 174–92.

Tushnett, Mark (1991) 'Change and Continuity in the Concept of Civil Rights: Thurgood Marshall and Affirmative Action', *Social Philosophy and Policy*, 8(2): 150–71.

Tuttle, Lisa (1987) *Encyclopedia of Feminism*. London: Arrow.

Van Loon, R.J. and Whittington, M.S. (1981) *The Canadian Political System: Environment, Structure, and Process* (3rd edn). Toronto: McGraw-Hill.

Veldman, Albertine (1991) '"The Rule of Power": The Implementation of Equal Employment Opportunity Law in a Corporate Setting', *Living Law in the Low Countries*, Special Issue of the Dutch and Belgian *Law and Society Journal*: 69–78.

Verba, S. and Orren, G. (1985) *Equality in America: The View from the Top*. Cambridge, MA: Harvard University Press.

Verleggen, G. (1991) *Moving Borders: Women and the Trade Unions in the Netherlands*. Amsterdam: Netherlands Trade Union Confederation (FNV).

Vickers, Jill, Rankin, Pauline and Appelle, Christine (1993) *Politics As If Women Mattered: A*

Political Analysis of the National Action Committee on the Status of Women. Toronto: University of Toronto Press.

Wagner, J. (1990) 'Groups, Individuals and Constitutive Rules: The Conceptual Dilemma in Justifying Affirmative Action', *Polity*, 23(1): 77–103.

Ware, Vron (1992) *Beyond the Pale: White Women, Racism and History.* London, Verso.

Wasserstrom, Richard (1976) 'The University and the Case for Preferential Treatment', *American Philosophical Quarterly*, 13(2): 165–70.

Webster's Seventh New Collegiate Dictionary (1967). Toronto, Ontario: Thomas Allen & Son Ltd.

Weedon, Chris (1987) *Feminist Practice and Poststructuralist Theory.* Cambridge, MA: Blackwell.

Weisstein, Naomi (1970) 'Women as Nigger' in Leslie B. Tanner (ed.) *Voices from Women's Liberation.* New York: Signet. pp. 296–303.

Whitehouse, Gillian (1990) 'Unequal Pay: a Comparative Study of Australia, Canada, Sweden and the UK', *Labour and Industry*, 3(2&3): 354–71.

Widerberg, Karin (1991) 'Reforms for Women – On Male Terms', *International Journal of Sociology of Law*, 19: 27–44.

Wiebrens, Casper (1988) 'The Netherlands', in Alfred J. Kahn and Sheila B. Kamerman (eds) *Child Support: From Debt Collection to Social Policy.* Newbury Park, CA: Sage.

Wilenski, Peter (1977) *Directions for Change: Review of New South Wales Government Administration.* Sydney: P. West.

Williams, Cynthia (1986) 'The Changing Nature of Citizen Rights', in Alan Cairns and Cynthia Williams (eds), *Constitutionalism, Citizenship and Society in Canada.* Toronto: University of Toronto Press. pp. 99–131.

Williams, Patricia J. (1991) *The Alchemy of Race and Rights.* Cambridge, MA: Harvard University Press.

Williams, Toni (1990) 'Re-forming "Women's" Truth: A Critique of the Report of the Royal Commission on the Status of Women in Canada', *Ottawa Law Review*, 22(3): 725–59.

Williams, Wendy (1981) 'Firing the Woman to Protect the Fetus: The Reconciliation of Fetal Protection with Employment Opportunity Goals under Title VII', *Georgetown Law Journal*, 69(1): 641–704.

Wilson, William Julius (1987) *The Truly Disadvantaged: the Inner City, the Underclass, and Public Policy.* Chicago, IL: University of Chicago Press.

Winn, Conrad (1985) 'Affirmative Action for Women: More Than a Case of Simple Justice', *Canadian Public Administration*, 28(1): 24–46.

Winters, Sylvia (1987) 'Women and the Future of Unions', in S.J. Frenkel (ed.) *Union Strategies and Industrial Change.* Kensington, NSW: NSW University Press. pp. 155–68.

Wistrand, Birgitta (1981) *Swedish Women on the Move.* Stockholm: The Swedish Institute.

Wittig, Monique (1982) 'The Category of Sex', *Feminist Issues*, Fall: 63–8.

Wollstonecraft, Mary (1978) *Vindication of the Rights of Women.* Harmondsworth: Penguin.

Women's Emancipation Council (1985) *Advisory Report.* Amsterdam.

Wyzan, Michael L. (ed.) (1991) *The Political Economy of Ethnic Discrimination and Affirmative Action.* New York: Praeger.

Yeatman, Anna (1990) *Bureaucrats, Technocrats, Femocrats.* Sydney: Allen & Unwin.

Young, Iris (1990) *Justice and the Politics of Difference.* Princeton, NJ: Princeton University Press.

Young, Iris (1994) 'Gender as Seriality: Thinking about Women as a Social Collective', *Signs*, 19(3): 713–38.

Index